Popular dissent, such as street demonstrations and civil disobedi-ence, has become increasingly transnational in nature and scope. As a result, a local act of resistance can acquire almost immediately a much larger, cross-territorial dimension. This book draws upon a broad and innovative range of sources to scrutinise this central but often neglected aspect of global politics. Through case studies that span from Renaissance perceptions of human agency to the collapse of the Berlin Wall, the author examines how the theory and practice of popular dissent has emerged and evolved during the modern period. Dissent, he argues, is more than just transnational. It has become an important 'transversal' phenomenon: an array of diverse political practices which not only cross national boundaries, but also challenge the spatial logic through which these boundaries frame international relations.

Roland Bleiker is Senior Lecturer and Coordinator of the Peace and Conflict Studies Program at the University of Queensland. He has also taught at the Australian National University, Pusan National University, and the University of Tampere. He is the author of a number of articles in scholarly journals.

CAMBRIDGE STUDIES IN INTERNATIONAL RELATIONS: 70

POPULAR DISSENT, HUMAN AGENCY AND GLOBAL POLITICS

Cambridge Studies in International Relations is a joint initiative of Cambridge University Press and the British International Studies Association (BISA). The series will include a wide range of material, from undergraduate textbooks and surveys to research-based monographs and collaborative volumes. The aim of the series is to publish the best new scholarship in International Studies from Europe, North America and the rest of the world.

CAMBRIDGE STUDIES IN INTERNATIONAL
RELATIONS

Series list continues after index

Popular Dissent, Human Agency and Global Politics

Roland Bleiker

CAMBRIDGE
UNIVERSITY PRESS

#4118816

PUBLISHED BY THE PRESS SYNDICATE OF THE UNIVERSITY OF CAMBRIDGE
The Pitt Building, Trumpington Street, Cambridge, United Kingdom

CAMBRIDGE UNIVERSITY PRESS
The Edinburgh Building, Cambridge CB2 2RU, UK
http://www.cup.cam.ac.uk
40 West 20th Street, New York, NY 10011-4211, USA   http://www.cup.org
10 Stamford Road, Oakleigh, Melbourne 3166, Australia

© Roland Bleiker 2000

First published 2000

Printed in the United Kingdom at the University Press, Cambridge

Typeset in Palatino 10/12.5 pt. [wv]

A catalogue record for this book is available from the British Library

Library of Congress cataloguing in publication data

Bleiker, Roland
    Popular dissent, human agency, and global politics/Roland Bleiker
        p. cm. – (Cambridge studies in international relations; 70)
    ISBN 0 521 77099 8 (hardback) ISBN 0 521 77829 8 (paperback)
    1. Government, Resistance to. 2. Civil disobedience.
    3. Demonstrations. 4. Dissenters. 5. International relations.
    I. Series.
    JC328.3.853 2000
    303.6′1 –dc21 99-26115 CIP

ISBN 0 521 77099 8 hardback
ISBN 0 521 77829 8 paperback

Meinen Eltern in Dankbarkeit

Contents

Contents

Acknowledgements

The contours of this book have emerged gradually, during what seems today like a dozen, belatedly started Wanderjahre. In some ways these nomadic years were as transversal as the book's theoretical themes, for the journey has led from Zürich to Brisbane, via Paris, Panmunjom, Seoul, Toronto, Vancouver, Boston, Canberra, Flagstaff, Tampere and Pusan, to mention only the long-term resting places. During the early stages of the journey I was fortunate to receive intellectual stimulation from Nibaldo Galleguillos, Kal Holsti, Julia Schtivelman, Guy Willy Schmeltz and Richard Stubbs. A pre-doctoral fellowship with the Program on Nonviolent Sanctions at Harvard University's Center for International Affairs first gave me the opportunity to explore issues of dissent and global politics in a systematic way. The genealogical chapters of this book are in some sense a conversation with my colleagues and friends in Cambridge: Doug Bond, Joe Bond, Chris Krugler, Lee Myung Soo, Gene Sharp, Beth Kier, Paul Routledge and Bill Vogele.

A first draft of this book was researched and written between 1993 and 1996, and handed in as a Ph.D. thesis at the Australian National University. The ANU has provided me with a stimulating institutional home and financial assistance. Particular thanks go my supervisor, Jim George, and to the members of my advisory committee, Andrew Mack and Jim Richardson. At all stages of the project I could count on their encouraging criticism and support. Many others in Canberra also made my stay rewarding. The list would be endless, omissions do not signify lacking gratitude: Tony Burke, Greg Fry, Subhash Jaireth, Kate Krinks, Stephanie Lawson

Rodd McGibbon, Cindy O'Hagen, Meredith Patton, Simon Philpott, Paul Rutherford, John Ravenhill and Larbi Sadiki.

Intellectual debt also accumulated during the various research trips I embarked upon. In Paris and Zürich I particularly recall discussions with Didier Bigot, Theodor Brönnimann, Urs Leimbacher, Max Rieser, as well as the Hubmanns, Straubes and Würmlis. In Berlin I would like to thank my cousin Helga for her hospitality and Ralf Bönt for the on-going conversation and for introducing me to the city's literary scene. In Leipzig I would like to acknowledge Gert Neumann and his reading at the Bürgerforum, which was at least as insightful as his pivotal Wenderoman *Anschlag*. Thanks go as well to countless librarians who, unfortunately, have mostly remained anonymous, to Fiona Sampson for her splendid Aberystwyth International Poetry Fest, to Ahmed, Dave and Steve for the Wednesday night breaks from writing during my winter in Arizona, and to Osmo Apunen, Ron Duncan, Chun Hongchan, Vivienne Jabri, Kim Sang Yong, Lee Kab-soo and Tarja Väyrynen for support during the later stages of my journey. Bronwyn Evans-Kent provided useful help with work on the index. I also appreciated the opportunity to air some of my ideas, tentative as they were, to audiences at the Universities of Lund, Tampere and Woollongong and The Danish Institute of International Affairs.

I benefited greatly from comments by Paul Patton and two anonymous referees. Their thorough and empathetic engagement with the manuscript pushed me much further than I had planned to go at the beginning of my journey. Without them, this book would look quite different today. John Girling, Barry Hindess, Ben Kerkvliet, Claus Offe, Jindy Pettman and Nikolas Rose offered insightful comments on drafts of chapters. Many thanks as well to John Haslam and Steve Smith, for their trust in and unwavering support of my project.

Finally, a few extra thanks. First to three exemplary international relations scholars, David Campbell, Mike Shapiro and Rob Walker, for their innovative work and their unusually generous personal support. The intellectual spaces they have opened up gave me permission to apply an old passion of mine – Nietzsche – to the study of global politics.

Words, even poetic ones, fail to capture Christine Sylvester's role in my lifelong task of trying to become who I am. As my 'Reader' she has pushed me further each time I thought I had arrived at an end point, and as my Liebensgefährte she has deepened the journey beyond not only with art and letters and medieval chants, but also, and above all, with a vie-à-deux that is as much exhilarating as it is comforting.

This book is dedicated to my parents, Lucia and Hans Bleiker. They have always wondered why, instead of taking over their barber shop or continuing a seemingly promising career as town notary in Zürich, I moved to places foreign simply to spend many a year hunched over obscure books and flickering computer screens. But no matter how strange this behaviour appeared, they have never lost trust in me.

Note on Sources
Certain passages in this book are drawn from two articles in *Alternatives: Social Transformation and Humane Governance* – 'Forget IR Theory' (Volume 22, Number 1, 1997, pp. 57–86); and 'Retracing and Redrawing the Boundaries of Events: Postmodern Interferences with International Theory' (Volume 23, Number 4, 1998, pp. 471–97). © 1997 and 1998 by Lynne Rienner Publishers.

Prologue **Theorising transversal dissent**

> The question is no longer one that opposes the *global* and the *local*,
> or the *transnational* and the *national*. It is, above all, a question of
> the sudden temporal commutation which blurs not only inside and
> outside, the boundaries of the political territory, but also the before
> and after of its duration, of its history.[1]

Manifestations of popular dissent, such as street demonstrations,
social movements and civil disobedience, have for long occupied central positions in most political landscapes. The processes through
which they exert human agency, however, have recently undergone
important transformations. In previous epochs, popular protests had
a mostly local nature, that is, their dynamic was one that directly
opposed ruler and ruled. By the late twentieth century the nature of
dissent has changed fundamentally. The presence of mass media can
transform a local act of resistance almost immediately into an event
of global significance. Images of a protest march may flicker over television screens worldwide only hours after people have taken to the
street. As a result, the protest soon takes on a much larger, trans-
territorial dimension.

This book theorises the changing nature of dissent in the context of
several historical and contemporary case studies. Among them is a
detailed scrutiny of the protest forms that contributed to the collapse
of the Berlin Wall and, ultimately, to a series of substantial transformations in global politics. East German popular resistance against
authoritarian rule, which peaked in the autumn of 1989, illustrates
how an act of dissent can draw immediate worldwide attention and

---

[1] Paul Virilio, *La Vitesse de Libération* (Paris: Galilée, 1995), p. 31.

1

lead to strong outside pressures on the authorities against which the protest was directed. The events in East Germany were extraordinary by any standard. They marked perhaps the key turning point in the transition from the Cold War to a new phase in international politics. In their dynamic, though, these protests were not necessarily unique. There are countless other, comparable instances of dissent today. Consider, for example, the regular interventions by Greenpeace or Amnesty International, the so-called people power revolution against Ferdinand Marcos in the Philippines, the dissident movement led by Aung San Suu Kyi in Myamar, the riots that forced Indonesia's president Suharto to step down in 1998, or the actions of the Zapatista rebels who voice their discontent from the Chiapas mountains of Southeast Mexico via cyberspace across the world.

Dissent has become a significant transnational phenomenon, reflecting and shaping various aspects of global politics. In fact, dissent has become what could be called a *transversal* phenomenon – a political practice that not only transgresses national boundaries, but also questions the spatial logic through which these boundaries have come to constitute and frame the conduct of international relations.

The term transversal draws attention to various political transformations that are currently taking place. It has emerged in response to a growing need to rethink the manner in which the domain of international relations has traditionally been conceptualised. David Campbell, for instance, argues convincingly that globalised life is best seen 'as a series of transversal struggles rather than as a complex of inter-national, multi-national or transnational relations'.[2] The latter, he points out, are modes of representation that have strong investments in the very borders that are currently being questioned. By contrast,

---

[2] David Campbell, 'Political Prosaics, Transversal Politics, and the Anarchical World', in Michael J. Shapiro and Hayward R. Alker (eds.), *Challenging Boundaries: Global Flows, Territorial Identities* (Minneapolis: University of Minnesota Press, 1996), p. 24. The term transversal was used briefly by Michel Foucault to denote forms of struggle against authority that 'are not limited to one country'. See 'The Subject and Power', an afterword to H.L. Dreyfus and P. Rabinow, *Michel Foucault: Beyond Structuralism and Hermeneutics* (New York: Harvester Wheatsheaf, 1982), p. 211. Richard Ashley then introduced the concept of transversal struggle to the study of international politics. 'The term is useful,' he says, 'because it conveys much that attaches to the term *transnational*, while avoiding the latter's tendency to invest authority in the national boundaries that are being traversed.' Richard K. Ashley, 'Living on Border Lines: Man, Poststructuralism, and War', in J. Der Derian and M.J. Shapiro (eds.), *International/Intertextual Relations: Postmodern Readings of World Politics* (Lexington, Mass: Lexington Books, 1989), pp. 270, 296–99, 314.

to conceptualise global politics as a site of transversal struggles is to draw attention to the multiple and multi-layered interactions that make up contemporary life. It is to recognise the complex cross-border flow of people, goods, ideas, capital – in short, 'the increasing irruptions of accelerated and nonterritorial contingencies upon our horizons'.[3]

What follows is an attempt to grapple with the consequences that emerge from viewing global politics as a series of transversal struggles. More specifically, the challenge consists of understanding the role of dissent at a time when old certainties are giving way to a continuously unfolding array of seemingly disparate political dynamics. Two interrelated objectives are central to this endeavour:

1 To scrutinise the phenomenon of transversal dissent through several concrete case studies: How have practices of popular dissent achieved transversal dimensions? How have we come to understand these practices and how has this understanding affected the manner in which they operate in practice? Are prevalent perceptions of dissent still adequate to appreciate the complex political dynamics of a world that operates increasingly along transversal lines?

2 To theorise questions of agency that inevitably arise with a conceptualisation of transversal dissent: What is the potential and limit of protest movements that transgress and challenge national boundaries? How can we understand the processes through which various forms of dissent shape – and are shaped by – the social and political struggles they seek to engage?

Before embarking on this double task, a relatively elaborate prologue is necessary to outline how an understanding of transversal dissent intersects with concerns that are, or at least ought to be, central to the study of global politics. Traditional approaches to international relations theory have treated dissident practices largely in repressive terms. In a nuclear age dominated by fierce Cold War rivalries, most theories of global politics were implicitly concerned with maintaining order, security and stability – to the point that manifestations of dissent have come to be seen as mere disruptive and disorderly phenomena, as 'breakdowns of otherwise regular processes in national and

---

[3] Campbell, 'Political Prosaics, Transversal Politics, and the Anarchical World', p. 9.

international society'.[4] Expressed in other words, the potential of dissent to engender transformation has remained largely unexplored by a field of study that treats the very notion of revolution with a mixture of 'disdain and neglect'.[5] It is through an extensive set of preliminary remarks that this book seeks to break this silence, so that alternative transversal voices can be heard and acted upon in the chapters that follow.

The level of analysis problem, or how to legitimise transversal stories about global politics

An attempt that seeks to demonstrate the relevance of transversal dissent to the study of international relations is immediately confronted with the so-called level of analysis problem. Which issues, actors, institutions and phenomena belong to the domain of global politics? What is the proper subject matter of international relations, and how is it distinguished from other spheres of inquiry, such as domestic politics or political theory?[6] Indeed, are such conceptual divisions useful at all at a time when mental and geopolitical boundaries are being increasingly transgressed and challenged?

Realism, which is arguably the most important tradition in international theory, has defined the discipline's purview in a rather specific way. In his influential analysis of international politics, Kenneth Waltz differentiates among three approaches to the study of interstate conflict. Depending on whether the causes of war are seen in 'man' (i.e., individuals), the attributes of specific states, or the nature of the international system, he labels them first, second and third image analysis.[7] According to Waltz's neo-realist interpretation, international theory ought to be concerned only with the third, systemic level of analysis. The main task thus consists of theorising how the anarchic structure

---

[4] Fred Halliday, 'The Sixth Great Power: On the Study of Revolution and International Relations', *Review of International Studies*, 16, 1990, 207.

[5] Ibid., 207.

[6] For a summary of this debate see Barry Buzan, 'The Level of Analysis Problem in International Relations Reconsidered', in Ken Booth and Steve Smith (eds.), *International Relations Theory Today* (University Park: Pennsylvania State University Press, 1995), pp. 198–216; Martin Hollis and Steve Smith, *Explaining and Understanding International Relations* (Oxford: Clarendon Press, 1990), pp. 92–118.

[7] K.N. Waltz, *Man, the State and War* (New York: Columbia University Press, 1959).

of the international system affects the behaviour of states.[8] The result is a rather narrowly perceived understanding of global politics, one that assumes, as K.J. Holsti summarises, that the proper focus of study is the causes of war and that the main units of analysis are the diplomatic-military behaviours of the only essential actors, nation-states.[9]

Realism is, of course, not the only approach to international theory. Neither has its exclusive focus on war and states remained unchallenged. Various authors have recognised for long that 'the state has not always been the primary actor in global politics and has never been the sole actor'.[10] In North America, neo-liberal contributions have drawn attention to the importance of such factors as trade, interdependence, international institutions, multinational corporations or the ability of states to engage in cooperative behaviour.[11] In Europe, the so-called English school has always held a broader, more historical and philosophical understanding of international politics.[12] Some scholars have, indeed, explicitly acknowledged the transnational, that is, 'cross-frontier-relations involving "non-state" actors and forces,' as a legitimate aspect of inquiries into international relations.[13]

While opening up the study of global politics to a variety of new domains, most efforts to rethink the international have not gone as far as they could have, or, indeed, should have gone. Here too, questions of conceptualisation and representation are of crucial importance.

[8] K.N. Waltz, *Theory of International Politics* (Reading, Mass,: Addison-Wesley, 1979), esp. pp. 38–59.
[9] K.J. Holsti, *The Dividing Discipline: Hegemony and Diversity in International Theory* (Boston, Mass: Unwin Hyman, 1985), p. 10.
[10] Richard W. Mansbach, Yale H. Ferguson and Donald E. Lampert, *The Web of World Politics: Nonstate Actors in the Global System* (Englewood Cliffs, NY: Prentice-Hall, 1976), p. 25.
[11] See, for instance, R.O. Keohane and J.S. Nye, 'Transnational Relations and World Politics', special issue of *International Organization*, 25, 3, Summer 1971; Robert Keohane, *After Hegemony: Cooperation and Discord in the World Political Economy* (Princeton: Princeton University Press, 1984); Lisa Martin, *Coercive Cooperation: Explaining Multilateral Economic Sanctions* (Princeton: Princeton University Press, 1992); Peter Haas, *Saving the Mediterranean: The Politics of International Environmental Cooperation* (Cambridge: Cambridge University Press, 1996).
[12] See, for instance, Hedley Bull, *The Anarchical Society: A Study of Order in World Politics* (London: Macmillan, 1977); Adam Watson, *The Evolution of International Society: A Comparative Historical Analysis* (London: Routledge, 1992); R.J. Vincent, *Human Rights and International Relations* (Cambridge: Cambridge University Press, 1986).
[13] Fred Halliday, 'The Pertinence of International Relations', *Political Studies*, 38, 1990, 503; See also R. Maghroori and B. Ramberg (eds.), *Globalism versus Realism: International Relations' Third Debate* (Boulder, Col.: Westview Press, 1982); James N. Rosenau, *Turbulence in World Politics: A Theory of Change and Continuity* (Princeton: Princeton University Press, 1990).

Campbell stresses that for all their efforts to understand a wide range of global phenomena, most approaches to international theory have displayed a remarkably persistent compulsion to anchor an understanding of the complexities of global life in a 'something-national' formulation – whether it is 'international', 'multinational', or 'transnational'.[14] Representative for such forms of conceptualising is Mark Zacher's seemingly sensible claim that 'non-state actors such as multinational corporations and banks may increase in importance, but there are few signs that they are edging states from centre stage'.[15]

Debates about the role of human agency display similar state-centric tendencies. There are disagreements on various fronts, but virtually all discussions on agency in international theory remain focused on conceptualising state behaviour. Alexander Wendt, who has been instrumental in bringing issues of agency to the study of international relations, has been equally influential in directing ensuing discussions on a state-centric path. He explicitly and repeatedly acknowledges 'a commitment to states as units of analysis' and constructs much of his theoretical work around an examination of states and the constraints within which they operate.[16] Here too, the logic behind adapting a state-centric form of representation rests on the assumption that 'as long as states are the dominant actors in international politics, it is appropriate to focus on the identity and agency of the state rather than, for example, a transnational social movement'.[17]

Questions of agency in international theory should not and cannot be reduced to analyses of state behaviour. This book demonstrates how an instance of transversal dissent may influence global politics at least as much as, say, a diplomatic treatise or a foreign policy decision. At a time when processes of globalisation are unfolding and national boundaries are becoming increasingly porous, states can no longer be

---

[14] Campbell, 'Political Prosaics, Transversal Politics, and the Anarchical World', p. 11.

[15] Mark W. Zacher, 'The Decaying Pillars of the Westphalian Temple: Implications for International Order and Governance', in J.N. Rosenau and E.O. Czempiel (eds.), *Governance without Government: Order and Change in World Politics* (Cambridge: Cambridge University Press, 1992), p. 64.

[16] Alexander Wendt, 'Constructing International Politics', in *International Security*, 20, 1, Summer 1995, 72; 'The Agent–Structure Problem in International Relations Theory', *International Organization*, 41 (1987), p. 364; 'Anarchy is What States Make of It: The Social Construction of Power Politics', *International Organization*, 46, 2, Spring 1992, 424.

[17] Mlada Bukovansky, 'Identity and Agency in the International System', in Eun Ho Lee and Woosang Kim (eds.), *Recasting International Relations Paradigms: Statism, Pluralism, Globalism* (Seoul: Seoul Press, 1996), p. 245.

viewed as the only consequential actors in world affairs. Various scholars have thus begun to question the prevalent spatial modes of representation and the artificial separation of levels of analysis that issues from them. They suggest, as mentioned above, that global life is better understood as a series of transversal struggles that increasingly challenge what Richard Ashley called 'the paradigm of sovereign man.' Transversal struggles, Ashley emphasises, are not limited to established spheres of sovereignty. They are neither domestic nor international. They know no final boundaries between inside and outside.[18] And they have come to be increasingly recognised as central aspects of global politics. James Rosenau is among several scholars who now acknowledge that it is along the shifting frontiers of transversal struggles, 'and not through the nation state system that people sort and play out the many contradictions at work in the global scene'.[19]

Once one accepts the centrality that transversal struggles play in today's world it becomes impossible to differentiate between political dynamics that take place in local, national or international spheres. It is the very transgressions of these spheres that drive and shape much of global life today. And once one has accepted the presence of these transgressions and the ensuing spatial contingencies, then, Campbell stresses, the levels of analysis problem is no more.[20]

If we are to gain an adequate understanding of contemporary dissent, and of global life in general, we must look beyond the lines that have been arbitrarily drawn into the sand of international politics. We must think past the current framing of the levels of analysis problem. It is the steady breeze, the gusty bursts of energy, the transversal forms of agency, that are gradually transforming the lines and shapes of contemporary global life. Expressed in more prosaic words, a multitude of actors, actions, spheres and issues must be recognised and discussed as legitimate parts of international relations debates. Needless to say, there are countless forms of dissent and agency that are

---

[18] Ashley, 'Living on Border Lines', pp. 296, 299. See also his 'Untying the Sovereign State: A Double Reading of the Anarchy Problematique', in *Millennium*, 17, 2, 1988, 227–62.

[19] James N. Rosenau, *Along the Domestic–Foreign Frontier: Exploring Governance in a Turbulent World* (Cambridge: Cambridge University Press, 1997), pp. 5–6. See also J. Agnew and S. Corbridge, *Mastering Space: Hegemony, Territory and International Political Economy* (London: Routledge, 1995); and Gearóid Ó Tuathail, *Critical Geopolitics: The Politics of Writing Global Space* (London: Routledge, 1996).

[20] Campbell, 'Political Prosaics, Transversal Politics, and the Anarchical World', p. 22.

operative within transversal struggles. Various authors have already identified the international in spheres hitherto unseen, unappreciated and untheorised. Feminist scholars, for instance, have located women and their influence on the global economy in such spaces as households, assembly lines, sweat shops, farms, secretariats, guerrilla wars and brothels that have sprung up around foreign military bases.[21]

To expand the scope of international theory and to bring transversal struggles into focus is not to declare the state obsolete. States remain central actors in international politics and they have to be recognised and theorised as such. In fact, my analysis will examine various ways in which states and the boundaries between them have mediated the formation, functioning and impact of dissent. However, my reading of dissent and agency makes the state neither its main focus nor its starting point. There are compelling reasons for such a strategy, and they go beyond a mere recognition that a state-centric approach to international theory engenders a form of representation that privileges the authority of the state and thus precludes an adequate understanding of the radical transformations that are currently unfolding in global life. Michael Shapiro is among an increasing number of theorists who convincingly portray the state not only as an institution, but also, and primarily, as a set of 'stories' – of which the state-centric approach to international theory is a perfect example. It is part of a legitimisation process that highlights, promotes and naturalises certain political practices and the territorial context within which they take place. Taken together, these stories provide the state with a sense of identity, coherence and unity. They create boundaries between an inside and an outside, between a people and its others. Shapiro stresses that such state-stories also exclude, for they seek 'to repress or delegitimise other stories and the practices of identity and space they reflect.' And it is these processes of exclusion that impose a certain political order and provide the state with a legitimate rationale for violent encounters.[22]

---

[21] Maria Mies, *Patriarchy and Accumulation on a World Scale: Women and the International Division of Labour* (London: ZED Books, 1986), Cynthia Enloe, *Bananas, Beaches, and Bases: Making Feminist Sense of International Politics* (London, Pandora, 1989); Jan Jindy Pettman, *Worlding Women* (London: Routledge, 1996); Christine Sylvester, *Feminist Theory and International Relations in a Postmodern Era* (Cambridge: Cambridge University Press, 1994).

[22] Michael Shapiro, 'Sovereign Anxieties', in Lee and Kim, *Recasting International Relations Paradigms*, p. 212. See also his *Violent Cartographies: Mapping Cultures of War* (Minneapolis: University of Minnesota Press, 1997) and William Connolly, *Identity/*

Transversal dissident practices can be seen as forms of thought and action that not only transgress, but also challenge the political order which has developed around the assertion of national sovereignty. They either question the arbitrariness of this division and its corresponding system of exclusion, or simply reveal how inadequate it has become in a world that has undergone fundamental change since the state system emerged with the Peace of Westphalia in 1648. This is why transversal alternatives to prevalent state-centric perspectives must be recognised as legitimate aspects of international theory. To dismiss them as reductionist, as Waltz suggests,[23] and to relegate them to some other sphere of inquiry, is to run the risk of entrenching the very dilemmas that international relations scholars are trying to address and overcome. It is thus with both an analytical and a normative objective that the present inquiry seeks to demonstrate the relevance of transversal dissent to an international relations audience. This effort is as much an expression of the need to understand the complexities and the changing nature of contemporary global politics, as it is a desire to heed and engage a variety of counter-narratives that may well give rise to ideas and practices that engender political transformation in international spheres.

Beyond objectivism and relativism, or how to move the structure–agency debate into discursive terrains

Once brought into the purview of international theory, transversal forms of dissent must be submitted to detailed scrutiny. What is their exact relevance to global politics? Where and under what circumstances can they influence the course of events? In other words, how do transversal forms of dissent exert human agency?

Questions of agency have been discussed extensively in international theory, mostly in the context of the so-called structure–agency debate. Although strongly wedded to a state-centric view, this debate nevertheless evokes a number of important conceptual issues that are relevant as well to an understanding of transversal dynamics. The roots of the structure–agency debate can be traced back to a feeling of

Difference: Democratic Negotiations of Political Paradox (Ithaca: Cornell University Press, 1991), p. 207.
[23] Waltz, *Theory of International Politics*, p. 60–78.

discontent about how traditional approaches to international theory have dealt with issues of agency. Sketched in an overly broad manner, the point of departure looked as follows: At one end of the spectrum were neorealists, who explain state identity and behaviour through a series of structural restraints that are said to emanate from the anarchical nature of the international system. At the other end we find neoliberals, who accept the existence of anarchy but seek to understand the behaviour of states and other international actors in terms of their individual attributes and their ability to engage in cooperative bargaining. If pushed to their logical end-point, the two positions amount, respectively, to a structural determinism and an equally far-fetched belief in the autonomy of rational actors.²⁴

The structure–agency debate is located somewhere between these two poles. Neither structure nor agency receive analytical priority. Instead, the idea is to understand the interdependent and mutually constitutive relationship between them. The discussions that have evolved in the wake of this assumption are highly complex and cannot possibly be summarised here.²⁵ Some of the key premises, though, can be recognised by observing how the work of Anthony Giddens has shaped the structure–agency debate in international relations. Giddens speaks of the 'duality of structure,' of structural properties that are constraining as well as enabling. They are both 'the medium and outcome of the contingently accomplished activities of situated

²⁴ For reasons to be articulated in more detail later, the task of this book is not to engage and explore treatments of agency in international relations theory. Hence, this overly sketchy portrayal inevitably does injustice to the complexities that make up the interaction between neorealist and neoliberal approaches to international theory. It also overlooks issues of agency that have been addressed in the context of foreign policy decision making. For a summary and juxtaposition of current realist and liberal approaches see, for instance, D.A. Baldwin (ed.), *Neorealism and Neoliberalism: The Contemporary Debate* (New York: Columbia University Press, 1993); Charles W. Kegley (ed.), *Controversies in International Relations Theory: Realism and the Neoliberal Challenge* (New York: St. Martin's, 1995). Examples of literature that deal with issues of agency in foreign policy include Graham T. Allison, *Essence of Decision: Explaining the Cuban Missile Crisis* (Boston: Little Brown, 1971); Alexander L. George, *Presidential decision making in foreign policy* (Boulder: Westview, 1980).

²⁵ Contributions include Wendt, 'The Agent–Structure Problem', pp. 335–70; David Dessler, 'What's at Stake in the Agent–Structure Debate?', in *International Organization*, 43, 3, Summer 1989, 441–473; Martin Hollis and Steve Smith, 'Beware of Gurus: Structure and Action in International Relations', *Review of International Studies*, 17, 4, 1991, 393–410; Walter Carlsnaes, 'The Agency–Structure Problem in Foreign Policy Analysis', *International Studies Quarterly*, 36, September 1992, 245–70; Vivienne Jabri, *Discourses on Violence: Conflict Analysis Reconsidered* (Manchester: Manchester University Press, 1996).

actors'.[26] Expressed in other words, neither agents nor structures have the final word. Human actions are always embedded in and constrained by the structural context within which they form and evolve. But structures are not immutable either. A human being, Giddens stresses, will 'know a great deal about the conditions of reproduction of the society of which he or she is a member'.[27] The actions that emerge from this awareness then shape the processes through which social systems are structurally maintained and reproduced.

Applying Giddens to international theory entails investigating how social structures and state actions mutually influence each other. Such a position rests, in Wendt's words, on the recognition that '(1) human beings and their organisations are purposeful actors whose actions help to reproduce or transform the society in which they live; and (2) that society is made up of social relationships, which structure the interaction between these purposeful actors'.[28] The state is thus perceived neither as a self-contained unit nor as an impotent object of structural necessity. A state's response to such aspects as wars, trade or technological change forms its sense of identity. And it is this sense of identity that then shapes a state's behaviour and its agency.

While appreciating these basic assumptions about contemporary global politics, my conceptualisation of transversal dissent embarks on a different path, and this not only because of the problematic state-centric nature around which the structure–agency debate has developed. Instead of articulating issues of agency in relation to structures, my approach relies on what could be called a discourse–agency axis.

Discourses are, in their broadest meaning, frameworks of knowledge and power through which we comprehend (and constitute) the world around us. Because the conceptual range of a discursive approach is broader than that of a structural one, it is better suited to scrutinise transversal struggles. The notion of structure, especially as applied in international theory, is intrinsically linked to neorealist, statist and spatial perceptions of world politics. But even outside the realist paradigm, structures often remain too closely identified with institutional practices and the type of societal order they sustain. The

---

[26] Anthony Giddens, *The Constitution of Society: Outline of the Theory of Structuration* (Berkeley: University of California Press, 1984), pp. 191, 297–304.
[27] Anthony Giddens, *Central Problems in Social Theory: Action, Structure and Contradiction in Social Analysis* (London: Macmillan, 1979), p. 5.
[28] Wendt, 'The Agent–Structure Problem', pp. 337–8.

notion of discourse, by contrast, encapsulates not only the structural terrains of rules and norms, but also a variety of other aspects, such as language and culture, that interfere with the mutually constituted and transversal production of power and knowledge.[29]

But posing questions of transversal dissent and human agency in relation to discourses breaks theoretical taboos. It creates various forms of anxieties. There are possible objections from those who employ the concept of discourse in their work. Neither Heidegger nor Foucault, for instance, nor many of their subsequent interpreters, have dealt with questions of agency in an explicit and systematic way. This omission has often been equated with an image of the world in which human beings are engulfed by discursive webs to the point that action becomes no more than a reflection of externally imposed circumstances. Towards such interpretations my challenge will consist in demonstrating that it is feasible as well as worthwhile to conceptualise the notion of human agency. In fact, my analysis will seek to show how this alleged inability or unwillingness to speak of agency is more often than not a reflection of anti-postmodern polemic, rather than a position that is inherent to or advocated by most authors who have sought to apply a discursive approach to the study of global politics.[30]

There are also possible objections from those who already pursue questions of agency. They often bestow the human subject and his/ her actions with a relatively large sense of autonomy. This remains, at least according to an insightful analysis by Roxanne Doty, a prime tendency even within the structure–agency debate. She claims that the dualism between structure and agency has not been solved in international theory. Existing solutions 'either end up reverting to a structural determinism or alternatively to an understanding of agency which presumes pregiven, autonomous individuals.'[31] This

[29] Although Wendt ('Constructing International Politics', p. 73) comes nominally close to a discursive position when defining social structures as 'shared knowledge, material resources, and practices', his epistemological stance contradicts, as will be shown below, the tenets of a discursive understanding of social dynamics.
[30] Representative here is the work of David Campbell and Michael Shapiro, who have taken on questions of ethics – and by extension of agency – through an explicitly discursive approach. See, for instance, David Campbell, 'Why Fight: Humanitarianism, Principles and Post-structuralism', *Millennium*, 27, 3, 1998, 497–521; Michael J. Shapiro, 'The Events of Discourse and the Ethics of Global Hospitality', *Millennium*, 27, 3, 1998, 695–713.
[31] Roxanne Lynn Doty, 'Aporia: A Critical Exploration of the Agent–Structure Problematique in International Relations Theory', *European Journal of International Relations*, 3, 3, 1997, 366.

tendency epitomises a fear of relativism that permeates much of international theory – a fear that is expressed in the belief that an analytical focus on discourses would produce a form of fatalism that can do no more than express bewilderment at the complexities of contemporary global politics. Theorising discourse, in other words, would undermine objective knowledge. It would open up the floodgates to a mass of relativistic ravings, according to which 'anything goes' and 'any narrative is as valid as another'.[32] Such a path, it is said, prevents the opportunity to ground human knowledge and action in stable and objective foundations – anchoring devices deemed necessary to exert human agency and ward off the lurking spectre of nihilism. Towards scholars who represent such positions, my task will consist in demonstrating that discourse is, indeed, a concept that can be highly useful to theorise human agency.

Departing from both a discursive fatalism and an overzealous belief in the autonomy of human action, I search for a middle ground that can draw together positive aspects of both opposing traditions of thought. I am, in this sense, following authors such as Pierre Bourdieu and Richard Bernstein, for whom the central opposition that characterises our time, the one between objectivism and relativism, is largely misleading and distorting. It is itself part of a seductive dichotomy that is articulated in either/or terms: either there is an ultimate possibility of grounding knowledge in stable foundations, or there are no foundations at all, nothing but an endless fall into a nihilist abyss.[33] But there are no Either/Or extremes. There are only shades of difference, subtleties that contradict the idea of an exclusionary vantage-point.

My own attempt at overcoming the misleading dichotomy between objectivism and relativism revolves around two major propositions, which I will sustain and expand throughout this book: (1) that one can theorise discourses and still retain a concept of human agency; and (2) that one can advance a positive notion of human agency that

---

[32] Øyvind Østerud, 'Antinomies of Postmodernism in International Studies', in *Journal of Peace Research*, 33, 4, November 1996, 386. Among the authors who express various concerns about postmodern scholarship are Fred Halliday, *Rethinking International Relations* (Vancouver: UBC Press, 1994); p. 39; K.J. Holsti, 'Mirror, Mirror on the Wall, Which are the Fairest Theories of All?', *International Studies Quarterly*, 33, 3, 1989, 255–61; Robert O. Keohane, *International Institutions and State Power: Essays in International Relations Theory* (Boulder, Col.: Westview, 1989).

[33] Pierre Bourdieu, *The Logic of Practice*, tr. R. Nice (Stanford: Stanford University Press, 1990/1980); Richard Bernstein, *Beyond Objectivism and Relativism: Science, Hermeneutics, and Praxis* (Oxford: Basil Blackwell, 1983).

is neither grounded in a stable foundation nor dependent upon a pre-supposed notion of the subject. The point of searching for this middle ground is not to abandon foundations as such, but to recognise that they are a necessary part of our effort to make sense of an increasingly complex and transversal world. We need foundations to ground our thoughts, but foundations impose and exclude. They should not be considered as stable and good for all times. They must be applied in awareness of their function and with a readiness to adjust them to changing circumstances.

Postmodernism versus constructivism, or how to legitimise a discursive understanding of human agency

A post-positive understanding of social dynamics is necessary to appreciate transversal forms of dissent and their ability to influence global politics. One may even call this endeavour 'postmodern', although I will, for reasons to be explained later, largely refrain from employing this overused and highly politicised term.

A post-positivist understanding of agency runs counter to currently influential 'constructivist' contributions to questions of agency in international theory. Constructivists share various traits with post-modernists. Among them is a common concern with the social construction of meaning, state identity and international politics in general. Both approaches reject, even at an analytical level, the notion of autonomous and rational actors. Instead, they scrutinise how rules, norms and values shape actors and issues in global affairs. Wendt, for instance, declares himself a 'constructivist', which is to say that he acknowledges that the world is 'socially constructed', that the structures of international politics are social, rather than merely material, and that these structures shape the identity and interests of actors.[34]

With regard to questions of epistemology, though, postmodernists and constructivists differ sharply. The former are sceptical of all forms of positivist knowledge while the latter remain faithful, at least to some extent, to traditional scientific and causal principles. Nicholas Onuf stresses that 'constructivists need not repudiate positivism just because it is liable to criticism'. Only through a systematic analysis,

---

[34] Wendt, 'Anarchy is What States Make of It', p. 393; 'Constructing International Politics', pp. 71–2.

he insists, can we hope to understand the behaviour of agents and the workings of social arrangements.[35] Although rejecting the strict tenets of logical positivism, Wendt too acknowledges the importance of causal and scientific analyses. It is through the methodological principles of scientific realism, espoused by writers such as Roy Bhaskar, that Wendt hopes to assess the influence of social structures in a systematic and scientifically legitimate manner. As opposed to a more narrow empiricist approach, scientific realism provides a legitimate way of recognising the crucial causal impact of unobservable phenomena, such as structures.[36] So-called 'bracketing' is the method through which Wendt and other constructivists attempt to achieve this objective. This is to say that they take 'social structures and agents in turn as temporarily given in order to examine the explanatory effects of the other'.[37] Various authors have investigated questions of agency in international relations along this path. David Dessler, for instance, has tried to supply a more explicit basis for the empirical applicability of a constructivist approach, and Martha Finnemore has, most recently, embarked on such an application through an alternate bracketing of agency and structure.[38]

While offering various insightful contributions, the constructivist reliance on scientific perceptions of international politics detracts from, rather than adds to our understanding of transversal forms of human agency. For all their efforts to reach beyond the dominant neorealist and neoliberal interpretations of international relations, Wendt and other constructivists exhibit, as Campbell notes, 'an overwhelming but underrecognized commitment to many of the general tenets of that disposition'.[39] Doty draws attention to some of them. For her, the process of bracketing presupposes, by its very logic, the existence of pre-given units – be they structures or agents. Combined with the analytical separation between object and subject, which is

---

[35] Nicholas Onuf, 'A Constructivist Manifesto', in Kurt Burch and Robert A. Denemark, *Constituting International Political Economy* (Boulder, Col.: Lynne Rienner, 1997), p. 8. See also his *World of Our Making: Rules and Rule in Social Theory and International Relations* (Columbia: University of South Carolina Press, 1989).

[36] Wendt, 'The Agent–Structure Problem', pp. 351–6, and, for a discussion of his usage of scientific realism, Hollis and Smith, 'Beware of Gurus', pp. 396–8; Doty, 'Aporia', pp. 368–75.

[37] Wendt, 'The Agent–Structure Problem', pp. 364–5.

[38] Dessler, 'What's at Stake in the Agent–Structure debate?', pp. 441–73; Martha Finnemore, *National Interest in International Society* (Ithaca, NY: Cornell University Press, 1996).

[39] Campbell, 'Political Prosaics, Transversal Politics, and the Anarchical World', p. 12.

implied in scientific realism, constructivists thus re-establish the very oppositional conceptualisation that the structure–agency debate was initially supposed to overcome.[40] To draw attention to these and other positivist pitfalls is not to invalidate constructivist approaches or scientific inquiries as such. There are many domains in which systematic empirical analyses of international relations can be useful. The conceptualisation of agency, however, is not among them.

Human agency is not something that exists in an a priori manner and can be measured scientifically in reference to external realities. Strictly speaking, there is no such thing as human agency, for its nature and its function are, at least in part, determined by how we think about human action and its potential to shape political and social practices. The mutually constituted and constantly shifting relationship between agents and discourses thus undermines the possibility of observing social dynamics in a value-free way. To embark on such an endeavour nevertheless is to superimpose a static image upon a series of events that can only be understood in their fluidity. It is to objectivise a very particular and necessarily subjective understanding of agency and its corresponding political practices. The dangers of such an approach have been debated extensively. Authors such as Richard Ashley, Jim George and Steve Smith have shown how positivist epistemologies have transformed one specific interpretation of world political realities, the dominant realist one, into reality per se.[41] Realist perceptions of the international have gradually become accepted as common sense, to the point that any critique against them has to be evaluated in terms of an already existing and objectivised world-view. There are powerful mechanisms of control precisely in this ability to determine meaning and rationality. 'Defining common sense', Smith thus argues, is 'the ultimate act of political power'.[42] It separates the possible from the impossible and directs the theory and practice of international relations on a particular path.

Dissent in global politics is precisely about redirecting this path. It is about interfering with the very manner in which international

---

[40] Doty, 'Aporia', esp. pp. 370–5.
[41] Jim George, *Discourses of Global Politics: A Critical (Re)Introduction to International Relations* (Boulder, Col.: Lynne Rienner, 1994), p. x; Richard Ashley, 'The Poverty of Neorealism', in *International Organization*, 38, 2, 1984, 225–86; Steve Smith, 'Positivism and Beyond', in S. Smith, K. Booth, and M. Zalewski (eds.), *International Theory: Positivism and Beyond* (Cambridge: Cambridge University Press, 1996), pp. 11–44.
[42] Smith, 'Positivism and Beyond', p. 13.

relations have been constituted, perceived and entrenched. The point, then, is not to 'rescue the exploration of identity from postmodernists',[43] but to explore questions of agency and identity in the context of an understanding of social dynamics that takes into account how ideas and practices mutually influence each other. This is to accept and deal with the recognition 'that our rationalisation of the international is itself constitutive of that practice'.[44] The purpose and potential of such an approach are well recognised at least since Robert Cox introduced a distinction between critical and problem-solving approaches to world politics. The latter, exemplified by realist and positivist perceptions of the international, take the prevailing structures of the world as the given framework for action. They study various aspects of the international system and address the problems that they create. The problem with such approaches, according to Cox, is that they not only accept, explicitly or implicitly, the existing order as given, but also, intentionally or not, sustain it.[45] Critical theories, by contrast, problematise the existing power relations and try to understand how they have emerged and how they are undergoing transformation. They engage, rather than circumvent, the multi-layered dynamics that make up transversal struggles. The notion of discourse, I shall demonstrate, is the most viable conceptual tool for such a task. It facilitates an exploration of the close linkages that exist between theory and practice. It opens up possibilities to locate and explore terrains of transversal dissent whose manifestations of agency are largely obscured, but nevertheless highly significant in shaping the course of contemporary global politics.

Disruptive writing, or how to approach transversal dissent in interdisciplinary terms

What has become clear, at this stage, is that my approach towards understanding transversal dissent diverges in significant ways from the manner in which international theory has dealt with questions of agency. My analysis does not take the state as a starting point. Neither

---

[43] Jeffery T. Checkel, 'The Constructivist Turn in International Relations Theory', in *World Politics*, 50, January 1998, p. 325.

[44] Steve Smith, 'The Self-Images of a Discipline: A Genealogy of International Relations Theory', in Booth and Smith, *International Relations Theory Today*, p. 3.

[45] Robert W. Cox, 'Social Forces, States and World Orders: Beyond International Relations Theory', in *Millennium*, 10, 2, 1981, pp. 128–9.

does it conceptualise agency in spatial terms or in relation to structures.

What follows may thus be called 'disruptive writing', a process that
Shapiro describes as tackling an issue not by way of well-rehearsed
debates, but through an alternative set of texts and narratives.[46] My
analysis juxtaposes familiar images of agency in global politics, such
as the collapse of the Berlin Wall, with relatively unusual sites of
investigation, such as Renaissance perceptions of dissent or contemporary poetics. The objective of this disruptive process is not to
declare alternative forms of knowledge true or even superior, but to
reveal what has been discussed above: that the nature of international
relations is intrinsically linked to the stories that are being told about
it, and that an unsettling of these stories has the potential to redirect
the theory and practice of global politics.

Disruptive writing disturbs. It inevitably creates anxieties. Max
Horkheimer observed half a century ago that widespread hostility
emerges as soon as theorists fail to limit themselves to verifying facts
and ordering them into familiar categories – categories which are
indispensable for the sustenance of entrenched forms of life.[47] Likewise, a disruptive reading of agency in global politics will not be met
with uniform approval. There are those who are concerned with maintaining the proper epistemological boundaries of a coherent and self-
contained discipline. Jack Levy, for instance, defends a distinct separation between the work of historians and international relations
scholars. The former, he points out, use theory 'primarily to structure
their interpretations of particular events'. The latter, by contrast, are
political scientists whose task is to 'formulate and test general theoretical propositions about relationships between variables and classes of
events'.[48] Ensuing methodological principles, which are strongly
influenced by a positivist understanding of social dynamics, have
often been discussed in the context of the level of analysis problem.
That is, they have been evoked to determine what is and is not a
proper subject-study of international relations. Barry Buzan convincingly points out that such approaches, which have become particularly influential in North American academia, fail to see that there are

---

[46] Shapiro, *Violent Cartographies*, pp. ix, 38.

[47] Max Horkheimer, *Traditionelle und kritische Theorie* (Frankfurt: Fischer Taschenbuch,
1992/1937), p. 249.

[48] Jack S. Levy, 'Too Important to Leave to the Other: History and Political Science in
the Study of International Relations', *International Security*, 22, 1, 1997, 32.

two different issues at stake. On one side are ontological questions that have to do with determining the proper units of analysis (individuals, state, system, etc.), and on the other side are epistemological questions that concern the proper research method, the manner in which one explains the units' behaviour.[49] By combining these two forms of delineating theoretical and analytical activities, the discipline of international relations has turned into a rather narrowly sketched field of inquiry. A focus that is all too often confined to states and systemic factors is further restricted by limits imposed on the types of knowledge that are considered legitimate to understand global politics. Consider how a group of highly influential scholars argue that the objective of proper research is 'to learn facts about the world' and that all hypotheses about them 'need to be evaluated empirically before they can make a contribution to knowledge'.[50] As soon as these epistemological boundaries are transgressed, anxieties emerge and defensive mechanisms become operative. The warning against such transgressions is loud and clear: 'A proposed topic that cannot be refined into a specific research project permitting valid descriptive or causal interference should be modified along the way or abandoned.'[51]

A disruptive reading and writing of the agency problematique in international theory combines a commitment to methodological pluralism with an interdisciplinary and multi-layered understanding of transversal struggles. International relations, then, is to be treated primarily as a broadly sketched theme of inquiry, rather than a disciplinary set of rules that determine where to locate and how to study global politics.

Gazing beyond the boundaries of disciplinary knowledge is necessary to open up questions of transversal dissent and human agency. Academic disciplines, by virtue of what they are, discipline the production and diffusion of knowledge. They establish the rules of intellectual exchange and define the methods, techniques and instruments that are considered proper for this purpose. Such conventions not only suggest on what ground things can be studied legitimately, but also decide what issues are worthwhile to be assessed in the first place.

---

[49] Buzan, 'The Level of Analysis Problem', pp. 203–5. See also Hollis and Smith, 'Beware of Gurus', pp. 394–5.
[50] Gary King, Robert O. Keohane and Sidney Verba, *Designing Social Inquiry: Scientific Interference in Qualitative Research* (Princeton: Princeton University Press, 1994), pp. 6, 16.
[51] Ibid., p. 18.

Thus, as soon as one addresses academic disciplines on their own terms, one has to play according to the rules of a discursive 'police' which is reactivated each time one speaks.[52] In this case, one cuts off any innovative thinking spaces that exist on the other side of this margin.

By consciously side-stepping highly specialised debates and by drawing upon less explored bodies of literature I seek to escape the constraining intellectual rules of conduct that have been established by academic disciplines and their framing of theoretical inquiries. The potential of such an approach to understanding transversal dissent lies in drawing together insights advanced by fields of knowledge that have so far existed in relative isolation from each other. Various authors, such as R.B.J. Walker, Chris Brown and Steve Smith, have already demonstrated how political theory and international theory are intrinsically linked.[53] The present analysis accepts this premise and further draws upon insights that stem from history, comparative politics, sociology, literary criticism, feminist theory, geography, cultural studies, philosophy, linguistics and poetics. Needless to say, to embark on such an interdisciplinary endeavour is to orient oneself in a vast array of knowledge fields. Relevant literatures are so extensive that difficult selections have to be made.

The very nature of the arguments presented in this book is thus intrinsically linked to the process of sorting out the discussions that are to be engaged from those that are not. As a result, there will be no sustained engagement with several themes one may expect to find in a book on dissent, human agency and global politics. For instance, there will be occasional references to, but no systematic analysis of the structure–agency debate that has come to take a prominent place in international theory. Such an engagement would have to revolve around issues that include the levels of analysis problem or the relative merits of conceptualising international structures and state behaviour. These discussions, even if conducted in a critical manner, would amount to replications of various dualisms, most notably the binary opposition between state and non-state actors, and between international and domestic spheres of inquiry.[54] By contrast, a disrupt-

---

[52] Michel Foucault, *L'Ordre du Discours* (Paris: Gallimard, 1971), p. 37.
[53] R.B.J. Walker, *Inside/outside: International Relations as Political Theory* (Cambridge: Cambridge University Press, 1993); Smith, 'The Self-Images of a Discipline', pp. 7–9; Chris Brown, *International Relations Theory: New Normative Approaches* (New York: Columbia University Press, 1992) p. 6.
[54] For a discussion of dualisms in international theory see, for instance, Ashley, 'Living on Border Lines', pp. 259–321; Campbell, 'Political Prosaics, Transversal Politics, and the Anarchical World', pp. 7–31.

ive and multi-disciplinary reading of transversal dissent is all about conceptualising global politics beyond the dualisms that have already disciplined our minds. Its task is to draw upon a novel set of theoretical and practical sources in order to explore the interconnected, multi-layered and constantly shifting nature of transversal struggles in global politics.

Outline

The introductory chapter that follows this prologue provides a rough map of my research itinerary. It outlines the logic of my approach, introduces the case studies, and discusses in more detail what is entailed in conceptualising human agency through a set of post-positivist lenses. What follows subsequently is divided into three main parts.

Part I (chapters 1–3) investigates the historical dimensions of popular dissent. It follows the dictum of a disruptive reading by starting neither with international theory nor with familiar sites of revolutionary ideologies. Instead, practices of dissent are traced back to a relatively unknown sixteenth-century French text, Étienne de la Boétie's *Anti-One*, or *Discourse of Voluntary Servitude*. This endeavour is genealogical insofar as it observes how, and with what consequences, a marginal and relatively localised idea has gradually given rise to practices of popular dissent that have taken on significant transversal dimensions. The analysis focuses on continuities and discontinuities during three historical epochs, the Renaissance, the Romantic period and the twentieth century. More specifically, the inquiry investigates (1) how this modern tradition has come to shape contemporary practices of dissent and (2) whether or not it remains adequate to understand the political dynamics that are unfolding in an increasingly complex and globalised world.

Part II (chapters 4–6) further explores these questions in the context of an influential transversal struggle in world politics: the events that led to the collapse of the Berlin Wall in 1989. Multiple readings of these events will scrutinise the transversal dynamics that were operative in between various sites of politics (local, national, intranational, transnational and international – to use state-centric terms). Emerging from this endeavour is a methodological move away from ahistoric modes of representing dissent towards a discursive understanding of power and human agency. Entailed in this shift is also an approach to social change that focuses less on spectacular revolutionary events and more on the slow transversal transformation of values that precedes them.

Part III (chapters 7–9) builds upon the insights gained by the previous two parts and portrays transversal dissent as working in discursive ways, that is, by transgressing political boundaries and interfering with the construction and reconstruction of societal values. Such a perspective creates opportunities to appreciate a range of alternative, hitherto largely unrecognised practices of resistance. A reading of East German dissident poetry serves as an example to illustrate the potential and limits of everyday forms of transversal dissent. By self-consciously stretching the boundaries of existing linguistic and political conventions, poetry reveals how it is possible to engender human agency – not by causing particular events, but by creating possibilities to think and act in more inclusive ways.

The conclusion reflects on what an appreciation of transversal dissent entails for our understanding of human agency in global politics. It emphasises, in particular, the need to conceptualise agency in a way that does justice to the transformative nature of global politics.

Finally, a note of caution about the structure of this book, and the manner in which it seeks to deal with circles of revealing and concealing. A structure is like a straitjacket. It is another form of framing. It protects a coherent and bounded whole. It paralyses thoughts and squeezes them, against their own inclination, into particular directions. Or so at least claims Wittgenstein, when justifying his preference for unstructured aphorisms.[55] The most central puzzles this book seeks to engage cannot be contained in water-tight compartments. They cannot be tackled chapter after chapter and be put to rest in proper order, one after the other. Some key dilemmas, like the search for a middle ground between objectivism and relativism, will cyclically reappear, penetrating the core of virtually every topic. Each chapter will have to discover anew the fine line between suffocating in the narrow grip of totalising knowledge claims and blindly roaming in a nihilistic world of absences. Hence, what follows is to be seen less as a linear progression towards a peak, but more as series of meditations, a circular journey around a cluster of pivotal transversal problematiques.

---

[55] Ludwig Wittgenstein, *Philosophische Untersuchungen*, in *Werkausgabe Band 1* (Frankfurt: Suhrkamp, 1993/1952), p. 231.

Introduction **Writing human agency after the death of God**

> God is dead; but given the way people are, there may still be caves for thousands of years in which his shadow will be shown. – And we – we still have to vanquish his shadow, too.[1]

The concept of human agency occupies a central position in the history of Western thought. From Aristotle onwards countless leading minds have philosophised how people may or may not be able to influence their social environment. Do our actions, intentional or not, bear upon our destiny? Or are we simply creatures of habit, blind followers of cultural and linguistic orders too large and too powerful to be swayed?

Today, the echoes of these questions resonate more than ever. Can there be human agency in an increasingly globalised and transversal world, an epoque of rapid change and blurring boundaries between nations, cultures, knowledges, realities? Who or what shapes the course of social dynamics at a moment when new communicative technologies constantly redefine time, space and the ways in which people relate to each other? Can shifting social designs and their designers be discerned at all?

These are difficult theoretical questions and they must be posed in an investigation that seeks to understand the role of transversal dissent in global politics. Human agency, this book argues, is a concept and a field of inquiry that should be retained despite the existence of a number of serious obstacles. But outlining the long and sometimes crooked path that leads to this position is far more intricate than

---

[1] Friedrich Nietzsche, *The Gay Science*, tr. W. Kaufmann (New York: Vintage Books, 1974/1882), § 108, p. 167 (translation altered).

merely presenting its affirmative endpoint. It requires a fundamental rethinking of what human agency is and how we could possibly understand it without imposing our preconceived ideas upon far more complex social phenomena. The present introductory chapter provides a rough map of the journey that emerged from this premise. It deals with the method and logic of my case studies, presents the major theoretical puzzles that lie ahead, and outlines how each chapter will in turn grapple with them.

The task of a genealogy of popular dissent

How to begin rethinking human agency in a way that does justice to the increasingly complex and interdependent nature of global politics today? How to scrutinise the effects of dissident practices that have come to transgress national boundaries? Martin Heidegger's study of Being offers some advice. Before even addressing the substantive aspects of this topic, Heidegger emphasises that we always already live in a preconceived understanding of what Being is, and that this understanding is part of the meaning of Being. He thus rejects an approach that relies upon an a priori notion of Being. Instead, he stresses that the question of Being must be posed by investigating the very process of posing the question of Being.[2]

Likewise, questions of human agency cannot be understood independently of how they have arisen in the first place. The concept of human agency is as elusive as the concept of Being. Human agency, accordingly, cannot be apprehended as part of a natural order of things, as something that exists out there, waiting to be unveiled through the right methodological tools. Human agency is, at least in part, determined by what is asked about it in the process of imbuing human action with socio-linguistic meaning.

An inquiry into dissent and human agency is thus a process that must begin by investigating how we have come to think about this issue. Expressed in Heideggerean terms, we must find out how, if we ask what *is* dissent, and what *is* human agency, we already have a certain preconceived understanding of the 'is'. Exploring this framing of questions is only possible in the context of an historical account. Heidegger's approach to this task takes the form of *Destruktion*, a process of deconstructing history, of disclosing what a tradition of

---

[2] Heidegger, *Sein und Zeit* (Tübingen: Max Niemeyer, 1993/1927), § 2, pp. 5–11.

thought transmits and how it does so.[3] While accepting the overall spirit of this endeavour, my own inquiry relies more upon Nietzsche's method of genealogy, expanded and popularised through the work of Michel Foucault. [4]

Genealogies attempt to trace the processes by which we have come to accept our world as natural and meaningful. They are historical investigations into the ideas and events that have shaped our thinking, speaking and acting. The task of genealogies, however, is not to discover a single meaning in history or an authentic origin, an *Ursprung*. Nietzsche employs the terms *Entstehung* and *Herkunft* to explain the task of genealogies. These terms do not indicate an authentic starting point, a source to which everything can be traced back. Genealogies, by contrast, focus on the process by which we have constructed origins and given meaning to particular representations of the past, representations that continuously guide our daily lives and set clear limits to political and social options.

Genealogies have become a widely accepted method of inquiry into various domains of global politics. To name just a few examples: Jean Elshtain has examined practices of warfare and observed how patriarchal discourses have assigned women the task of life givers and men the one of life takers, despite empirical cases that confound these assignments.[5] James Der Derian has reread the history of diplomacy because, as he argues, its contemporary practices cannot be understood without knowledge of its origins.[6] Authors such as R.B.J. Walker, Jens Bartelson, Cindy Weber and Michael Shapiro have in one way or another scrutinised how centuries of modern political discourses have shaped the concept of sovereignty and entrenched rigid boundaries between domestic and international spheres.[7]

[3] Ibid., §6, p. 20.
[4] See, in particular, Nietzsche, *Zur Genealogie der Moral* (Frankfurt: Insel Taschenbuch, 1991/1977); and Foucault, 'Nietzsche, Genealogy, History', in P Rabinow (ed.), *The Foucault Reader*, tr. D.F. Bouchard and S. Simon (New York, Pantheon Books, 1984/1971), pp. 76–100.
[5] Jean Bethke Elshtain, *Women and War* (New York: Basic Books, 1987).
[6] James Der Derian, *On Diplomacy: A Genealogy of Western Estrangement* (Oxford: Basil Blackwell, 1987).
[7] R.B.J. Walker, *Inside/Outside: International Relations as Political Theory* (Cambridge: Cambridge University Press, 1993); Jens Bartelson, *A Genealogy of Sovereignty* (Cambridge: Cambridge University Press, 1995); Cynthia Weber, *Simulating Sovereignty: Intervention, the State and Symbolic Exchange* (Cambridge: Cambridge University Press, 1995); Michael J. Shapiro, *Violent Cartographies: Mapping Cultures of War* (Minneapolis: University of Minnesota Press, 1997).

What, then, can a genealogy of dissent tell us about human agency in contemporary global politics? A great deal, for questions of agency are above all questions of power relations. And power relations are best understood, Michel Foucault argues convincingly, by examining specific attempts that are made to uproot them.[8] Dissent thus becomes a field of inquiry that has the potential to reveal far more about power and agency than one may think initially. The process of undermining authority says as much, for instance, about the values and functioning of the existing social and political order as it does about the urge to break out of it.

The first part of this book thus engages in a genealogical inquiry that seeks to understand how we have come to think about dissident practices such as street demonstrations and civil disobedience campaigns. In keeping with the principles of a disruptive reading that is essential to a genealogy, the analysis does not begin with historical texts or practices that are normally recognised as lying at the origin of dissent or current international politics. Instead, it commences with a relatively unfamiliar Renaissance treatise, Étienne de la Boétie's *Discourse of Voluntary Servitude*,[9] known also under its alternative and perhaps more adequate title of *Contr'un*, or *Anti-One*.[10] La Boétie claimed, in 1552, that any form of rule is dependent upon popular consent. In the context of its articulation, sixteenth-century France, this was a radical claim. But the idea that people hold the key to social change, which is implied in la Boétie's treatise, was also part of a larger humanist movement that started to challenge the prevalent medieval order. In this sense, the *Anti-One* symbolised the re-emergence of the concept of human agency, which had been celebrated in ancient Greece, but was largely pushed into obscurity during the Middle Ages.

Although la Boétie's *Anti-One* is a relatively unknown text today, it played a significant role in shaping practices of popular dissent during

---

[8] Foucault, 'The Subject and Power', in H.L. Dreyfus and P. Rabinow (eds.), *Michel Foucault: Beyond Structuralism and Hermeneutics* (New York: Harvester Wheatsheaf, 1982), pp. 210–11.

[9] Étienne de la Boétie, *Discours de la Servitude Volontaire*, ed. P. Bonnefon in *Oeuvres Complètes* (Genève: Slatkine Reprints, 1967/1552).

[10] La Boétie's supporter, the famous essayist Michel de Montaigne, said about his friend's text that 'it is a discourse that he named *Voluntary Servitude*, but those who have not known him have since renamed it properly *Anti-One*'. This practice has largely remained intact until today. Montaigne, *Essais* (Paris: Gallimard, 1950), book I, chapter 28, p. 219.

some of the preceding centuries.[11] Comparable to Niccolò Machiavelli's humanist texts, which became catalysts for the burgeoning literature on international relations and the art of governing the state,[12] la Boétie's more obscure *Anti-One* gave rise to a body of literature that deals with radical resistance to existing forms of authority. Chapters 1–3 carefully retrace the history of this tradition of dissent. The task is to observe how la Boétie's text was interpreted at various historical intersections and how these interpretations have given rise to currently influential forms of popular dissent.

A genealogical task cannot be fulfilled without attention to detail. Indeed, genealogies are all about detail, about the meticulous collection of a multitude of source materials.[13] Shifts in historical consciousness and their bearing upon political practice cannot be assessed adequately through sweeping statements about philosophical trends. Such shifts do not occur as factual events that can be understood on their own terms. They are shaped by the ways in which historical observers interpret events around them.[14] A genealogy of popular dissent cannot be separated from the individuals who, in various time periods, ruminated about the subject in question. This is why I examine closely the work of several authors who wrote directly or indirectly in the wake of la Boétie's *Anti-One*; among them are Michel de Montaigne, Félicité de Lamennais and, as the legacy of this French text grew more international, Henry David Thoreau, Leo Tolstoy, Mohandas Gandhi, Martin Luther King Jr and Gene Sharp. What is human agency for them? How does dissent function? Who is endowed with the capacity of agent? What values are implied in these respective views and how did they differ from other, more dominant approaches at the time? These are the questions to be asked of the la Boétien tradition in its various evolutionary stages from the sixteenth century to the present.

[11] La Boétie still featured prominently in Pierre Mesnard's path-breaking work on early modern thought, *L'Essor de la Philosophie Politique au XVIe Siècle* (Paris: J. Vrin, 1951/1935), pp. 389–406. By contrast, many contemporary historians of political thought do not deal with the influence of la Boétie. His work barely warrants a mention, for instance, in Quentin Skinner's influential *The Foundations of Modern Political Thought* (Cambridge: Cambridge University Press, 1978).
[12] See Michel Foucault, 'Governmentality', in G. Burchell *et al.* (eds.), *The Foucault Effect: Studies in Governmentality* (London: Harvester Wheatsheaf, 1991/1978), pp. 87–104.
[13] Foucault, 'Nietzsche, Genealogy, History', pp. 76–7.
[14] Paul de Man, *Romanticism and Contemporary Criticism* (Baltimore: Johns Hopkins University Press, 1993), pp. 95–6.

The la Boétiean tradition, which developed at times in a close relationship with anarchist thought, is of course not the only story about
popular dissent in the modern period. Countless other and often
better-known stories could be narrated too. There are influential liberal and Marxist narratives of resistance and social change. There are
structural and functional approaches to revolutionary upheavals, psychological analyses of the crowd or, more recently, inquiries into social
movements.[15] There are even more investigations into the nature of
human agency. Virtually every philosopher and theorist has dealt
with this issue in one way or another. Ensuing ruminations range
from questions of intentionality, causality and responsibility to
reflections about the evaluation of desire or the moral dimensions of
human action. All of these different stories are part of how we have
come to perceive dissent and human agency today. Rather than trying
to synthesise all of them in a sweeping intellectual *tour de force* – a
task that would be doomed from the start – a genealogy must aim at
appreciating the complexities and multiplicities of our past. Its power
lies in telling different stories about our world, in making room for
voices that have been silenced by conventional historiography. In this
sense a genealogy reveals, as Michael Shapiro notes, the arbitrariness
of the constitution of meaning 'by producing unfamiliar representations of persons, collectivities, places, and things, and by isolating the
moments in which the more familiar representations have merged'.[16]

The la Boétiean story is one of many that have been laid to rest in
the graveyards of our collective memory. It is a story about dissent
that is worth unearthing, worth being retold in a different light – not
to be exhaustive, not to be true or even representative, but to

---

[15] For key contributions to the sociology of action see Talcott Parsons, *The Structure of
Social Action* (Glencoe, Ill: The Free Press, 1949/1937); Alain Touraine, *Sociologie de
l'Action* (Paris: Éditions du Seuil, 1965); Jürgen Habermas, *Theorie des kommunikativen
Handelns* (Frankfurt: Suhrkamp, 1988). For analysis of the psychological and social
impact unleashed by the gathering of large crowds see Elias Canetti, *Masse und Macht*
(Frankfurt: Fischer, 1994/1980); Gustave le Bon, *Psychologie des Foules* (Paris: Félix
Alcan, 1911) and George Rude, *The Crowd in History* (London: Lawrence And Wishart,
1981). Among the many works that deal with collective action and new social movements are Alberto Melucci, *Nomads of the Present* (London: Hutchinson Radius, 1989);
Mancur Olson, *The Logic of Collective Action* (Cambridge, Mass.: Harvard University
Press, 1965); Sidney Tarrow, *Power in Movement: Social Movements, Collective Action
and Politics* (New York: Cambridge University Press, 1994); Charles Tilly, *From Mobilization to Revolution* (Reading, Mass.: Addison-Wesley, 1978); and Alain Touraine, *La
Voix et le Regard* (Paris: Seuil, 1978).
[16] Michael J. Shapiro, *Reading the Postmodern Polity: Political Theory as Textual Practice*
(Minneapolis: University of Minnesota Press, 1992), p. 2.

problematise what has been constituted as unproblematic, to illustrate the framing of dominant narratives, to scrutinise how and with what consequences we have come to think about popular dissent today.

Modern continuities: the recurring search for foundational authority

Genealogy, Jens Bartelson states, 'must start from an analysis of the present, and explain the formation of the present in terms of its past'.[17] The prologue began this task, but an additional brief look ahead into the results of my genealogical inquiry is necessary before the remaining course of rethinking dissent and agency in global politics can be mapped out.

The la Boétiean theory and practice of popular dissent proved to be not nearly as subversive as its outspoken anti-authoritarian message suggested at first sight. While standing in radical opposition to dominant ideas and political practices, it shared with them similar basic assumptions about the world. In a mirror image of mainstream modern discourses, the theory and practice of popular dissent has been characterised by the recurring inability to come to terms with what Nietzsche called the death of God – the disappearance, at the end of the medieval period, of a generally accepted world-view that provided a stable ground from which it was possible to assess nature, knowledge, common values, truth, politics; in short, life itself. The la Boétiean tradition of dissent was one of many humanist attempts to find replacements for the fallen God, to search for new foundations from which humanity could safely reflect upon itself and the world. Details on this will follow later. Suffice it at this point to mention that the compulsion to anchor perceptions of popular dissent in Archimedean foundations took various superseding forms. Painted in broad strokes they include: an unbounded Renaissance trust in the ability of human beings to elevate themselves to the measure of all things (chapter 1); an Enlightenment belief in reason and science; a romantic reassertion of human agency grounded in the notion of an autonomous Self (chapter 2); and more contemporary endeavours to master the question of popular dissent by reducing complex social dynamics to a few universal and empirically assessable laws (chapter 3).

These superseding attempts to ground an understanding of the

---

[17] Bartelson, *A Genealogy of Sovereignty*, pp. 7–8.

world in stable foundations are not just linearly unfolding events, historical epoques with a clear beginning and end. They are, rather, overlapping layers of contemporary consciousness, sets of carefully crafted lenses that are still used to look at today's world. This is why an investigation into their formation is of utmost importance to gain a more inclusive view of dissent and human agency in contemporary global politics.

The larger picture that emerges from such a genealogy of popular dissent is, of course, neither new nor particularly surprising. The right to criticism has been recognised, at least since Hegel, as a key feature of modernity. Thus, the existence of strong similarities between radical dissident movements and the political practices they oppose only confirms the larger boundaries that surround modernity's celebration of diversity. And that these boundaries are drawn, at least in part, by the inability to come to terms with the death of God, has been discussed extensively since Nietzsche first tried to capture the modern condition with this metaphor. William Connolly is among those who have most convincingly elucidated the long struggle in a world where there is no longer a God that serves as a unifying centre for humanity. He shows that while successive attempts to ground certainty in other external sources run into grave difficulties, the insistence that such foundations must be found has remained a prominent modern theme. This quest for a grounded and perfectly ordered world, Connolly argues, can only be sustained by treating everything that does not fit into this order as irrational, perverse, in need of punishment or destruction.[18] It is self-evident that systems of exclusion emerge from such practices, even if they engage, as the la Boétiean tradition does, in the very attempt to resist domination.

Postmodern discontinuities: transversal dissent and processes of globalisation

While displaying a strikingly consistent attachment to key modern themes, the practice of popular dissent is also characterised by strong discontinuities. What began as a rhetorical idea in Renaissance France and later became a series of localised forms of resistance eventually turned into a tradition of dissent that acquired global dimensions. The

[18] William E. Connolly, *Political Theory and Modernity* (Ithaca: Cornell University Press, 1993/1988), p. 13–14.

writings of Thoreau, Tolstoy and Gandhi, in particular, have contributed to an ever-more widespread application of la Boétiean principles of resistance. By the twentieth century, popular dissent began to play an important role in virtually all parts of the world, from independence struggles in South Africa and India to the civil rights movements in the United States or the velvet revolutions in East-Central Europe.

But the practice of popular dissent has not only spread beyond national boundaries, it has also changed in nature. Processes of globalisation have radically transformed the manner in which dissent engenders human agency.

Globalisation is an important and much debated contemporary phenomenon. At the minimum it signifies 'a coalescence of varied transnational processes and domestic structures, allowing the economy, politics, culture, and ideology of one country to penetrate another'.[19] For some commentators, though, globalisation has far greater implications. It is a process that has fundamentally reorganised the relationship between space and time.[20] Advances in economic, technological and informational domains have led to what could be called a 'deterritorialisation' of the world – a series of transformations that are characterised, according to Gearóid Ó Tuathail, by the diminishing power of states.[21] Deterritorialisation is particularly far-reaching in the domains of finance and production, but it is perhaps with regard to the flow of information that processes of globalisation most evidently transgress the boundaries of the territorial state system:

> [G]lobal political space is skimmed twenty-four hours a day and produced as a stream of televisual images featuring a terrorist attack here, a currency crisis there, and a natural disaster elsewhere. Global space becomes political space. Being there live is everything. The local is instantly global, the distant immediately close. Place-specific political struggles become global televisual experiences, experiences structured by an entertainmentized gaze in search of the dramatic and the immediate.[22]

There is considerable debate about the nature of these phenomena and

---

[19] James H. Mittelman, 'The Dynamics of Globalization', in Mittelman (ed.), *Globalization: Critical Reflections* (Boulder, Col.: Lynne Rienner, 1996), p. 3.

[20] See, for instance, Paul Virilio, *Vitesse et Politique* (Paris: Éditions Galilée, 1977); David Harvey, *The Condition of Postmodernity* (Oxford/Cambridge, MA: Blackwell, 1989).

[21] Gearóid Ó Tuathail, *Critical Geopolitics: The Politics of Writing Global Space* (London: Routledge, 1996), pp. 228–9.

[22] Ibid., pp. 250, 228–9.

the extent to which they have led to a qualitative transformation of global politics. Chapter 3 will engage some of the ensuing discussions. Indisputable, though, is the fact that processes of globalisation have substantially altered the functioning of popular dissent.

As remarked at the outset of this book, dissident practices no longer take place in a purely local context. The presence of global media networks now provide a protest march or a civil disobedience campaign with the potential of an immediate worldwide audience. Dissent has become transversal in nature, for it now has the ability to transgress the political and mental boundaries erected by existing practices of international relations. The local, in Ó Tuathail's words, is instantly global. The ensuing dynamics, of course, call into question the very spatial organisation of the interstate system, that is, the key pillars of 'state sovereignty, territorial integrity and community identity'.[23]

Once one has recognised the transversal nature of contemporary global politics a number of questions immediately arise. The most obvious one is whether or not a long tradition of modern thought can still adequately account for political dynamics that are unfolding in a fundamentally transformed global space. More specifically, does the la Boétiean vision of human agency, which is based on an ahistoric and spatial understanding of relationships between ruler and ruled, remain adequate to assess the changing nature of dissent in a media-infused contemporary world?

An instance of transversal dissent: reading and rereading the collapse of the Berlin Wall

Part II of this book addresses some of these and other questions that have emerged in the context of the genealogical inquiry conducted in part I. For this purpose the focus rests on a close scrutiny of a specific contemporary transversal struggle: the events that led to the disintegration of East Germany and, eventually, to a transition into a new, post-Cold War international order.

The massive street demonstrations that preceded the collapse of the Berlin Wall were undoubtedly key manifestations of popular dissent. They may, at least at first sight, also be read as endorsements of the la Boétiean image of human agency. During the autumn of 1989, after decades of harsh authoritarian rule, hundreds of thousands of East

---

[23] Ibid., p. 230.

Germans took to the streets and demanded political reform. Day after day, their monophonic battle cry 'we are the people' echoed throughout the country, in East Berlin, Dresden, Leipzig, Karl-Marx-Stadt and many other cities. These protests attracted immediate world-wide attention and triggered a series of discursive maelstroms that defied the political logic of national boundaries. The effects were startling: one of the most repressive regimes in East-Central Europe collapsed like a house of cards. Jürgen Habermas, one of Germany's best known philosophers and political commentators, remarked that 'the presence of large masses gathering in squares and mobilizing on the streets managed, astonishingly, to disempower a regime that was armed to the teeth'.[24] The scenes of common citizens walking through the Berlin Wall remain one of the key images – televised around the world – that symbolised the end of the Cold War and the transition into a new era of international politics. A sense of optimism was in the air. It was a time of crumbling walls and falling dictators. It was a time of turmoil and change. It was a time when dissent not only transgressed, but also uprooted the spatial constitution of global politics. Decades of entrenched political structures were swept away by popular resistance. The romantic subject re-emerged, inflated with unbounded confidence. History was once more open to be shaped by human agency.

But was all this really the result of popular dissent? Can the East German revolution be explained, for instance, by the la Boétiean proposition that any form of rule, no matter how authoritarian, crumbles as soon as people withdraw their consent? Does human agency work so directly and so consensually? Can it be understood in the context of spatial and relational linkages between ruler and ruled?

A critical look at the events in East Germany reveals a much more complex picture (chapter 4). A whole range of transversal factors – political maelstroms that unravelled in-between local, domestic and international spheres – contributed to the fall of the regime. The political contexts within which the events unfolded were far too intricate to be assessed by a parsimonious model of power relations, yet alone by a grand theory of popular dissent or a rigid spatial separation into different levels of analysis. The events that led to the fall of the Berlin Wall are best characterised as a series of diverse but interconnected occurrences that transgressed the spatial and political givenness of

---

[24] Jürgen Habermas, 'The Rectifying Revolution and the Need for New Thinking on the Left', in *New Left Review*, 183, 1990, 7.

both East German and Cold War international politics. This reading is, of course, consistent with an already widespread Foucauldian position that views power as working in a diffused and stratified way, constantly intersecting with the production and diffusion of knowledge.[25] What, then, are the consequences that emerge from such a transversal interpretation?

At first sight, the East German revolution seems to vindicate a well-known image of popular dissent: a spectacular unfolding of social change through great events. But such events are often far less potent than their dramatic appearance suggests. This is not to say that the East German revolution was ineffective. It did, after all, uproot a dictatorial regime, tear town the Iron Curtain and redraw the boundaries of Cold War geopolitics. But in doing so it also entrenched more subtle and persistent forms of domination that are embedded in discursive practices. A second, gender-oriented reading of the events of 1989 reveals a different picture (chapter 5). Despite their unusually active participation in the protest movement, East German women suffered disproportionately from the subsequent process of unification. For them the democratic dawn ushered in drastic setbacks in such realms as reproductive rights, access to day care or employment opportunities. A revived civil society, which identifies men with the public and women with the private sphere, further increased the masculinist character of post-Wall German politics. Whether or not other emerging benefits for women will outweigh these setbacks in the long run remains to be seen. At this point, however, the East German revolution underlines that patriarchy is a discursively embedded system of exclusion that cannot simply be overthrown by popular dissent.

A transversal interpretation of the East German revolution suggests that we must understand issues of dissent, agency and social change from a variety of different perspectives. Chapter 6 thus reads the collapse of the Berlin Wall from yet another vantage point – one that focuses not on the role of spectacular popular dissent, but on the slow transformation of values that preceded them. Transversal dynamics now become particularly evident, for one notices how a porous Iron Curtain permitted a constant cross-border flow of information, and how the ensuing presence of international media sources influenced the thoughts and actions of the East German populace. Such a

---

[25] See Michel Foucault, *Power/Knowledge: Selected Interviews and Other Writings 1972–1977*, ed. Colin Gordon (New York: Pantheon, 1980).

discourse-oriented approach to power and social change creates various possibilities to rethink human agency. It not only recasts agency as a transversal process of interfering with the constitution of social and spatial practices, but also resists the temptation of subsuming unique features into a universalised and foundationalist narrative. But as soon as this thinking space is ripped open, new puzzles and dilemmas start to flood through its gaping doors.

The problem of grounding an understanding of human agency: (1) the usefulness of the concept of discourse

A transversal interpretation of the collapse of the Berlin Wall implies that practices of dissent in global politics should be viewed in discursive terms. This is to say that dissent exerts human agency not primarily through localised spatial dynamics, but through a transformation of values that takes place across a variety of political territories. Viewing dissent in discursive terms opens up possibilities to recognise practices of resistance that have hitherto been obscured. The third and last part of this study explores their potential and limits. But before such a task can begin, a number of difficult conceptual questions must be confronted. How to lift a concept of human agency out of a genealogical critique? How to ground thought, critique, action, norms, transversal life itself, if there are no universal values that can enable such a process of grounding? How to retain a positive approach to the problem of agency without having to anchor one's position in stable foundations?

Evoking the notion of discourse as a way of investigating the framing of global politics often elicits suspicion. Is discourse not merely a faddish term, destined to wax and wane with fleeting intellectual trends of the postmodern and poststructural kind? Does the concept of discourse, as many fear, reduce the world to playful interactions of texts and meanings that are void of any relevance to the so-called 'real', the concrete daily aspects of our lives?

These questions are being posed very often today, and they must be taken seriously. The prologue has already shown how many international relations theorists are sceptical of authors who employ the concept of discourse. They fear that such an approach cannot but lead, in Robert Keohane's representative words, to 'an intellectual and moral disaster'.[26] This scepticism goes far beyond the domain of international relations. Critics of so-called postmodern scholarship often draw attention to the pitfalls of discursive approaches, particularly their alleged inability to speak of agents and agency. Seyla Benhabib represents many concerned scholars when arguing that a postmodern position mistakenly dissolves the subject into chains of signification that lie beyond human influence.[27] We would find ourselves in a conceptual order dominated by overarching discursive systems. People would be reduced to mere bystanders, passive, impotent, irrelevant. Crushed into oblivion. But is this elusive spectre called postmodernism really so menacing that it must be warded off at any cost? Is it leading us into an apocalyptic world in which 'man would be erased', as a famous Foucauldian passage speculates, 'like a face drawn in the sand at the edge of the sea'?[28]

Taking on these important critiques of postmodern theory is a tall order. There are no easy answers to the above questions, and there are certainly no ready-made solutions. Each chapter will address these complex questions, and each will seek to demonstrate in one way or another how a discursive understanding of transversal dissent can contribute to a conceptualisation of human agency in global politics. At this stage a short illustration, taken from a rather unexpected source, must suffice to underline the usefulness of discourse theory. Consider how no other than Plato works with an implied concept of discourse, even though his search for an ahistoric form of truth is often taken to counter Nietzschean and Foucauldian elaborations on the power-knowledge nexus. Consider the strategy through which Plato dismisses his chief philosophical rivals, the Sophists. *The Republic* is divided into ten so-called books, all of which revolve around dialogues. Peculiar about this structure is that only book I, in which Plato refutes his Sophist rival Thrasymachus, is set against a larger public. In all of the remaining books Glaucon and Adeimantus are the only respondents. Cornelius Castoriadis argues that this crucial difference is to be explained by Plato's inability to dismiss the Sophists through rational argumentation.[29] Thrasymachus' claim that 'justice is

---

[26] Robert O. Keohane, 'International Relations Theory: Contributions of a Feminist Standpoint', *Millennium*, 18, 2, 1989, p. 89.

[27] Seyla Benhabib, 'Feminism and Postmodernism', in *Feminist Contentions* (New York: Routledge, 1995), p. 20.

[28] Michel Foucault, *Les Mots et les Choses* (Paris: Gallimard, 1966), p. 398.

[29] Cornelius Castoriadis, 'Ontologie et Anthropologie', seminar presented at the École Normale Supérieure, Paris, 26 October 1995.

the interest of the stronger' cannot be dismissed on objective grounds by Plato's position that 'justice is goodness'.[30] Hence Plato needed a cheering public to support his critique, he needed a discursive context that rendered his position rational. Thrasymachus is portrayed as wild, noisy, offensive, irrational. Plato then strengthened his position in the dialogues by discursive reinforcements from the gallery, like 'Glaucon and the others backed up my request' or 'it was clear to everyone that his [Thrasymachus] definition of justice had been reversed'.[31] Once the discursive order and its corresponding power relations were established, at the end of book I, there was no more need for a gallery. Plato could go on and dismiss on newly established rational grounds what was left of the Sophist challenge.

Discursive dynamics in the realm of global politics function not unlike those in Plato's rhetorical dialogues. Foreign policy decisions, for instance, are not taken based on purely objective grounds, they are formed, articulated and justified in relation to a set of transversally recognised values that render these decisions rational – or irrational, depending on the issue and the perspective.

Transversal forms of dissent are the thoughts and actions that interfere with these rationalisations. They are discursive in nature, but they do not necessarily operate in a void of values. Discursive interventions do not preclude formulations of critique or advancements of specific political positions. A discursive understanding of transversal struggles does, however, engender the need for a more differentiated approach to the problem of anchoring thought and justifying action.

The problem of grounding an understanding of human agency: (2) the role of contingent foundations

We know of proclamations that herald the return of the actor.[32] Most of them were advanced against the determinism of structuralist scholarship. Structuralist positions, be it in international theory or in scholarship about revolutions, locate the emergence of social change not in agents and their actions, but in the structural conditions within which their behaviour is confined. Revolutionary change is said to be

---

[30] Plato, *The Republic*, tr. D. Lee (London: Penguin, 1987/1955), pp. 90, 95.
[31] Ibid., pp. 74–84.
[32] Most notably Alain Touraine, *Le Retour de l'Acteur* (Paris: Fayard, 1984).

dependent not upon conscious subjectivity, but upon the underlying logic of functional and structural necessity.[33]

Parallel to this defence of the actor against structural determinism I attempt to salvage the notion of human agency from postmodern annihilations of the subject. However, I advance this position not against, but *through* the body of knowledge referred to, in the largest sense, as postmodernism. I elaborate what could be called a postmodern position on human agency, except that I discard the actual term postmodernism as an unfortunate misnomer. It is misleading in designating a new historical epoch, not only because we have hardly transgressed the parameters of modernity, but also because the act of compartmentalising history expresses an inherently modern urge to control our environment. The term postmodernism may be more useful to indicate a certain epistemological or ontological stance. Yet, many of the authors who are labelled postmodern, such as Foucault, Derrida, Deleuze or Cixous, do not actually use this term. And those who do barely have enough in common to be lumped together into the same category. If anything unites them, it is the acceptance of difference and the ensuing willingness to come to terms with the death of God.

Affirming from negation and grounding an understanding of human agency in nothingness is not as problematic as it may appear at first sight. Judith Butler has demonstrated this convincingly. For her, the recognition that power pervades all aspects of society, including the position of the critic, does not necessarily lead to a nihilistic relativism. It merely shows that political closure occurs through attempts to establish foundational norms that lie beyond power. Likewise, to reopen this political domain is not to do away with foundations as such, but to acknowledge their contingent character, to act with more awareness of their function, to illuminate what they authorise, exclude and foreclose.[34]

One must come to terms with how the subject and its agency are

---

[33] Representative are Barrington Moore, *Social Origins of Dictatorship and Democracy* (Boston: Beacon Press, 1966) and Theda Skocpol, *States and Social Revolutions* (Cambridge: Cambridge University Press, 1979). Among the most influential structuralist positions in international theory are K.N. Waltz, *Theory of International Politics* (Reading, Mass.: Addison-Wesley, 1979) and Immanuel Wallerstein, *The Modern World-System*, vols. I and II (New York: Academic Press, 1974 and 1980).

[34] Judith Butler, 'Contingent Foundations: Feminism and the Question of 'Postmodernism'', in J. Butler and J.W. Scott (eds.), *Feminists Theorize the Political* (New York: Routledge, 1992), pp. 3–7.

constituted and framed by specific regimes of power. But this is not the end of human agency. Quite to the contrary. Butler argues persuasively that 'the constituted character of the subject is the very precondition of its agency'.[35] To appreciate the practical relevance of this claim one must investigate the possibilities for agency that arise out of existing webs of power and discourse. One must scrutinise how social change can be brought about by a reworking of the power regimes that constitute our subjectivity.[36]

It is in this constantly shifting mesh of power, discourse and dissent that I ground my own attempt to rethink human agency in global politics. This approach explicitly recognises the transversal nature of contemporary life, the manner in which dynamics that evolve in various political spheres, from the local to the global, are intrinsically linked with each other. It is an approach that explicitly engages transversal struggles in a way that goes past the levels of analysis problem which has come to frame current understandings of international relations. But what happens if we try to grasp our elusive and multi-layered subject status, and build a notion of human agency upon contingent foundations? How to deal with the urge to order and control our lives? How to avoid superimposing preconceived ideas, inadequate as they are, upon a set of highly complex and maybe incomprehensible transversal phenomena? How to act on the Wittgensteinean warning 'to say no more than we know'? [37]

The problem of grounding an understanding of human agency: (3) 'how to say no more than we know'

The present rethinking of transversal dissent and human agency is anchored not in a systematic theory, but in a specification of what Michel de Certeau called 'operational schemes'.[38] Attempts to establish a systematic theory of human action will always run the risk of objectifying the elusive subject they are trying to capture. A theory is

---

[35] Ibid., p. 12.
[36] Ibid., p. 13.
[37] Ludwig Wittgenstein, *The Blue and Brown Books: Preliminary Studies for the 'Philosophical Investigations'* (New York: Harper Torchbooks, 1964), p. 45.
[38] Michel de Certeau, *Arts de Faire*, vol. I of *L'Invention du Quotidien* (Paris: Gallimard, 1990/1980), p. 51.

a method of delineation. It freezes what should be understood in its fluidity.

An approach that specifies operational schemes recognises these limits to cognition. Instead of establishing a new and better theory of agency, it is content with formulating a framework that facilitates understanding of how human agency is incessantly constituted and reconstituted in the context of transversal struggles. Expressed in de Certeau's language, one must comprehend forms of action in the context of their regulatory environment. Such an approach departs from ways in which traditional philosophy (and, by extension, international theory) has framed the understanding of human action. This framing process has revolved around three ways of explaining action: teleological, causal and intentional.[39] My analysis breaks with most elements that are entailed in this mode of analysis. It does not assume that agency can be assessed only by establishing links between means and ends. It does not assume that every form of agency needs an identifiable agent that causes an identifiable outcome. It does not assume that agency occurs only if it stands in a relationship with a declared intention.

What is left of the concept of human agency if one no longer relies upon causal, teleological and intentional explanations? The Interlude situated between chapters 7 and 8 deals with this question at a conceptual level. Its objective is to outline a framework that facilitates an understanding of the discursive conditions that are necessary for the exertion of human agency. From this vantage point, the most potent forms of transversal dissent operate in tactical, rather than strategic ways. They move along an indeterminate trajectory, transgress political boundaries and slowly transform values. They becomes visible and effective only through maturation over time and space.

A further deconstruction of the notion of discourse is necessary to appreciate the unfolding of transversal dissent through tactic and temporality. Despite their power to frame the world, discourses are not monolithic forces that crush everything in sight. They are often thin, unstable, fragmented. They contain cracks. By moving from epistemological to ontological levels of analysis, the inquiry explores the ways

---

[39] See Rüdiger Bubner, *Handlung, Sprache und Vernunft: Grundbegriffe praktischer Philosophie* (Frankfurt: Suhrkamp, 1982/1976), pp. 125–56. This tripartite mode of analysis has also become central to constructivist approaches to questions of agency in international relations. See Alexander Wendt, 'The Agent–Structure Problem in International Relations Theory', *International Organization*, 41 (1987), 364.

in which people can resist discursive domination (chapter 7). Human beings have hyphenated identities. Furthermore, these identities are not frozen in time, but part of a constantly unfolding process of becoming. By tapping into these multiple and shifting dimensions of Being, individuals are able to think and act beyond the narrow confines of the established discursive order. They engage in everyday forms of resistance that allow them to reshape the social context in which they are embedded. Such forms of discursive dissent can be found in countless seemingly insignificant daily acts of defiance. They transform values, transgress boundaries and may eventually promote social change far more effectively than the so-called great events of international politics.

An instance of transversal dissent: linguistic interferences with the social and spatial constitution of East German politics

Part III of this book scrutinises everyday forms of resistance that appear once one views global politics as a series of transversal and discursively driven struggles. More specifically, the focus rests on examining forces of domination and resistance entailed in one of our most daily activities, speaking and writing (chapter 8).

Language penetrates all aspects of transversal struggles. Whatever we think and do is framed by the language within which these acts are carried out. Hence, an engagement with the philosophy of language must be part of an adequate approach to questions of agency in global politics, especially if this approach rests upon a view of human life as constituted by self-understanding.[40] From such a vantage point language must be seen not as an image of the world or a way of representing realities, but, as Wittgenstein's famous dictum holds, as 'part of an activity, a way of life'.[41] This position has far-reaching consequences. If language expresses a particular way of life it is also responsible, at least in part, for the constitution of this way of life. Human agency cannot take place outside language, in some pre- or extra-linguistic realm. It can only take place through language.

[40] See Charles Taylor, *Human Agency and Language* (Cambridge: Cambridge University Press, 1995/1985), pp. 3–4, 9.
[41] Ludwig Wittgenstein, *Philosophische Untersuchungen*, in *Werkausgabe Band 1* (Frankfurt: Suhrkamp, 1993/1952), p. 250, § 23.

Expressed differently: languages are not just frameworks to assess actions. They are themselves forms of action.

There are, of course, countless domains in which language interferes with transversal struggles. We live at a time when ever-increasing communicative capabilities account for an ever-shrinking globe. Moreover, transversal politics revolves not only around interactions between various national languages, but also between different types of speech. When a liberal, a realist, a defence technician or a peace movement member describes the same event, they use very different languages to interpret the realities they see. Each of these languages has its own set of rules. Each embodies a world-view that implicitly promotes certain social values and certain political, ethical and spatial perceptions of global politics. The clash between these forms of speech is the domain where domination and resistance is carried out. It is the process that engenders human agency.

How exactly can linguistic interferences transform values and turn into a transversal form of dissent? Chapter 9 embarks on one more rereading of East German politics in order to probe this question. The focus now rests with a young generation of poets who engaged in critique of language during the decade that led up to the fall of the Berlin Wall. Epitomising their activities is the area around Prenzlauer Berg, a former workers' quarter in East Berlin, which turned into a Bohemian artist and literary scene during the 1980s. What characterised this generation of poets was the fact that they were born into an already established socialist state. They felt that the existing language was inadequate to express their feelings and experiences; in short, the frustrations of living in a suffocating society. Young poets in East Berlin, but also in many other parts of the country, began to draw attention away from the heroics of politics to the subtleties of everyday life. Most of their work was published in small and illegal underground magazines.

Heidemarie Härtel, a poet from Leipzig, not only anticipated the role that mass protests would play in the fall of 1989, but also draws attention to the complex everyday processes that take place against the backdrop of historical discontinuities and so-called great events in global politics. From her poem 'the street':

> i can roll my cigarettes
> late into the night. history
> is made by the masses

in which i swing because i
know to observe the streets'
most minuscule movements [42]

Much of the work produced by the young East German poets of the 1980s can be read as attempts to stretch the German language such that it became possible to speak again, critically and dialogically. The objective was 'to be multiple', to 'formulate what language does not yet contain'. Or so proclaimed, quite representatively, one of the small underground magazines published illegally at Prenzlauer Berg.[43] It is in this sense that these poets were pursuing forms of dissent that R.B.J. Walker portrayed as central to critical social movements.[44]

But were these poetic dissident activities, as some fear, a mere play with words, intellectual games devoid of social significance? Not necessarily. Language is always already politics. The links between words and what they signify may not be authentic, but they are constituted as real through the language in which they are embedded. And the ensuing forms of representation, partial and subjective as they are, become our social and political realities. Hence, to engage with language is to engage directly in social struggle. In this sense, poetic dissent is as real and often as effective as the practices of international *Realpolitik*.

In attempting to stretch the boundaries of language, the East German poets of the 1980s practised a form of discursive dissent. They searched for words to describe the undersides of daily life in East Germany: the urban and industrial wastelands that had no place in the official ideological discourse. They celebrated multiplicities, they made ambivalence part of their language, and by doing so challenged the state's promotion of a black-and-white, one-dimensional and teleological approach to history.

But what rendered such poetic forms of dissent transversal? Were

---

[42] Heidemarie Härtel, 'die strasse', in K. Michael and T. Wohlfahrt (eds.), *Vogel oder Käfig sein: Kunst und Literatur aus der unabhängigen DDR 1979–1989* (Berlin: Galrev, 1991), p. 79. 'ich kann zigaretten drehen/bis morgen früh. die geschichte/wird von den massen gemacht//in denen ich schwinge weil ich/gelernt habe auf die kleinsten/regungen der strasse zu achten'.

[43] ariadnefabrik, IV/1987, cited in Olaf Nicolai, 'die fäden der ariadne', in Heinz Ludwid Arnold, *Die Andere Sprache: Neue DDR-Literatur der 80er Jahre* (Munich: Text und Kritik, 1990), p. 92.

[44] R.B.J. Walker, *One World, Many Worlds: Struggles for a Just World Peace* (London: Zed Books, 1988).

they not everyday forms of resistance whose impact remains confined, by and large, to local political struggles? Not necessarily. David Campbell convincingly argues that everyday life is not 'a synonym for the local level, for in it global interconnections, local resistances, transterritorial flows, state politics, regional dilemmas, identity formations, and so on are always already present'.[45] Indeed, the formation and impact of poetic dissent in East Germany was intrinsically linked with various transversal processes. For instance, the strategy of the poets was decisively shaped by representations in Western mass media and by trends in French literary theory. A substantial part of their work was printed and subsequently celebrated in West Germany. More importantly, much of the substance of their poetry dealt with the dilemmas imposed by state sovereignty, with the desire to gaze and live beyond national boundaries. It is in this sense that the Prenzlauer Berg scene not only transgressed, but also questioned the spatial constitution of East German and, indeed, Cold War international politics.

And yet, the transversal features that drove the younger East German poets were bound by limits too. While demonstrating the potential of language-based dissent, their work also epitomised the difficulties of challenging existing forms of domination. A couple of years after the fall of the Berlin Wall, declassified documents revealed that some of the leading underground poets at Prenzlauer Berg had actively collaborated with the state's notorious security service. Language-based dissent clearly had not been enough to create a critical distance from the authoritarian regime. But rather than invalidating the project of poetic resistance altogether, as some suggest, these revelations underline the need to come to terms with the complexities that are entailed in breaking through existing webs of power and discourse.

What, then, can a case study of poetic dissent in East Germany exactly tell us about language, agency and transversal struggles? Needless to say, poetry is a form of speaking whose impact will always remain very limited. It certainly cannot single-handedly change the course of global politics. Poetry is mostly an elitist form of speaking and writing that is only read by a small segment of the

---

[45] David Campbell, 'Political Prosaics, Transversal Politics, and the Anarchical World', in Michael J. Shapiro and Hayward R. Alker (eds.), *Challenging Boundaries: Global Flows, Territorial Identities* (Minneapolis: University of Minnesota Press, 1996), p. 23.

population. The relevance of poetic dissent to our understanding of transversal dynamics lies in the processes through which it engages with the linkages between language and politics. It is in this domain that poetry demonstrates how the content of speech is inseparable from the form through which it is expressed, how world political dynamics cannot be understood outside of the discursive context within which they unfold.

Poetry does, in a sense, what critical international theory seeks to do: instead of accepting prevailing structures of the world as given, it questions them in an effort to create space for alternative and perhaps more inclusive ways of organising global life.[46] Poetry reveals how important political transformations may occur through practices of dissent that deliberately and self-consciously stretch, even violate existing linguistic rules. 'Inventions from the unknown', Arthur Rimbaud says, 'demand new forms'.[47] The present, relatively limited analysis of the Prenzlauer Berg poetry scene should thus be seen as a case study that illustrates how, in a much larger context, discursive forms of dissent have the potential to transgress boundaries and engender human agency, not by directly causing particular events, but by creating a language that provides us with different eyes, with the opportunity to reassess anew the spatial and political dimensions of global life.

Discursive and transversal forms of dissent unleash their power only through a long process that entails digging, slowly, underneath the foundations of authority. They work through a gradual and largely inaudible transformation of values. A poetic search for thinking space, for instance, acknowledges that there are no quick and miraculous forms of dissent to discursive domination. Poetry resists the temptation to provide 'concrete' answers to 'concrete' questions. It does not bring certainty. In fact, poetry generates more questions, creates ambivalence and doubt. And in doing so it comes to terms with the death of God, makes room for a more tolerant politics, recognises that a society is oppressive and closed if all major questions either have an answer or are considered irrational, absurd, taboo.[48]

---

[46] See Robert W. Cox, 'Social Forces, States and World Orders: Beyond International Relations Theory', in *Millennium*, 10, 2, 1981, pp. 129–30.

[47] Arthur Rimbaud, 'Letter to Paul Demeny, 15 May 1871', *Collected Poems*, tr. O. Bernard (London: Penguin, 1986), p. 16.

[48] Cornelius Castoriadis, 'Ontologie et Anthropologie'.

Language and human agency: the problem of translation

Inevitable problems arise with a move that links human agency with language. If human agency can only be understood in the context of language, then this understanding is never absolute. It never escapes language. If form is substance, then the language through which a rethinking of human agency takes place is itself linked to a particular representation of human agency. This dilemma cannot be avoided. It can only be recognised. And it engenders a long needed modesty to engage in less ambitious and more tolerant forms of theorising.

An investigation into the role of language in transversal dynamics creates major problems for a critically inquiring mind, especially if the project entails, as the present one does, a series of translations across several national languages. The unity of form and substance that characterises the poetic imagination is particularly difficult to translate. If poetry engages in discursive dissent by transgressing the boundaries of specific linguistic practices, then its main message is, by definition, untranslatable. Each language has its own grammatically and syntactically entrenched systems of exclusion and each must be addressed on its own terms. Poetry, then, can be seen as 'the fateful uniqueness of language'.[49] But there is also room for optimism. Mikhail Bakhtin, for example, reminds us that translation, broadly perceived, is the essence of all human communication. We are always crossing language boundaries, not just among different national languages, but between language games that exist within a single culture, a single speaking community.[50]

How can we preserve as much substance as possible in the process of transgressing linguistic boundaries? Walter Benjamin has carved out a convincing and well-used path. I have pursued it as faithfully as possible in the research for this book. According to Benjamin, translation is a provisional way of grappling with the foreignness of a language. A translation must reproduce the echo of the original. It does so by focusing not primarily on meaning and sense, but on the original's way of representing and signifying. It approximates, as closely

---

[49] Paul Celan, 'Antwort auf eine Umfrage der Librairie Flinker, Paris, 1961', in *Gesammelte Werke*, vol. III (Frankfurt: Suhrkamp, 1986), p. 175.
[50] Caryl Emerson, 'Editor's Preface' to Bakhtin's *Problem of Dostoevsky's Poetics* (Minneapolis: University of Minnesota Press, 1993), p. xxxi.

46

as possible, the syntax of the original. A translation should not try to produce a smooth and stylistically flawless English text. Instead, it should be as syntactically literal as possible and retain, at the risk of sounding awkward, the spirit of the foreign language.[51]

I drew the following practical consequences from this insight: If possible, I based my research on original texts, not to unveil some authentic meaning in them, but to acknowledge the links between form and substance. When directly citing foreign language passages, I use official translations, unless they are unavailable or depart too drastically from the above principles. In the latter case, I either present my own translation or alter the official one while indicating that I am doing so. The original text of all self-translated citations that are central to my analysis can be found in footnotes, providing the reader with the opportunity to retrace my journey within and across linguistic boundaries. It should also be noted that my translations and comments throughout part I of this book concur with the common practice of using male gendered nouns and pronouns to denote human beings in general. I am concurring with this practice not to sanction its semantic form of exclusion, but to emphasise that the tradition of dissent I am analysing is by and large a story of men talking about men. Subsequent parts of this book, especially chapter 5, will then further problematise the gender dimensions of popular dissent.

From proofs to traces, or how to evaluate a disruptive reading of global politics

The present effort to reframe questions of agency in global politics relies largely on texts and case studies that may be unfamiliar to many scholars of international relations. What, then, are the criteria by which one could evaluate the usefulness of such a rethinking process? Charles Kegley represents a widely shared view when arguing that 'a theory of international relations must perform four principal tasks. It should describe, explain, predict and prescribe'.[52] Not only is my approach, for reasons explained above, not a 'theory', but its usefulness must be judged in relation to a different set of criteria.

---

[51] Walter Benjamin, 'Die Aufgabe des Übersetzers', in *Illuminationen: Ausgewählte Schriften 1* (Frankfurt: Suhrkamp, 1995/1923), pp. 50–62.

[52] Charles W. Kegley (ed.), *Controversies in International Relations Theory: Realism and the Neoliberal Challenge* (New York: St. Martin's, 1995), p. 8. See Scott Burchill *et al.*, *Theor-*

Prediction, in particular, is a highly problematic standard to evaluate the adequacy of theoretical propositions. Indeed, most international relations theories do not fare well when judged by such a measuring device. Consider, once more, the case of East Germany. None of the influential contributions to international theory was able to anticipate, let alone predict, the momentous transformations that took place when the Berlin Wall crumbled and the Soviet-led alliance system fell apart. If existing theories revealed anything, it was how closely they were intertwined with the Cold War and ensuing perceptions of world politics. 'An empire collapsed,' Jean Elshtain points out, 'and many, if not most, practitioners of international relations were entirely unprepared. It seems that precisely when theories of international politics should have best served us, they failed rather strikingly, overtaken, as it were, by politics itself.'[53] For Elshtain this crucial failure demands a rethinking of what theory is and does. 'If 1989 taught us nothing else,' she stresses, 'it should have taught us humility.'[54] For others, such as Martin Hollis and Steve Smith, the inability of international theory to anticipate the collapse of the Cold War system calls for a more specific, but equally fundamental, rethinking of the agency problematique'.[55] This book is devoted to the latter task – and reassessing questions of evaluation is an integral part of it.

The very notion of prediction does, by its own logic, annihilate human agency. To assert that international relations is a domain of political dynamics whose future should be predictable through a convincing set of theoretical propositions is to assume that the course of global politics is to a certain extent predetermined. From such a vantage-point there is no more room for interference and human agency, no more possibility for politics to overtake theory. A predictive approach thus runs the risk of ending up in a form of inquiry that imposes a static image upon a far more complex set of transversal political practices. The point of a theoretical inquiry, however, is not to ignore the constantly changing domain of international relations. Rather, the main objective must consist of facilitating an understand-

ies of International Relations (New York: St. Martin's Press, 1995), pp. 22–6, for a more widely sketched discussion of how to evaluate theoretical propositions.
[53] Jean Bethke Elshtain, 'International Politics and Political Theory', in Ken Booth and Steve Smith, *International Relations Theory Today* (University Park: The Pennsylvania State University Press, 1995), p. 272.
[54] Ibid., p. 272.
[55] Martin Hollis and Steve Smith, 'Two stories about structure and agency', in *Review of International Studies*, 20, 3, 1994, 241.

ing of transversal struggles that can grapple with those moments when people walk through walls precisely when nobody expects them to do so.

Prediction is a problematic assessment tool even if a theory is able to anticipate future events. Important theories, such as realist inter-pretations of international politics, may well predict certain events only because their theoretical premises have become so objectivised that they have started to shape decision makers and political dynamics. Dissent, in this case, is the process that reshapes these entrenched perceptions and the ensuing political practices.

Describing, explaining and prescribing may be less unproblematic processes of evaluation, but only at first sight. If one abandons the notion of Truth, the idea that an event can be apprehended as part of a natural order, authentically and scientifically, as something that exists independently of the meaning we have given it – if one abandons this separation of object and subject, then the process of judging a particu-lar approach to describing and explaining an event becomes a very muddled affair. There is no longer an objective measuring device that can set the standard to evaluate whether or not a particular insight into an event, such as the collapse of the Berlin Wall, is true or false. The very nature of a past event becomes indeterminate insofar as its identification is dependent upon ever-changing forms of linguistic expressions that imbue the event with meaning.[56]

The inability to determine objective meanings is also the reason why various critical international relations scholars stress that there can be no ultimate way of assessing human agency. Roxanne Doty, for instance, believes that the agent–structure debate 'encounters an aporia, i.e., a self-engendered paradox beyond which it cannot press'. This is to say that the debate is fundamentally undecidable, and that theorists who engage in it 'can claim no scientific, objective grounds for determining whether the force of agency or that of structure is operative at any single instant'.[57] Hollis and Smith pursue a similar line of argument. They emphasise that there are always two stories to tell – neither of which is likely ever to have the last word – an inside

---

[56] See Paul Patton, 'The World Seen From Within: Deleuze and the Philosophy of Events', in *Theory and Event*, 1, 1, January 1997, http://muse.jhu.edu/journals/t+ae, § 6.

[57] Roxanne Lynn Doty, 'Aporia: A Critical Exploration of the Agent-Structure Prob-lematique in International Relations Theory', *European Journal of International Rela-tions*, 3, 3, 1997, 375–777, 387.

story and an outside story, one about agents and another about structures, one epistemological and the other ontological, one about understanding and one about explaining international relations.[58]

The value of an insight cannot be evaluated in relation to a set of objectively existing criteria. But this does not mean that all insights have the same value. Not every perception is equally perceptive. Not every thought is equally thoughtful. Not every action is equally justifiable. How, then, can one judge?

Determining the value of a particular insight or action is always a process of negotiating knowledge, of deciding where its rotating axes should be placed and how its outer boundaries should be drawn. The actual act of judging can thus be made in reference to the very process of negotiating knowledge. The contribution of the present approach to understanding transversal dissent could, for instance, be evaluated by its ability to demonstrate that a rethinking of the agency problematique has revealed different insights into global politics. The key question then revolves around whether or not a particular international event, like the fall of the Berlin Wall, appears in a new light once it is being scrutinised by an approach that pays attention to factors that had hitherto been ignored. Expressed in other words, knowledge about agency can be evaluated by its ability to orient and reorient our perceptions of events and the political actions that issue from them. The lyrical world, once more, offers valuable insight. René Char:

> A poet must leave traces of his passage, not proofs. Only traces bring about dreams.[59]

---

[58] Martin Hollis and Steve Smith, *Explaining and Understanding International Relations* (Oxford: Clarendon Press, 1990), pp. 1–15; and 'Two stories about structure and agency', pp. 241–51.

[59] René Char, *La bibliothèque est en feu*, in *Oeuvres complètes* (Paris: Gallimard, 1983), p. 382.

Part I: A genealogy of popular dissent

> People are always shouting they want to create a better future. It's not true. The future is an apathetic void, of no interest to anyone. The past is full of life, eager to irritate us, provoke and insult us, tempt us to destroy or repaint it. The only reason people want to be masters of the future is to change the past.[1]

The first part of this book examines the historically constituted dimensions of transversal dissent. The focus rests, in particular, with theories and practices of popular dissent. More specifically, the inquiry investigates how ideas about popular dissent have emerged and evolved during the modern period, and how the political practices that issued from them have come to transgress boundaries of national sovereignty. The main objective of this endeavour is to understand how centuries of practising and thinking about resistance have shaped the nature of dissent and its role in contemporary global politics.

This history of the present, to use Foucault's well-known terminology, takes the form of a genealogy. Its purpose is to illuminate relatively unknown aspects of our past to then illustrate how they have gradually grown into ideas and practices that are more familiar to us. The inquiry begins with a sixteenth-century French text, Étienne de la Boétie's *Contr'un*, or *Anti-One*. Despite its relative obscurity today, this text played a significant role in shaping practices of dissent in the early and middle stages of the modern period. Its legacy – together with various other influences – has given rise to a tradition of radical resistance to authoritarian rule. I retrace the evolution of this tradition

---

[1] Milan Kundera, *The Book of Laughter and Forgetting*, tr. M. H. Heim (New York: HarperCollins, 1994/1978), p. 22.

by focusing on images of human agency that it espoused at several historic turning points, the Renaissance (chapter 1), the Romantic period (chapter 2), and the twentieth century (chapter 3).

During the latter two epoques, European dissident practices have spread beyond national boundaries and turned into an increasingly significant aspect of global politics. They were part of a process through which many ideas and modes of life that emerged in modern Europe have achieved worldwide significance. Consider, for instance, the impact of capitalism, a key feature of modernity. Its quintessential features, such as the continuous strife for profit, the inherent tendency to revolutionise modes of production and communication, or the constant search for raw materials and cheap labour markets, have resulted in a continuous dissemination of European values, practices and institutions. The outcome of this globalisation process has received multifarious terms, including 'global village', 'universal international society', and 'time-space compression'.[2] In the wake of this phenomenon, Eurocentric perceptions of dissent and human agency have come to influence political dynamics on a much wider spatial scale. To understand their form and dynamic one must thus look into the values that facilitated their emergence. This is what the following chapters set out to do. In this sense, the present genealogical inquiry into the framing of transversal dissent is less a historical investigation than an assessment of the political consequences that issue from the spread of European cultural hegemony.

---

[2] Hedley Bull and Adam Watson (eds.), *The Expansion of International Society* (Oxford: Clarendon Press, 1984); Anthony Giddens, *The Consequences of Modernity* (Stanford: Stanford University Press, 1990); David Harvey, *The Condition of Postmodernity* (Oxford/Cambridge, MA: Blackwell, 1989); Serge Latouche, *The Westernization of the World*, tr. R. Morris (Cambridge: Polity, 1996); Marshall McLuhan, *Understanding Media: The Extensions of Man* (London: Ark Paperbacks, 1987/1964).

1   Rhetorics of dissent in Renaissance Humanism

Quoniam Dominus excelsus, terribilis:
rex magnus super omnem terram.
Subiecit populos nobis:
et gentes sub pedibus nostris.

[For the Lord is high, terrible;
a great king over all the earth.
He hath subdued the people under us;
and the nations under our feet][1]

After a celebratory spree in ancient Greece, particularly among the Sophists, the concept of human agency all but vanished in the Middle Ages. Life was said to be governed by laws that lie beyond human influence. The medieval world-view revolved around an undisputed theological core that left little room for privileges associated with subjecthood. Common people were reduced to spectators, impotent onlookers in a unfolding human drama. They were caught in an immense mesh of fate and sacrifice, spun by the hands of God and his quasi-divine earthly embodiments. Or so at least resonates a common image of the medieval period. Somewhat correct, but oversimplified. Black and white, with black prevailing most of the time. But there was, of course, much more to the Middle Ages than an omnipotent God. The theocentric vision was only the frame within which a whole range of complex and highly diverse dynamics took place. Even in the

---

[1] Psalm 46, 11th–12th century version, Gregorian Chant Gaudete, Sung by the Benedictine Nuns of St Cecilia's Abbey, Ryde, Isle of Wight (Farnham, Surrey: Herald AV Publications, 1992), p. 7.

pre-modern period strong ideas about popular sovereignty existed.[2] The transition from the medieval to the early modern period is equally complex. It is a long and gradual evolution that cannot be grasped satisfactorily by rehearsing a few key events deemed crucial by subsequent historical interpretations. Indeed, some argue that the respect for and interest in the individual, a key theme of modern thought, had its origin as far back as the second half of the twelfth century.[3]

Despite this blurring image one can identify a number of shifts that occurred in the transition from the medieval to the modern period. With the rise of Humanism during the Italian Renaissance, in the fourteenth and fifteenth centuries, the prevalent theocentric vision of the world came under increasing challenge. A good century later, the new humanist message gradually penetrated the remaining parts of Europe. It resurrected the notion of human agency and challenged God's monopoly to anchor all aspects of human existence. Humanism placed the subject at the centre of history and expressed a profound belief in people's dignity, in their own ability to solve problems.

The present chapter demonstrates how these emerging humanist ideas provided the foundations for a tradition of popular dissent that espouses a strong belief in human agency. Turn the clock back to 1552. We are in early modern France. Writing is Étienne de la Boétie, a young student who expresses profound disgust with all forms of governing that entail some people dominating others. He protests against divine authority, against royal absolutism and, maybe most importantly, against the deprivation of subjecthood:

> Is this a happy life? Can this be called living?. . . What condition is more miserable than to live such that nothing is one's own, such that one derives from someone else one's entire well-being, one's freedom, one's body & one's life?[4]

La Boétie's work first lingered in obscurity. But the rhetorical reflections that followed his initial fury eventually influenced the emergence of a tradition of dissent that deals with radical resistance to authoritarianism.

---

[2] See Walter Ullmann, *A History of Political Thought: The Middle Ages* (Harmondsworth: Penguin Books, 1965), pp. 200–228.

[3] Colin Morris, *The Discovery of the Individual: 1050–1200* (London: SPCK, 1972).

[4] Étienne de la Boétie, *Discours de la Servitude Volontaire*, ed. P. Bonnefon in *Oeuvres Complètes* (Genève: Slatkine Reprints, 1967/1552), p. 49. 'Cela eft ce viure heureufement? cela f'appelle il viure?. . . Quelle condition eft plus miferable que de viure ainfi, qu'on n'aie rien à foy, tenant d'autrui fon aife, fa liberté, fon corps & fa vie?'

In subsequent centuries, la Boétiean assumptions about power, domination and resistance will play a significant, albeit often unrecognised role in shaping practices of popular dissent. While Machiavelli's *The Prince* helped to define sovereignty, state power and the ensuing international order, la Boétie's *Anti-One* contributed to the emergence of forces that came to circumvent and undermine the spatial and political logic of this order. The present chapter takes the first step in retracing the ensuing tradition of dissent.

Because la Boétie, and early modern thought in general, provided the foundation for various transversal dissident dynamics that are operative today, my genealogical inquiry engages in a relatively extensive reading of the *Anti-One* and its relationship to ideas and political practices in sixteenth-century France. Placing la Boétie in the context of larger discursive trends entails searching for unpronounced assumptions that are entailed in his work, assumptions about society, power, the subject and, above all, human agency. But analyses of social dynamics, especially if they date as far back as the sixteenth century, can never be authentic representations of events. My reconstruction of the context within which la Boétie's work unfolded is inevitably coloured by my views of history, by the sources I have chosen to investigate, and by the motivations that lie behind my effort to come to terms with them. Hence, a reconstruction of historical dynamics must be sensitive to multiple voices from the past and compare various subsequent interpretations of them.

From heaven to earth: the new humanist vision

Étienne de la Boétie was born in 1530 in Sarlat, a small town in the south-west of France. He grew up in a well-placed aristocratic family.[5] La Boétie wrote his main political text as a student at the University

---

[5] The text that comes closest to a serious biography of la Boétie remains Paul Bonnefon's introduction to the 1892 edition of la Boétie's *Oeuvres complètes*, pp. xi–lxxxv. In researching the context of la Boétie's life I also drew upon Jacques Joseph Desplat, *La Boétie: le magistrat aux nombreux mystères* (Le Bugue: PLB Editeur, 1992); Jean-Michel Delacompté, *Et q'un seul-soit l'ami: la Boétie* (Paris: Gallimard, 1985) and several introductions to French and English editions of la Boétie's writings, especially Simon Goyard-Fabre, 'Introduction', *Discours de la Servitude Volontaire* (Paris: Flammarion, 1983), pp. 17–127; Nadia Gontarbert, 'Présentation', *De la Servitude Volontaire ou Contr'un* (Paris: Gallimard, 1993), pp. 12–45; and Murray N. Rothbard, 'The Political Thought of Étienne de la Boétie', *The Politics of Obedience: The Discourse of Voluntary Servitude*, tr. H. Kurz (New York: Free Life Editions, 1975), pp. 9–35.

of Orléans. It is a relatively short polemical treatise, officially entitled *Discours de la Servitude Volontaire*. I will refer to its widely used and more adequate alternative title *Contr'un*, or *Anti-One*.[6]

La Boétie addresses his main theme without hesitation. The *Anti-One*'s opening lines reveal the author's profound abhorrence of all forms of governing that are based on some people ruling over others:

> [I]t must be said that the domination of several could not be good for the power of one alone, as soon as he acquires the title of master, is harsh & unreasonable. . . it is extremely unfortunate to be subjected to one master, whose kindness one can never be assured of, since it is always in his power to be cruel whenever he desires; & as for having several masters, the more one has, the more extremely unfortunate it is.[7]

What precisely is the object of la Boétie's rage? We are, as mentioned, in the south-west of France, in the middle of a century that is characterised by rapid change, radical turmoil, and bloody civil wars. All power is claimed by the King, but he does not have the ability to enforce it. The regional gentry is seeking to profit from the power vacuum, the Catholic Church desperately attempts to hold on to at least some of its fading strength, peasants rebel and religious strife is soon to bring the entire country to a standstill.

As he was writing, la Boétie may have had the rebellion of Guyenne in mind, which dominated politics in the region at the time.[8] In 1548, when la Boétie was eighteen years old, thousands of repressed peasants of the Guyenne region opposed the *gabelle*, a salt tax, and started to rebel. In August the insurgents entered Bordeaux. Meeting up with sympathetic commoners, they soon took control of the city. Its authorities first entered into a dialogue with the protesting population and

---

[6] For a non-specialist in medieval French language, the subtleties of this sixteenth-century text are not easy to decipher. Besides using specialised dictionaries, I contrasted the original text (or what comes closest to it, the so-called manuscript of de Mesmes), with various versions transcribed into modern French. I also compared my translations with the ones by Harry Kurz in la Boétie, *The Politics of Obedience*.

[7] La Boétie, *Discours de la Servitude Volontaire*, pp. 1–2. '[I]l falloit dire que la domination de plufieurs ne pouuoit eftre bonne, puifque la puiffance d'vn feul, deflors qu'il prend ce tiltre de maiftre, eft dure & defraifonnable . . . c'eft vn extreme malheur d'eftre fubiect à vn maiftre, duquel on ne fe peut iamais affeurer qu'il foit bon, puifqu'il eft toufiours en fa puiffance d'eftre mauuais quand il voudra; & d'auoir plufieurs maiftres, c'eft, autant qu'on en a, autant de fois eftre extremement malheureux.'

[8] See Jules Jolly, *Histoire du Mouvement Intellectuel au XVIe Sciècle*, vol. I. (Genève: Slatkine Reprints, 1969), pp. 35–6.

actually revoked the *gabelle*, but this conciliatory approach was soon replaced by an extremely brutal crackdown. Local authorities called upon Henri II, the King of France, whose army then crushed the rebellion and established an extended reign of terror. The leaders of the uprising were executed in various tortuous ways – decapitated, burned, broken, impaled or torn apart by horses – as part of a carefully orchestrated public display of vengeance and intimidation that lasted for weeks.

If la Boétie indeed wrote about the 1548 uprising, the first of a series of big peasant revolts in France, then he did it without direct reference to the events. But even in its abstraction the message of the *Anti-One* was clear. Its description of servitude, violence and suffering under a tyrant reflected the frustrations of a whole generation of commoners and captured the spirit of popular protest that soon was to take hold of France.[9]

With or without the repressive regime of King Henri II in mind, la Boétie's essay was a devastating critique of existing practices of governance. Its condemnation of one man rule fundamentally opposed the prevailing absolutist theory of monarchy, which rested on the idea of a *princeps*, a ruler who has a divine mission and to whom unlimited obedience is due. Consider Charles de Grassaille's influential *Regalium Franciae*, published in 1538. It portrays the King of France as 'imperator in suo regno', as 'quidem corporalis Deus': a prince of divine appointment, a ruler whose power extends to virtually all domains except the law of his own succession. He reigns as an earthly embodiment of God, entirely independent of popular consent.[10]

La Boétie attacked the very core of these doctrinal foundations of royal absolutism by linking power and consent:

> The one who controls you so much has only two eyes, has only two hands, has only one body & has nothing more than what the large and infinite number of men in your villages have. All he has is the means that you give him to destroy you. From where does he get all these eyes to spy upon you, if you do not give them to him? How can he have so many hands to hit you with if he does not take them from you? The feet that trample down your cities, where does he get

---

[9] Henry Heller, *Iron and Blood: Civil Wars in Sixteenth-Century France* (Montreal: McGill-Queen's University Press, 1991), p. 40.
[10] J.W. Allen, *A History of Political Thought in the Sixteenth Century* (London: Methuen, 1941/1928), pp. 283–4, xiii–xxii.

them if not from among you? How can he have any power over you except through you?[11]

La Boétie's contention that any form of rule is dependent upon popular consent is both radical and subversive in the context of sixteenth-century France. A clear concept of human agency is implied in these lines, for la Boétie dares to speak of subjects and, even more courageously, of subjects who act independently of a divine will. Justifying this radical stance purely on secular grounds, particularly on the power of reason, logic and a natural right to freedom, he argues that sovereignty belongs to the people, and not to the King or to God. Before discussing the consequences of these claims in more detail it is necessary to place the *Anti-One* again in the context of larger discursive struggles that were waged at the time.

Some elements of la Boétie's writings reflect the ideas and assumptions of the humanist movement that started to take hold of France at the time. Humanism was anticipated by several medieval poets – Dante, Boccaccio and Petrarch among them – and it reached its heyday in fifteenth-century Italy. In its broadest meaning, Humanism refers to an 'interest in Latin and Greek literature which sets a high value on the lessons to be drawn from it'.[12] It is the gaze back to the classical period, the attempt to revive a long past culture, that gave the corresponding period, the Renaissance, its name. The revival of classical culture took on a specific form. Some commentators emphasise that the rereading of Hellenistic philosophy via Cicero, which was the most popular approach at the time, amounted to a revival of scepticism – the belief that 'man' is caught in a web of illusory perceptions, unable to gain secure knowledge of the physical world.[13] Hence, instead of searching for a Platonic truth, humanists were usually more concerned with rhetoric, with practising the art of convincing others by drawing on the power of persuasion. It is in the passion for rhetoric

---

[11] La Boétie, *Discours de la Servitude Volontaire*, pp. 12–13. 'Celui qui vous maiftrife tant n'a que deus yeulx, n'a que deus mains, n'a qu'vn corps, & n'a autre chofe que ce qu'a le moindre homme du grand & infini nombre de vos villes, finon que l'auantage que vous luy faites pour vous deftruire. D'où a il pris tant d'yeulx, dont il vous efpie, fi vous ne les luy bailles? comment a il tant de mains pour vous fraper, f'il ne les prend de vous? Les pieds dont il foule vos cites, d'où les a il, f'ils ne font des voftres? Comment a il aucun pouuoir fur vous, que par vous?'

[12] George Holmes, 'Humanism in Italy', in A. Goodman and A. MacKay (eds.), *The Impact of Humanism on Western Europe* (London: Longman, 1990), p. 118.

[13] Richard Tuck, 'Humanism and Political Thought', in Goodman and MacKay (eds.) *The Impact of Humanism*, pp. 43–4.

that they grounded their basic intellectual identity.[14] But the society at the time did not lend itself easily to such endeavours. Humanists first needed to carve out institutional and political spaces that allowed them to engage in rhetorical interactions. Universities provided these spaces. It is through them that Humanism gradually moved north and penetrated France towards the end of the fifteenth century.

When la Boétie commenced his studies, in the late 1540s, Humanism had already spread throughout most of Western Europe. The University of Orléans, one of the most prestigious universities in France, enjoyed an unusually wide range of intellectual freedom. Students read classical philosophy and waged debates about it. Criticism was encouraged. Within the confines of university life, a general atmosphere of free inquiry and discussion prevailed. Not surprisingly, la Boétie's *Anti-One*, composed during his student days in Orléans, bore the mark of this humanist environment. His opening argument, the condemnation of all tyranny, is presented as a critical dialogue with Ulysses, as narrated in Homer's Iliad. He continues to draw upon Greek philosophy, ruminates about the politics of Brutus or Nero, and illustrates his points by reference to ancient history and mythology. His style is abstract, theoretical, polemical. This is why many portray la Boétie's work as a typical Renaissance exercise in classical rhetoric.[15]

There was, of course, more to Renaissance Humanism than rhetoric, a spirit of free inquiry, and an interest in classical literature. Rhetoric was only the means to a much more ambitious political end: Humanism was a revolt against a long tradition of grounding truth and authority in religion. It fundamentally restructured the relationship among the individual, the church and the emerging state. The focus of attention moved from heaven to earth, from the truth prescribed by the holy scripts to the power of reason and persuasion, from the church's doctrinal morality to a loosening of norms and a secularisation of values.

La Boétie's *Anti-One* was deeply embedded in this humanist attempt to create a vision for the future, a vision that rested upon human dignity, to be fought for with rhetorical means. At the centre

---

[14] Jerrold E. Seigel, *Rhetoric and Philosophy in Renaissance Humanism* (Princeton: Princeton University Press, 1968).

[15] C.A. Sainte-Beuve, *Causeries du Lundi,* vol. XI (Paris: Garnier Frères, 1858/1856), p. 144; Paul Bonnefon, *Montaigne et ses Amis*, vol. I, (Paris: Armand Colin: 1898), p. 150; Pierre Mesnard, *L'Essor de la Philosophie Politique au XVIe Siècle* (Paris: J. Vrin, 1951/ 1935), p. 405.

of this tradition was Renaissance 'man', penetrating nature's secrets, venturing out into the sea to discover new worlds, producing stunning works of art that celebrate the human body. An unprecedented sense of optimism arose. People, unchained from the confines of God's will, became masters of their own destiny. Nothing seemed out of their reach. There was no hesitation. The subject was born and took responsibility. With it appeared an unlimited faith in human agency and in the ability to solve the world's problems.[16] Paradoxically, like so much in the Renaissance, this process of secularisation was accompanied by a new glorification of the church, a last resurrection before this institution faced the Reformation and embarked upon a journey that led towards what Nietzsche later called nihilism, or the death of God.

The rhetorical origins of popular dissent

The particular way in which la Boétie sought to confront the problem of freedom and human agency made the *Anti-One* a much-disputed essay in the centuries to come. His idea of freedom entails that no government can survive without the support of the population. He argues that there is not even a need to fight a tyrant, for 'he' is defeated as soon as the population refuses to consent to its enslavement.[17] Numerous passages in the *Anti-One* deal with this possibility of withdrawing consent. They later became the conceptual foundations of an entire literature on popular dissent. Here are its Renaissance roots, expressed in la Boétie's rhetorical Humanism:

> If one concedes nothing to them [the tyrants], if one refuses to obey them, then without fighting, without striking, they become naked & defeated & are no more, just as when the root is deprived of water and nourishment, the branch withers and dies.[18]
>
> Be resolved to serve no more & you will be free. I do not want you

---

[16] This new individualism and the trust in moral autonomy was, to simplify things, the essence of Jacob Burckhardt's influential *Die Kultur der Renaissance in Italien* (Berlin: Knauer, 1928). For one of the recently proliferating revisionist accounts of the period see Lisa Jardine, *Worldly Goods: A New History of the Renaissance* (London: Macmillan, 1996).

[17] La Boétie, *Discours de la Servitude Volontaire*, p. 9.

[18] *Ibid.*, pp. 10–11. '[F]i on ne leur baille rien [les tirans], fi on ne leur obeit point, fans combattre, fans frapper, ils demeurent nuds & deffaits & ne font plus rien, finon que comme la racine, n'aians plus d'humeur ou aliment, la branche deuient feche & morte.'

to hurt or unsettle the tyrant, but simply that you serve him no more, & you will see how he collapses under his own weight and breaks into pieces, just like a large Colossus whose base has been snatched away.[19]

By linking any form of government to popular consent and ruminating about the possibilities that could arise when this consent is withdrawn, la Boétie advances a fundamental proposition about the nature of power. Contrary to the prevalent view of the time, he does not perceive power as something stable and restraining, a privilege that some have and others do not. Power emerges from popular consent and it is relational, a constantly changing force field located in the interactive dynamics between ruler and ruled. Perhaps most importantly, power is enabling, it provides common people with the chance to create opportunities for social change.

La Boétie was, of course, not the only early modern voice that opposed domination. Already in the early Italian Renaissance, various authors, such as Marsiglio of Padua and Bartolus of Saxoferrato, had openly condemned tyranny and advocated government by the people. But most of these and subsequent writers did not question the foundations of existing regimes. Instead, they were concerned with the proper functioning of the machinery of government. Out of this concern emerged a long-lasting humanist tradition of giving advice to princes, kings and magistrates. Humanists from Niccolò Machiavelli to Justus Lipsius counselled their rulers on how to be virtuous, how to govern best, or how to retain a position of power in adverse circumstances.

La Boétie's clearly went further than these concerns with proper government, political stability and the functioning of power politics. The *Anti-One* was more radical not because of its claim that any form of rule is or should be dependent upon popular consent. This relational perspective on power was implied in most of the advice given to the princes of Renaissance Italy and France. Where the *Anti-One* differed sharply from the advice-book tradition was in its claim that popular consent can be withdrawn at any time and that this act disempowers even the most ruthless dictator. It was this identification with

---

[19] Ibid., p. 14. 'Soies refolus de not feruir plus, & vous voilà libres. Ie ne veux pas que vous le pouffies ou l'esbranflies, mais feulement ne le fouftenes plus, & vous le verres, comme vn grand coloffe à qui on a defrobé la bafe, de fon pois mefme fondre en bas & fe rompre.'

the people and their claim to sovereignty that made the *Anti-One* stand apart from more immediate contemporary concerns with the machinery of the newly emerging modern state.

The *Anti-One's* radicalism is best exemplified in its opposition to Machiavelli's *The Prince*, which was published in Rome two decades before la Boétie's student days in Orléans. It is likely that la Boétie knew *The Prince* since it was available in France at that time and constituted normal reading material for students. Parallels between la Boétie and Machiavelli are clearly visible, albeit not at first sight. Both situate power in the relationship between ruler and ruled, an idea that was alien to the preceding medieval period. Pierre Mesnard, in his classical study of Renaissance political theory, detects this common humanist trait but also draws attention to the above-mentioned important difference:

> For la Boétie as well as for Machiavelli, authority can only emerge through acceptance by the subjects: except that one teaches the prince how to enforce their acquiescence while the other reveals to the people the power entailed in refusing it. In other words, the remedy of the *Anti-One*, whose political effectiveness we know today, is passive resistance, civil disobedience, the refusal to collaborate with an order one disapproves of.[20]

Mesnard's summary makes clear that Machiavelli, at least in his best-known passages, was primarily operating within a framework of realist power politics. Viewing the world as a place where the struggle for power and the survival of the fittest determines the outcome of events, he advised the prince to abandon all precepts of morality if he is to retain his rule. La Boétie, of course, positioned himself at the other side of the social spectrum. His focus on withdrawing popular consent suggests that the *Anti-One* was written for the people and their quest for freedom, rather than for the prince and his attempts to cement authoritarian rule.

La Boétie's work represents the radical element of the emerging humanist movement. He dares to speak of a subject, places 'man' at the centre of attention, and displays an unbounded optimism in 'his' ability to exert human agency and change the course of history. But the *Anti-One* has other faces too, faces that cannot be classified easily, faces that do not fit neatly into preconceived intellectual spaces, at

---

[20] Mesnard, *L'Essor de la Philosophie Politique au XVIe Siècle*, p. 400.

least not the ones that existed in Renaissance France. These are the aspects of the *Anti-One* that most subsequent interpretations neglect. They are the pluralities of a text, the faces that grimace, mock, provoke; the ones that contradict, disturb and rebel. A short elucidation of them is necessary at this point.

La Boétie tried to open up possibilities to resist tyranny. But he was equally if not more concerned with explaining the puzzling lack of such resistance. Why is it that so many people serve a tyrant who, if the premises of the *Anti-One* are correct, they need not fear at all? A perplexed la Boétie exclaims:

> If two, if three, if four do not defend themselves against one, this is strange but nevertheless conceivable;... but a thousand, but a million, but a thousand cities, if they do not defend themselves against one, then this is not cowardice, for cowardice does not sink to such a low point.... What monstrous vice is this then that does not even deserve to be called cowardice?[21]

The vice has a name: voluntary servitude. La Boétie explains its existence in two ways, one deals with the force of customs, the other with a system of positive and negative privileges. Both of them entail, in essence, clear limits to human agency. The first is linked to a tyrant's ability to deprive his subjects of their memory of freedom:

> It is this, that men born under the yoke & thereafter nourished & brought up in servitude are content, without searching any further, to live like they are used to, & not being aware at all of any other situation or right than the one they know, they accept as natural the condition into which they were born.[22]

La Boétie's argument that the emergence of a quest for freedom requires a prior experience of it departs quite radically from his earlier polemics about a natural right to freedom. Facing the political reality of the time, he now admits that nature has less power over us than customs do. No matter how benevolent nature wanted us to be, our

---

[21] La Boétie, *Discours de la Servitude Volontaire*, pp. 5–6. 'Si deux, fi trois, fi quatre ne fe defendent d'vn, cela eft eftrange, mais toutesfois poffible... mais mille, mais vn million, mais mille villes, fi elles ne fe defendent d'vn, cela n'eft pas couardife, elle ne va point iufques là... Doncques quel monftre de vice eft cecy qui ne merite pas ancore le tiltre de couardife...?'
[22] Ibid., p. 22. 'C'eft cela, que les hommes naiffans foubs le ioug, & puis nourris & efleues dans le feruage, fans regarder plus auant, fe contentent de viure comme ils font nes, & ne penfans point auoir autre bien ni autre droict que ce qu'ils ont trouué, ils prennent pour leur naturel l'eftat de leur naiffance.'

environment shapes us to the point that, against our own disposition, we learn 'how to swallow, & not find bitter at all, the venom of servitude'.[23] When Cyrus took the Lydian city of Sardis, la Boétie illustrates, its citizens rebelled against the occupation. But instead of simply repressing the uprising, which would have entailed the problematic and continuous employment of an expensive army, Cyrus opted for a much more subtle and powerful form of domination: he established brothels, taverns, public games and then encouraged the people to go and enjoy them. This kind of garrison proved to be so effective that Cyrus henceforth could subjugate the Lydians without the least use of force.[24]

La Boétie mentions a second reason for the existence of voluntary servitude. It revolves around pyramidically structured systems of threats and privileges. Indeed, this is the secret of domination, he claims. The key to such a system lies in a tyrant's ability to corrupt his people, particularly those who strive for power and wealth. La Boétie explains how each ruler is dependent on his closest advisers, half a dozen men, at most. They are accomplices in 'his' cruelties and share the profits of 'his' plundering sprees. In this way, the system replicates itself endlessly, because:

> Those six have six hundred who profit under them & they proceed with these six hundred as they do with the tyrant. These six hundred have six thousand under them, they promote them in rank and give them the provinces to govern or the finances to manage, so that they too become entangled in avarice and cruelty. . . Devastating are the consequences of all this, & whoever is willing to follow this trace will realise that not six thousand, but hundred thousand, even millions are tied to the tyrant by this one cord.[25]

Implied in these lines is the suggestion that a ruler can only maintain 'his' position if a large number of people profit from the existing system and thus have an interest in maintaining the status quo. The tyrant, who lacks independent foundational sources of power, is able

---

[23] Ibid, p. 23.
[24] Ibid., pp. 35–6.
[25] Ibid., p. 45–6. 'Ces fix ont fix cent qui proufitent fous eus, & font de leurs fix cent ce que les fix font au tiran. Ces fix cent en tiennent fous eus fix mille, qu'ils ont efleué en eftat, aufquels ils font donner ou le gouuernement des prouinces, ou le maniement des deniers, afin qu'ils tiennent la main à leur auarice & cruauté. . . Grande eft la fuitte qui vient apres cela, & qui voudra f'amufer à deuider ce filet, il verra que, non pas les fix mille, mais les cent mille, mais les millions, par cefte corde, fe tiennent au tiran. . .'

to subjugate the people only through them. 'He' is protected by those who could easily end the charade if they had the courage to resist.

Despite its multiple faces, the *Anti-One* never loses sight of its radical humanist message. Even while elaborating on subtle systems of exclusion, la Boétie's main interest is not in analysing domination as such, but in demonstrating how it can be overcome. In perfect humanist rhetoric, he reasserts his faith in agency, practises the art of persuasion, tries to incite people to overcome voluntary servitude. He constantly reminds the reader that systems of domination are fragile and dependent upon popular consent. As long as there are thinking subjects a tyrant's position is in danger. And there will always be thinking minds, people who cannot be fooled easily, who sense the weight of the yoke, people who open their eyes and reclaim their natural right to freedom.[26] Renaissance 'man' looms around the corner, able to see it all, equipped with the vision, the will, and the strength to change the world. Will 'he' succeed?

Protestantism and the problem of free will

What was the immediate impact of la Boétie's writings? How were they received? How did they shape practices of dissent and perceptions of human agency?

It is important to distinguish between la Boétie as an author and the *Anti-One* as a text. After its composition, a text takes off in multiple directions and becomes an object of appropriation over which the author inevitably loses control. In Michel Foucault's words, 'writing unfolds like a game that invariably goes beyond its own rules and transgresses its limits'.[27] One must then locate and explore the spaces that are left by the author's disappearance. A text is read in many different ways, it becomes a political tool that continuously changes shape and content. A reader of a text is thus, as Roland Barthes emphasises, an active producer, rather than simply a passive consumer.[28] Readers constantly reinvent texts, view them in the light of particular experiences, note some passages and neglect others. Reading becomes appropriation. Appropriation becomes politics. Politics shapes our lives.

---

[26] Ibid., p. 30.
[27] Michel Foucault, 'What is an Author', in P. Rabinow (ed.), *The Foucault Reader*, tr. J.V. Harari, (New York: Pantheon Books, 1984), p. 102.
[28] Roland Barthes, *S/Z* (Paris: Éditions du Seuil, 1970), pp. 9–23.

Viewing the *Anti-One* as an object of appropriation is necessary to understand how its intellectual legacy has influenced the emergence of a tradition of popular dissent that later came to operate in the grey zones between domestic and international politics. Not long after its composition in the 1550s, the *Anti-One* and its author parted company. La Boétie turned into a conservative diplomat concerned with law and order while his text became part of a long crusade to promote the humanist concept of free will. The remaining sections of this chapter join the *Anti-One's* journey in its initial phase, the second half of the sixteenth century.

We are in a period that is dominated by one key phenomenon, the Reformation. Like Humanism, the Reformation is a complex set of ideas and events, susceptible to many different interpretations. At its most uncontested site, the Reformation was a movement that questioned the Pope's monopoly over the interpretation of the Bible. It tried to liberate Christianity from corrupt practices that the Roman Catholic Church had superimposed on it. It was a return to what was claimed to be the only authentic source of knowledge, the Bible. The Reformation was a second Renaissance, directed not at reviving classical Greek philosophy, but at reasserting the original faith, at halting the decay of Christianity. The Reformation's protagonist was the Augustinian monk Martin Luther, preaching and writing in the Saxon city of Wittenberg. Luther's famous posting of ninety five theses to the door of his church, on the eve of All Saints in 1517, marked the beginning of a turbulent period that undermined most of the Catholic Church's spiritual, jurisdictional and political power.

But the Reformation was more than just a fight against the corruption of the Catholic Church. At its core, the Reformation was, as one commentator puts it, 'a life-or-death attack on Humanism'.[29] From this perspective, the main battle was waged in 1524/5 between Luther and Erasmus, a Christian humanist writing in Basel. The focus of attack was not the Papacy, but Renaissance 'man', the secularisation of life, the faith in reason and free will, the very concept of human agency. Luther opposed Erasmus by arguing that true freedom cannot be reached by asserting human independence. Our own actions cannot lead to freedom or salvation because we are corrupt, helpless and entirely dependent upon God's grace. Luther's concern reflects a key

[29] John Carroll, *Humanism: The Wreck of Western Culture* (London: Fontana Press, 1993), p. 47.

dilemma that permeated Renaissance thought. Ever since Pico della Mirandola's celebration of the dignity of 'man', a double-edged message haunted the rising humanist movement. It was double-edged, 'for to be uniquely privileged man was also uniquely burdened'.[30] There was no longer an omnipotent God that could take over the responsibility for humanity's fate. Renaissance 'man' had put 'himself' into a state of suspense, having taken over command, but not yet assumed responsibility for it. Luther recognised this dilemma. Free will, for him, was an illusion that robbed us of all foundations for life. 'Man' was left with nothing to stand on, no fixed world-view, no certainty; only despair and sin. True freedom, he hailed, can only arise from faith, from obedience to God's will.

The tensions surrounding this dispute over religion and free will started to take hold of France at about the time when la Boétie ruminated about withdrawing consent at the University of Orléans. Protestant reformers, the Huguenots, were trying to practise their subversive form of Christianity. The Catholic Church and its secular representative, the deified French monarch, increasingly saw their authority undermined and started to adopt more hostile positions. France was about to turn into a battle ground between adherents of the Catholic status quo and its Huguenot opponent.

La Boétie finished his studies and was admitted to the Parliament of Bordeaux in 1554. By then religious strife had already come to dominate political issues. Six years later, in the midst of various controversies triggered by the persecution of Protestants, la Boétie was entrusted with a delicate diplomatic mission. He was asked to mediate between his own parliament in Bordeaux and the court of King Charles IX, who had just succeeded his father Henry II. Catherine de Médici, who had taken over the regency for her ten year old son Charles IX, initiated a politics of appeasement and gave la Boétie the task of returning to his Parliament, known for an inflexible Catholic stance, to explain this new, more tolerant approach towards the Huguenots. De Médici' first attempt at appeasement failed. Violent confrontations between Catholics and Protestants increased and in 1562 she signed the *Edit de Janvier*, which was intended to protect the Huguenots from persecution.

A long report, a *Mémoire*, that la Boétie wrote about this edict

---

[30] John Hale, *The Civilization of Europe in the Renaissance* (London: Fontana Press, 1993), p. 208.

reveals how much his opinions changed in comparison to the *Anti-One*, composed a decade earlier in his student days. La Boétie's rhetoric is gone, and so is the quest for freedom beyond the confines of the newly emerging state. His language is no longer one of anger, of defiance; it is the language of order, of discipline and of diplomatic manoeuvring. La Boétie defends the King and sanctions the use of force to restore peace and order. While the *Anti-One* aimed at unchaining the people, the *Mémoire* provided instructions about how to further enslave them.[31] La Boétie the student angrily and passionately condemned the forces of Henry II that crushed the revolt against the *Gabelle*, whereas la Boétie the diplomat defended and revered these very same instruments of repression. But la Boétie could not control the fate of his earlier, radical text. The *Anti-One* was about to embark on a different route than its author. It was to leave its assigned place and turn into an unpredictable instrument of rebellion.

Rage, rebellion and the voice of the sceptic

After la Boétie's death at the age of thirty-two (most likely of the plague), his intellectual legacy, including the radical *Anti-One*, was entrusted to his close friend, the famous essayist Michel de Montaigne.[32] Without Montaigne's protection and leverage, the *Anti-One* might have remained an unknown and obscure Renaissance text. La Boétie never saw his rhetorical treatise published. It only circulated as a manuscript among a small group of personal friends. In August 1570, seven years after la Boétie's death, Montaigne travelled to Paris to arrange the publication of some of his friend's writings, particularly poems and translations of classical Latin texts. But he decided against publishing la Boétie's more political *Anti-One*. Montaigne defended his editorial choice by arguing that this piece of writing was simply 'too delicate and subtle to be abandoned to the rough and dense climate of such a mischievous season'.[33]

The early 1570s were indeed a 'mischievous season', and this even by the standards of a century that was dominated by insecurity, civil

---

[31] Étienne de La Boétie, *Mémoire touchant l'Edit de Janvier 1562* (Paris: Editions Bossard, 1922), pp. 103–180.

[32] On the relationship between la Boétie and Montaigne see Bonnefon, *Montaigne et ses Amis*, vol. I, pp. 210–224 and Gérald Allard, *La Boétie et Montaigne sur les liens humains* (Québec: Le Griffon d'Argile, 1994).

[33] Montaigne, 'Advertissement av Lectevr', in la Boétie, *Oeuvres complètes*, p. 62.

wars, revolts and brutal repression. The tension between the entrenched, defensive Catholicism and the new, dissident Protestantism was at its peak. Reacting to a number of intricate domestic and foreign policy issues, King Charles IX was persuaded that the Huguenots were trying to overthrow him. On Saint Bartholomew's Day 1572 he ordered the execution of Protestant leaders. Events escalated dramatically when the Parisian militia precipitated a large and systematic massacre of Protestants, a slaughter that lasted for six days in Paris and even longer in some provincial towns. An estimated 16,000 Protestants were slain.[34]

The Saint Bartholomew massacre, publicly celebrated by Pope Gregory XIII, was an important turning point in terms of both political struggles and the history of ideas.[35] The civil war in France intensified again. Catherine de Médici, who had previously argued strongly for a politics of religious compromise, sanctioned the killing of Protestant leaders and adapted a much more combative stance. Huguenot activists too abandoned tolerance and moved towards an uncompromising defiance of all Royal authority. This constituted a dramatic shift away from earlier Protestant positions that advocated a strict doctrine of non-resistance to tyranny. The old position claimed that since God instituted princes, political authority was unquestionable and obedience to it was due as an act of religious faith. Calvin summarised this position perfectly when claiming that 'there can be no tyranny which in some respect is not a defence to conserve the society of men'.[36] But Luther had already abandoned this doctrine of non-resistance and argued that it is moral and lawful to oppose forcibly a ruler who turns tyrant.[37] Even Calvin eventually abandoned his conservative position and adapted what could be called a Hobbesian position that claimed a ruler must only be obeyed as long as he has the power to impose this obedience.[38] The Saint Bartholomew massacre clearly fuelled this

---

[34] See J.H.M. Salmon, *Society in Crisis: France in the Sixteenth Century* (London: Ernest Benn, 1975), pp. 183–195.

[35] Benedict Anderson, for example, argues that the selective forgetting and mythical representation of the Saint Bartholomew massacre played an important role in the creation of French national identity: *Imagined Communities: Reflections on the Origin and Spread of Nationalism* (London: Verso, 1991/1983), pp. 199–201.

[36] Calvin cited in Michael Walzer, *The Revolution of the Saints: A Study in the Origins of Radical Politics* (New York: Athenaeum, 1968/1965), p. 37.

[37] Quentin Skinner, *The Foundations of Modern Political Thought*, vol. II (Cambridge: Cambridge University Press, 1978), pp. 16–9, 74.

[38] Walzer, *The Revolution of the Saints*, p. 38.

more subversive and radical strand of Protestantism, which eventually turned it into a revolutionary political ideology. Pamphlets advocating radical forms of resistance started to emerge all over France: François Hotman's *Franco-Gallia* (1573), Théodore de Bèze's *De iure magistratuum in subditos* (1574) and Du Plessis-Mornay's *Vindiciae contra Tyrannos* (1579).

The Reformation, initially a conservative religious reaction, now began to look like a radical political movement. While trying to reassert Christian faith, it undermined the only theological authority and thus contributed to a further secularisation of Europe, to the eventual death of God. The most paradoxical aspect of this evolution was that Luther's doctrines, which were primarily aimed at undermining the humanist concepts of free will, turned out to be Humanism's most important catalyst. The Reformation became the ultimate affirmation of rebellious individualism. Liberated from the dogmatism of the Catholic Church, 'man' now stood alone in front of God. Out of these theoretical foundations emerged an unprecedented revolutionary movement that transformed the entire continent. The concept of human agency was no longer simply a rhetorical position. It was by now a radical political practice.[39]

La Boétie's political writings made their public début in the context of this emerging Huguenot radicalism. The *Anti-One* was first published in 1574, in French and in a Latin translation. Both were anonymous and ruthlessly mutilated versions of the original text. The pirated extracts were published as part of a militant Protestant pamphlet, the *Réveille-Matin des François*. It contained a detailed account of the Saint Bartholomew massacre and, directed personally against the King and his Regent, Catherine de Médici, called for the 'revolt of the many against the tyranny of one-man rule'.[40] The actual text of the *Anti-One* was reduced to a dozen pages that included all rhetorical condemnations of tyranny, but none of the more subtle discussions on systems of domination and the engineering of consent. Two years later, the *Anti-One* was printed again in a similarly combative collection of essays, *Les Mémoirs de l'Estat de France sous Charles Neufiesme*, edited by Simon Goulart, a Protestant pastor from Geneva.

---

[39] See Walzer, *The Revolution of the Saints*, pp. 1–21 and in Richard Tarnas, *The Passion of the Western Mind* (New York: Ballantine Books, 1991), pp. 237–43.
[40] *Réveille–Matin des François*, with comments by P. Bonnefon in la Boétie, *Oeuvres complètes*, pp. 402–7.

This publication, reprinted twice in Holland, not only condemned one man rule and feudal hierarchy, but also provided a much more sweeping criticism of contemporary society in general.[41]

By the mid 1570s the *Anti-One* was relatively widely known and associated with radical Huguenot positions. However, this originally complex rhetorical text was by now reduced to an anonymous political pamphlet, a battle cry for radical political action. The concept of human agency, which had emerged only recently in the transition from the Middle Ages to the Renaissance, became helplessly entangled in the religious strife of the Reformation.

Montaigne was clearly upset by this myopic usage of la Boétie's work. He initially intended to give the *Anti-One* a prominent place in his own *Essais*, but given its entanglement in political battles this was not to happen. When the first edition of the *Essais* appeared, in 1580, Montaigne again refused to publish la Boétie's controversial text.[42] To protect the *Anti-One* from being misused as a tool for radical political action, Montaigne downplayed its importance. He claimed that la Boétie wrote this essay 'in his infancy, by way of exercise, as a common subject that had already been treated in a thousand books'.[43] It is likely that Montaigne's position was informed by more than a conservative hostility to change. His work embodies the sceptical element of Renaissance Humanism. For him, the world is a place of diversities and idiosyncrasies, of unique events that cannot be assessed through a Platonic search for truth. There have never been two opinions alike, he claims, not any more than two hairs or two grains are alike. 'Their most universal quality is diversity'.[44] Knowledge of the world can never be absolute. People are deceived by appearances and hence cannot judge things objectively. Montaigne's philosophical scepticism questions people's abilities to reach a consensus about what is good for them.

---

[41] Heller, *Iron and Blood*, p. 75–6.
[42] See Montaigne, *Essais* (Paris: Gallimard, 1950), book I, chapter 28, pp. 231–2.
[43] Ibid, pp. 219, 231–2. For further comments on Montaigne's strategy to trivialise the *Anti-One* see Bonnefon, *Montaigne et ses Amis*, vol. I, pp. 143–5; Mesnard, *L'Essor de la Philosophie Politique au XVIe Siècle*, pp. 390–1.
[44] Montaigne, *Essais*, book II, chapter XXXVII, p. 881. Chapter XII (pp. 481–683), which is entitled 'Apology of Raymond Sebond', contains Montaigne's most explicit engagement with scepticism. See also Max Horkheimer, 'Montaigne und die Funktion der Skepsis', *Kritische Theorie*, vol. II (Frankfurt: Fischer Verlag, 1968/1938), pp. 201–59; and Paul de Man, 'Montaigne and Transcendence', in *Critical Writings, 1953–1978* (Minneapolis: University of Minnesota Press, 1989).

The dispute between Montaigne and radical Huguenots over the interpretation of the *Anti-One* set the framework for many subsequent debates about human agency. Huguenots employed la Boétie's message as a battle cry to support their rebellious individualism. Montaigne, by contrast, drew attention to the authoritarian aspects of the Huguenot revolution. His view implies that dogmatic political actions, even if they seek more freedom, are likely to create new forms of oppression. Hindsight clearly vindicated Montaigne. But in the late sixteenth century his critical voice drowned in the roaring of myopic political battles.

Summary

This chapter constituted the first step of an inquiry into the emergence and constitution of popular dissent. It has observed how rhetorical ideas about dissent have come to shape Renaissance perceptions of human agency. Such an investigation is of direct relevance to an understanding of contemporary transversal dissent, for the assumptions about power and agency that were formed in the early modern period continue to influence political dynamics today.

In a sixteenth-century world where the subject and the very notion of human agency barely existed, Étienne de la Boétie's *Anti-One* was a radical text. The prevailing sense of authority at the time consisted of 'a right to demand obedience as a duty to God'.[45] La Boétie broke radically with this deeply entrenched discourse. He condemned unequivocally all forms of governing that entail some people dominating others. The *Anti-One* claimed that people hold the key to social change, that any form of government, no matter how despotic, is dependent upon popular consent. Because people can withdraw this consent, they can precipitate the downfall of even the most tyrannical ruler.

La Boétie's rhetorical position was part of an emerging humanist challenge that symbolised the transition from the medieval to the modern period. Humanism defied the prevalence of God and placed humanity at the centre of attention. With it re-emerged the long lost notion of human agency, the idea that people are their own masters, equipped with the ability to change both the world and themselves.

The *Anti-One's* subversive message entered the public realm in the

---

[45] Allen, *A History of Political Thought in the Sixteenth Century*, pp. xiv–xv.

context of the civil war between rebellious Huguenots and defensive Catholic authorities. But la Boétie's text was immediately appropriated. It was bent, cut, mutilated. Virtually all of its rhetorical complexities vanished. Left were only the passionate condemnations of tyranny, which were then used to promote popular uprisings against the King of France. The *Anti-One* had turned into a political weapon for radical Huguenots, an instrument of resistance and revolution, an object of contempt and abhorrence. By the end of the sixteenth century, the *Anti-One* was reduced to a mere political pamphlet that did little more than inflate and dogmatise the concept of human agency.

The public appropriation of the *Anti-One* symbolises how dissent and human agency were constituted at the time. The Reformation, which challenged the newly emerging humanist concept of free will, paradoxically provided it with unprecedented momentum. Luther passionately believed that freedom can only arise out of obedience to God's will. If humanity is deprived of this foundation, it will inevitably plunge into a moral and spiritual abyss. But by trying to purify Christian doctrines, the Protestant reformers undermined the only theological authority, the Papacy. The Reformation became an expression of rebellious individualism that eventually led to a secularisation of Europe. Humanism emerged victorious. So victorious that it was to transform the entire Western world in the centuries to come. But one of Humanism's key components, the rhetorical concept of human agency, had become impoverished to a narrow and dogmatic political tool, a dangerously repressive affirmation of the newly gained independence from God and 'his' earthly embodiments.

2   **Romanticism and the dissemination of radical resistance**

> At certain moments in history a strong inspiration takes hold of the masses; then their breathing, their words, and their movements merge to the point that nothing can resist them'.[1]

The previous chapter has shown how Renaissance humanists stepped out of the theocentric medieval discourse and placed 'man' at the centre of the world. Taking Étienne de la Boétie's *Anti-One* as an example, it demonstrated how the notion of popular dissent re-emerged, first as a rhetorical argument, and then as a practice of political protest. The present chapter examines how this early and often tentative articulation of resistance turned into a coherent tradition of popular dissent – one that started to influence social dynamics far beyond the boundaries of Europe. The political dimensions of this tradition thus took on increasingly transversal characteristics – not yet in the sense that protest acts acquired an immediate global dimension, but insofar as the theory and practice of popular dissent gradually came to influence the thoughts and actions of an ever-wider populace.

The dissemination and maturation of popular resistance is observed as a way of continuing the genealogical inquiry into the framing of human agency and transversal dissent. The focus now lies with the period between the seventeenth and the nineteenth century. La Boétie remains central, or at least the dancing shadows of his quill.

Just as Machiavelli's work served as a catalyst for the burgeoning literature on the art of governing the State, la Boétie's intellectual legacy influenced the emergence of a body of knowledge that deals

[1] Simone Weil, 'Méditation sur l'obéissance et la liberté', in *Oeuvres complètes* vol. II (Paris: Gallimard, 1991/1934–7), p. 131.

74

with radical resistance to government. But before this was to happen, the *Anti-One* and its more eminent Renaissance rival, *The Prince*, plunged into relative anonymity. In an attempt to come to terms with this phenomenon, the inquiry will brush over broad discursive trends, particularly the Enlightenment, to then examine more carefully how the *Anti-One* re-emerged in the context of nineteenth-century Romanticism.

The intertwinement of popular dissent with romantic ideas is important because the ensuing characterisation of human agency has contributed substantially to how we perceive the interaction between domination and resistance today. Romanticism is more than simply an historical epoch. It is, as Paul de Man noted, a powerful source for our own contemporary consciousness,[2] a source that often does not receive sufficient attention, especially among social scientists. The same can be said of the tradition of dissent that emerged in the wake of the *Anti-One*. Most of the time it lingered in the margins of dominant discourses. Yet, because it has waged a constant struggle, both in theory and in practice, with dominant societal positions, the *Anti-One*'s intellectual legacy has shaped modern representations of popular dissent.

The human subject in Enlightenment thought

Before la Boétie's intellectual legacy could unfold, French history entered calmer waters and the *Anti-One* disappeared from the stage of political struggles. The coronation of Henri IV signified the advent of a more tolerant phase, albeit a short-lived one. The Edict of Nantes, pronounced in 1598, guaranteed freedom of worship and ended almost four decades of religious wars.

A combative text like the *Anti-One* found few interested readers in such a period of healing. It is unlikely that a marginal comment to an *Anti-One* manuscript, which reads 'seditious against the monarchy' and is dated 22 February 1602, reflected popular opinions at the time.[3] Devastated by decades of religious and political conflicts, Europe at the beginning of the seventeenth century was not looking for radical dissident ideas. People longed for a practical philosophy that could

[2] Paul de Man, *Romanticism and Contemporary Criticism* (Baltimore: Johns Hopkins University Press, 1993), esp. pp. vii–24, 95–100.
[3] Simone Goyard-Fabre, 'Introduction' to la Boétie, *Discours de la Servitude Volontaire* (Paris: Flammarion, 1983), pp. 34–5.

secure order and tranquillity. Neostoicism was among the emerging movements that provided such a stable framework through which people could orient themselves and deal with the problems of everyday life. Political Neostoicism, championed in particular by Justus Lipsius, a professor at Leiden University, stressed that order was needed for the development of the individual. People were expected to obey a ruler who could provide the discipline necessary for the maintenance of stability. The ruler, in turn, was supposed to honour this commitment and govern fairly.[4]

The concept of popular dissent vanished even more when the recently gained tolerance gave way to another wave of absolutism. The new authoritarian practices were epitomised by the governing style of cardinal Richelieu and the subsequent reign of Louis XIV. After the Catholic Church had lost most of its power during the Reformation, the king, as the remaining established authority, was able to profit from the power vacuum and further extend his rule. Jean Bodin had already provided the conceptual foundations for this new authoritarianism. His *Six Livres de la République* granted the sovereign – now installed within a modernised absolutist State – the unlimited power of making law for itself. The *Anti-One* literally drowned in a dominant societal discourse that once more elevated absolutism to the centre of political practice. On rare occasions curious minds still engaged the *Anti-One*, which suggests that its subversive flame was not entirely extinguished. A book by the cardinal of Retz, anonymously published in 1665, is said to be influenced by a reading of the *Anti-One*, and no lesser than Richelieu was trying to estimate its potential for subversion. Having read Montaigne's praise of la Boétie, he gave orders to search all libraries and book stores on rue Saint-Jacques in Paris for this obscure text.[5]

While political practices were confined within the parameters of seventeenth-century royal absolutism, the world of thought entered a highly innovative period. Expanding upon the propositions that Copernicus had advanced in the previous century, scholars such as Newton, Kepler and Galileo ushered Europe into an unprecedented

---

[4] John Hale, *The Civilization of Europe in the Renaissance* (London: Fontana Press, 1993), pp. 212–13. See also Gerhard Oestreich, *Neostoicism and the early modern state* (Cambridge: Cambridge University Press, 1982).

[5] Paul Bonnefon, *Montaigne et ses Amis*, vol. I (Armand Colin: Paris, 1898), pp. 167–9.

scientific revolution. Philosophers soon started to borrow the methods with which the spectacular scientific discoveries became possible. René Descartes' much-rehearsed 'cogito, ergo sum' symbolised the search for irrefutable knowledge. Although he agreed with Montaigne that much is uncertain in the world, Descartes asserted that the actual process of thinking cannot be doubted. 'I think, therefore I am'. The awareness of the thinker is a fact and 'his' capacity to reason opens up possibilities to understand the world.

The quest for objectivity culminated in the following century, the so-called Enlightenment. In an influential essay, first published in 1784, Immanuel Kant portrays this epoque as 'a way out', a process of emancipation, the liberation of humanity from a self-imposed state of immaturity.[6] It is not my intention to engage with the various complex debates that characterise the Enlightenment – a period that exerted a monumental influence on science and the history of ideas. My objective is merely to provide a rudimentary, and consequently somewhat stereotypical, image of this epoque, so that I can then analyse more carefully how la Boétie's intellectual legacy re-emerged in the subsequent romantic era. Both the seventeenth and the eighteenth century produced a range of enigmatic political philosophers (Spinoza, Hobbes, Rousseau, Hume and Kant, among others, spring to mind) whose writings not only shaped, but also defied the mainstream discursive patterns that I am painting here with broad and slightly rushed strokes.

The dominant strains of Enlightenment thought embody the victory of reason over superstition, science over mythology, progress over tradition and human kind over nature. They capture the death of God in the language and logic of physics, mathematics and modern rationality. But humanity now faced the problem Luther had anticipated one and a half centuries earlier: there was nothing left to stand on. Humanism had dismantled the theocentric universe and replaced it with rather shaky foundations, based upon honour and the dignity of man, upon what Machiavelli called virtue. The Enlightenment used a different strategy to regain the certainty that had existed during the medieval period. It now focused the word around an unbounded confidence in man's ability to reason. Mainstream Enlightenment thought

---

[6] Immanuel Kant, 'Beantwortung der Frage: Was ist Aufklärung?', *Werke*, vol. IV (Berlin: Bruno Cassirer, 1922), p. 169.

discovered the Archimedean foundation that modern 'man' had long searched for: an objectified Humanism, stripped of Renaissance rhetoric and scepticism.

La Boétie's radical portrayal of popular dissent stands in an ambivalent relationship with Enlightenment thought. Some of his ideas fit well into the new context, others contradict its most fundamental tenets. La Boétie's emphasis on natural rights, his belief in the power of logos and emancipation, clearly had some appeal to an audience who increasingly became captured by themes of reason, progress and the search for a secular autonomy of the Self. Not surprisingly, la Boétie's rhetoric slowly started to re-emerge. Several new editions of Montaigne's *Essais*, appearing between 1727 and 1745, now included the text of the *Anti-One*.[7] This brought la Boétiean rhetoric to an ever-wider circle of readers. In the revolutionary period, between 1789 and 1792, the *Anti-One* was reprinted several times on its own. But as radical Huguenots had done two centuries earlier, revolutionaries now appropriated the *Anti-One* to promote an activist celebration of human agency. The text appeared in various forms, alone or in annexes to other texts, prefaced and postscripted with combative introductions and comments. There is even good reason to believe that J.P. Marat's influential 1790 edition of *Les Chaînes de l'Esclavage* contains passages that are plagiarised from la Boétie.[8]

Despite this renewed interest in popular dissent, the *Anti-One* was unable to escape from the margins of Enlightenment thought, at least in part because la Boétie's rhetorical defence of human agency was incompatible with a quest for scientific objectivity. In a world of pure reason there was little scope for Renaissance scepticism, for ruminations about limits to cognition. Paradoxically, the Enlightenment became increasingly incompatible with the crux of Humanism, the concept of free will. In this sense Enlightenment and Humanism were, as Foucault notes, 'in a state of tension rather than identity'.[9] Expressed in a crass and simplified manner: if 'man' was still autonomous, then only as an observer, not as an agent. There was no place for human agency in a world that allegedly worked according to a

---

[7] See Goyard-Fabre, 'Introduction', pp. 45–6.
[8] J.P. Marat, *Les Chaînes de l'Esclavage* (Paris: Imprimerie de Marat, 1790), esp. the section on pp. 286–95, entitled 'how people enslave themselves'. See also Bonnefon, *Montaigne et ses Amis*, vol. I, pp. 169–71.
[9] Michel Foucault, 'What is Enlightenment', in P. Rabinow (ed.), *The Foucault Reader*, tr. C. Porter (New York: Pantheon Books, 1984), p. 44.

set of fixed, universal and ahistoric principles. 'Man' was alienated, depersonalised – a small and irrelevant part of a much larger, automatically functioning machine driven and controlled by pre-set scientific laws.

Romanticism and the aesthetic revival of human agency

Romanticism was, amongst other things, a reaction against Enlightenment determinism. It penetrated France towards the end of the eighteenth century and took hold of a disintegrating world characterised by the Napoleonic wars and turmoil. One of the key assumptions of the Enlightenment, the idea that the spread of reason and science would inevitably lead towards progress, towards a better world, had not materialised. With the failure of the French Revolution, the belief in linear progress was shattered. Disillusioned with their predecessors' trust in reason, some romantics were now looking for suppressed voices in their cultural heritage. Rousseau was remembered, or at least the passages in which he defies his contemporaries and portrays the achievements of civil society as leading humanity to nothing but further enslavement. Reason, Rousseau claimed, alienates 'man' from nature, engenders egocentrism (*amour propre*) and turns humanity against itself.[10]

Joining Rousseau in his philosophical journey back to the peaceful state of nature, romantics tried to escape the deterministic and suffocating world of scientific laws by creating space for self-expression and imagination. The focus now shifted from the realm of objectivity to the subjective, the unconscious and the mystical, from reason to emotion, passion and spontaneity. Truth no longer lay in science, but in aesthetics – which then comprised not just art or music or literature, but all aspects of human sensation and cognition. With this aesthetic move, predated by Kant, the whole register of human experiences suddenly appeared less marginal than before. The world centred again around the human subject.[11] Modern thought increasingly recognised, as Wolfgang Welsch points out, that our perceptions of the world are not

---

[10] Jean-Jacques Rousseau, *Discours sur l'origine et les fondements de l'inégalité parmi les hommes* (Paris: Gallimard, 1985/1755), p. 79.
[11] Terry Eagleton, *The Ideology of the Aesthetic* (Oxford: Basil Blackwell, 1990), p. 102.

authentic, but part of specific forms of life. 'Reality', in this sense, was acknowledged as being 'aesthetically constituted'.[12]

Being sceptical of universalised norms, romantics generally refused to rely upon rational and abstract notions of the subject – they opposed the Enlightenment themes of *liberté, egalité, fraternité*. Instead, romantics celebrated the diversities of the human drama, its destructive and creative moments, the idiosyncrasies of the individual mind. Although Romanticism is often considered to be Europe's last common cultural approach, it embraced a different mantle in each of the various countries, walks of life and intellectual circles it penetrated. One would be hard pressed to find a lowest common denominator that unites French Romanticism with German romantic pioneers like Goethe, Herder, Hölderlin, Schiller, Schlegel, Schelling and Schleimermacher, or with the Anglo-Saxon literary Romanticism of Byron, Wordsworth, Coleridge, Shelley and Yeats.

Romantic ideas are characterised by heterogeneity, rather than a set of common beliefs. This is why the present analysis does not claim to provide a representative account of a highly complex intellectual movement. Instead, the focus rests on a specific, activist form of Romanticism, one that has shaped practices of popular dissent and often lacks some of the more subtle nuances that were articulated in philosophical, literary and poetic circles.

In the realm of politics, Romanticism signified above all a strong re-emergence of the concept of human agency. The subject was no longer simply a perceiver in the world, but again an agent. History was once more open to be shaped by the will and actions of people.

The *Anti-One* surged back into prominence and became one of the textual sources that provided the foundation for a romantic celebration of human agency. In 1835, against the backdrop of an emerging proletarian struggle and a radical insurrection that stretched from Paris to Lyon, the Abbot Félicité de Lamennais revived some of la Boétie's ideas. Initially one of the Catholic defenders of the Bourbons, Lamennais became one of the period's most outspoken critics. He refused a cardinal's position, was repudiated by the Pope, and subsequently turned into a militant advocate of proletarian rights.[13] His journal *L'Avenir*, founded during the revolution of 1830, was a well-

---

[12] Wolfgang Welsch, *Ästhetisches Denken* (Stuttgart: Reclam, 1993), p. 7.
[13] See Jean-René Derré, *Lamennais, ses Amis, et le Mouvement des Idées à l'Époque Romantique* (Paris: Librairie Klincksieck, 1962).

known protest voice against the bourgeois monarchy and all forms of state intervention and repression. Lamennais published a new version of the *Anti-One*, hoping that its rhetoric would engender popular dissent and terminate the terror and despotism that had dominated France in the preceding forty years.

Lamennais' emotional and combative preface to the new publication of the *Anti-One* signifies Romanticism at its peak. We are in a world of turmoil, struggle and darkness, a world in which the subject heroically strives for freedom:

> You who have faith in the destiny of the human kind, summon up your courage, the future will be yours. You will be persecuted and tortured, but you will never be defeated. Each great cause requires great sacrifices to become triumphant.[14]

In the wake of this romantic passion for revolt, interest in the *Anti-One* surged. The same year, 1835, two more editions emerged and the following year Charles Teste, exiled from France for his subversive activities, published a version transcribed into modern and thus more widely accessible French. The *Anti-One* became increasingly prominent, especially in the context of protest movements that followed the December 1853 *coup d'état* by Napoleon II. La Boétie's essay was reprinted numerous times, read in ever wider circles, and discussed in various forums, such as the prominent *Journal des Débats*.[15] By the 1860s the *Anti-One* had escaped from the shadows of Montaigne's protective *Essais*. Although still stripped of its rhetorical complexities, a more popular *Anti-One* contributed to the emergence of a tradition of dissent that espouses a strong notion of human agency – a tradition that was no longer confined to the boundaries of France, but gradually shaped political practices on a much wider scale.

Rebellious individualism as a foundation of dissent

There are various ways through which one could observe how, during the second half of the nineteenth century, ideas about popular dissent

---

[14] Félicité de Lamennais, 'Préface de 1835', in la Boétie, *Le Discours de la Servitude Volontaire* (Paris: Payot, 1978), p. 39. 'Pour vous qui avec foi aux destinées du genre humain, prenez courage, l'avenir ne vous faillira point. Vous serez persécutés, tourmentés, mais jamais vaincus'.
[15] See Goyard-Fabre, 'Introduction', pp. 53–9, 123–24.

gradually turned into political practices that became highly significant in ever-more parts of the world. An illustrative example must suffice.

The American romantic Henry David Thoreau is one of the authors who popularised the notion of radical resistance to government. Some have argued that his ideas were directly influenced by la Boétie.[16] This claim is at best speculative. Thoreau's close friend, the poet Ralph Waldo Emerson, was certainly aware of la Boétie. The title of a poem and a notebook entry from early 1843 suggest that Emerson knew him, at least via a reading of Montaigne's *Essais*.[17] Thoreau's writings, however, are silent about the *Anti-One*, and so are most of his biographers.[18] But this is, in some sense, secondary to the fact that the idea of popular dissent, initially articulated by la Boétie, came to shape a variety of discursive practices. Genealogies do not attempt to trace ideas back to an authentic starting point. They observe how sets of common values, norms and behaviours have emerged from a multitude of sources and directions.

With or without drawing directly on the *Anti-One*, Thoreau almost literally re-articulated many of its key claims and then embedded them into a romantic world-view. His writings imply, like la Boétie's, that any form of government rests upon popular consent, and if this consent is withdrawn, even the most authoritarian regime will crumble like a house of cards. Passive withdrawal, so-called civil disobedience, is enough to trigger this process. Writing in protest against slavery and the war with Mexico, Thoreau argues in 1848:

> [I]f one thousand, if one hundred, if ten men whom I could name, – if ten honest men only, – aye, if one HONEST man, in this State of Massachusetts, *ceasing to hold slaves*, were actually to withdraw from this copartnership, and be locked up in the county jail therefor, it would be the abolition of slavery in America. . . A minority is powerless while it conforms to the majority; it is not even a minority then; but it is irresistible when it clogs by its whole weight. If the alternative is to keep all just men in prison, or give up war and slavery, the State will not hesitate which to choose.[19]

---

[16] Bart de Ligt, *The Conquest of Violence: An Essay on War and Revolution* (London: George Routledge, 1937), p. 104.

[17] Ralph Waldo Emerson, 'Etienne de la Boéce', in *The Complete Works*, vol. IX (Boston: Houghton Mifflin, 1918), p. 82; *The Journals and Miscellaneous Notebooks*, vol. IX, *1843–1847* (Cambridge: Harvard University Press, 1971), p. 28.

[18] Note, for example, la Boétie's absence in Robert Sattelmeyer's *Thoreau's Reading: A Study in Intellectual History* (Princeton: Princeton University Press, 1988).

[19] Henry David Thoreau, 'Civil Disobedience', in *Walden and Civil Disobedience* (New York: W.W. Norton, 1966/1848), p. 232–3.

Thoreau's concept of withdrawing consent is embedded in a theory of power that could literally have been lifted out of the *Anti-One*. His main focus, however, does not lie with the masses and their ability to overthrow a ruler. It is almost exclusively geared towards fighting for and protecting the autonomy of the individual.

Thoreau exemplifies the crux of political Romanticism, a Self that is autonomous and has priority over everything else. This tendency to deify the individual has been interpreted in various ways. Carl Schmitt called it subjectified occasionalism, a situation in which the romantic ego, embedding the final authority, relegates the world and everything else into a mere occasion.[20] René Girard talks of 'romantic lies' – illusions that consider the subject as the centre of everything. The romantic, he says, 'wants to be persuaded that his desire is inscribed into the nature of things or, which amounts to the same, that he is the emanation of a serene subjectivity, the creation *ex nihilo* of a quasi-divine Self'.[21]

While Enlightenment thought had employed science and reason to restore certainty in the world, Romanticism anchored its world-view in a sovereign subject and an unbounded trust in the power of human agency. The overall quest, however, remained the same: to fill the vacuum that had opened up after the death of God.

Thoreau argues that the state may have superior physical strength, but it can never interfere with an individual's intellectual or moral senses. The state, 'timid' and 'half-witted', can inflict punishment upon one's body, but this strategy is of no match to a Thoreau who proclaims that 'I will breathe after my own fashion. Let us see who is the strongest'.[22] While reconstructing the night he spent in jail for refusing to pay taxes, Thoreau stresses that the thick walls of solid stone, the iron door and grating, indeed, the entire power of the state's repressive apparatus could not reach him – a great waste of stone and mortar they were, he says.[23] For romantics, nothing can touch the autonomous Self, not the prison, not the repressive state, not even the subtle power of societal customs.

Awoke the romantic hero: the individual who rises to the occasion and challenges the repressive forces around 'him', the one who 'stands

---

[20] Carl Schmitt, *Politische Romantik* (München: Duncker & Humblot, 1925), p. 24.
[21] René Girard, *Mensonge romantique et vérité romanesque* (Paris: Bernard Grasset, 1961), p. 30.
[22] Thoreau, 'Civil Disobedience', p. 236.
[23] Ibid., pp. 236–9.

resolutely and incorruptly against decadence, evil and deceit, until they are exposed for what they are'.[24] It is, however, important to remember that the speculative idealism and the strong notion of human agency that is entailed in this deification of the Self was an important but not uncontested position within romantic thought. Other forms of Romanticism flourished at the same time. Consider, for example, the feminist Romanticism that evolved parallel to the canonical masculine one. This body of literature shared some of the above-mentioned themes, such as the hostility towards authority, a sense of identification with the victim, or a focus on emotions and the construction of subjectivities.[25] But feminine forms of Romanticism also differed in various crucial aspects. Most women writers, such as Mary Shelley, Jane Austen, Mary Wollstonecraft or Dorothy Wordsworth did not pursue the search for a visionary freedom beyond the confines of the state. Instead, they were concerned with the social constraints that had been imposed upon them. They employed the novel as a site of contestation, expressing the manner in which their female subjectivity was intertwined with and confined by concrete daily concerns, linked to such issues as family, community or female bodies.[26] This contrast is well reflected in the work of Margaret Fuller, Thoreau's contemporary and fellow Bostonian. Fuller clearly rejects the sense of autonomy and unboundedness that prevails in Thoreau's Romanticism. For her, the discursive prison walls are much thicker than they are for Thoreau. It is, consequently, the social construction of femininity and masculinity that is the subject of her inquiries.[27] Later parts of this book will return in detail to the themes opened up by Fuller and others. For the moment, however, the attention rests primarily with the dominant, masculine and activist heritage of Romanticism. This is not to suggest that this strain is more insightful or authentic than others, but to recognise that through its hegemonic status it has played a crucial role in shaping the formation of our contemporary consciousness.

The right to refuse allegiance to a government that engages in acts

[24] David Morse, *Perspectives on Romanticism* (London: MacMillan, 1981), p. 37.
[25] Julia Ellison, *Delicate Subjects: Romanticism, Gender, and the Ethics of Understanding* (Ithaca: Cornell University Press, 1990), p. 11.
[26] See, for example, Meena Alexander, *Women in Romanticism* (London: MacMillan, 1989), pp. 1–17; and Anne K. Mellor, *Romanticism and Gender* (New York: Routledge, 1993), pp. 2–11.
[27] See *The Essential Margaret Fuller*, ed. J. Steele (New Brunswick, NJ: Rutgers University Press, 1992).

of tyranny is a theme that resonates not just in romantic, but also in liberal discourses. Nancy Rosenblum, for example, interprets Thoreau's Romanticism as a combination of heroic individualism and liberal democracy. She argues that Thoreau advances a libertarian agenda that constantly oscillates between a liberal concern for the public sphere and a radical romantic detachment from it.[28] There are indeed parallels between liberalism and the la Boétiean tradition. The importance of the individual and a deep distrust towards government provides both of these strains of thought with an inherent anti-authoritarian core, at least in theory. But Thoreau also displays very strong anarchist traits. Disgusted with a state that endorses slavery and war, he wants to disengage altogether from this repressive institution, 'withdraw and stand aloof from it effectually'.[29] His two year stay at Walden Pond is, of course, the embodiment of this withdrawal, the classical Rousseauean return to nature. Implied in this withdrawal, and at times explicitly articulated, is a much deeper distrust towards the state, indeed, towards every societal organisation that controls the individual and 'his' mind. For Thoreau injustice is a necessary product of the machinery of government. An individual cannot be free as long as 'he' operates within the confines of the state. In some of his more combative moments, Thoreau assumes a passionate anarchist stance, declares war against the state and portrays government as a demonic force, a monster, 'a semi-human tiger or ox, stalking over the earth with its heart taken out and the top of its brain shot away'.[30] It is this anarchist element that sucks Thoreau right into the vortex of la Boétie's legacy.

But there are still several missing links between an individualistic anarchist revival of la Boétie and a theory of collective resistance. Romantic dissent focuses on the primacy of the perceiver and the poetisation of political practice. This pushes romantics, at least according to the influential opinion of Carl Schmitt, towards a situation in which conflicts are not addressed, but deferred, subjectified, transplanted into a higher realm of aesthetic imagination.[31] Some even claim that romantic thought contains, by definition, a conservative

---

[28] Nancy L. Rosenblum, *Another Liberalism: Romanticism and the Reconstruction of Liberal Thought* (Cambridge, Mass.: Harvard University Press, 1987), pp. 103–4.
[29] Thoreau, 'Civil Disobedience', p. 239.
[30] Thoreau cited in Rosenblum, *Another Liberalism*, p. 109.
[31] Schmitt, *Politische Romantik*, esp. pp. 115–52, 222–8.

core.[32] One can argue with such an interpretations, and I shall do so later. What matters at this point, however, is that the anarchist romantic generally does not seek political power, but despises and circumvents it. Thoreau engaged in the struggle around slavery by withdrawing from the state that endorses this repressive practice. He returned to the woods, to Walden Pond, retreating into the ultimate source of the romantic world-view, the Self. This anarchist form of individualism was subversive on many accounts, but it was perceived to lack the element of immediate and direct social engagement.

From theory to practice, from individual to collective action

Some of the later romantics tried to add a more direct political dimension to the already subversive Thoreauean foundations. They shifted the practice of withdrawing consent from detachment to engagement, and from individualism to collective action. With this move arose a coherent tradition of popular dissent and an equally powerful assertion of human agency – one that came to influence political dynamics in ever-more parts of the world.

The more la Boétie's legacy spread beyond national boundaries, the more it became intertwined with the emerging anarchist movement. By the end of the nineteenth century leading anarchist historians, such as Max Nettlau and Ernst Victor Zenker, portrayed la Boétie as an important intellectual precursor to the likes of Pierre Joseph Proudhon, Mikhail Bakunin, Petr Kropotkin, Max Stirner or Emma Goldman.[33] One can, indeed, hear la Boétie's voice resonating in Stirner's claim that if the labourer acts upon the insight that 'his' power is 'his' property, the state simply crumbles.[34] By the early twentieth century several anarchists started to draw directly upon la Boétie. Gustav Landauer, one of the key figures in the German anarchist movement, constructed his central arguments around a discussion of the *Anti-*

---

[32] Karl Mannheim, *Essays on Sociology and Social Psychology* (London: Routledge and Kegan Paul, 1953), esp. pp. 74–164.
[33] Ernst Viktor Zenker, *Anarchism: A Criticism and History of the Anarchist Theory* (London: Methuen, 1898), pp. 15–16; Max Nettlau, *Bibliographie de l'Anarchie* (New York: Burt Franklin, 1968/1897), p. 2.
[34] Max Stirner, *Der Einzige und sein Eigentum* (Leipzig: Verlag Otto Wigand, 1845), esp. pp. 244–8.

One. Bart de Ligt, a prominent Dutch anarcho-pacifist relied upon la Boétie, and so did Simone Weil in her unusual fusion of Anarchism, Marxism, Stoicism and Christian mysticism.[35] But to understand how radical popular dissent gained prominence in various parts of the world, we must reach further back and observe what precisely occurred when la Boétie's intellectual legacy came of age during the transition from the nineteenth to the twentieth century.

Various authors played a crucial role in transforming romantic individualism into a coherent tradition of popular dissent. I will focus primarily upon two of them, Leo Tolstoy and Mohandas Gandhi. Both operated within anarchist and neo-romantic frameworks. Both played a crucial role in bringing the la Boétiean legacy to a world-wide audience. Both were instrumental in transforming the concept of withdrawing consent into a mass phenomenon of far-reaching political significance. And, finally, both espoused a strong notion of human agency.

Tolstoy draws directly and extensively upon la Boétie's work. Violence, he argues, can never be enough to keep a ruler in place. Domination over the populace can only be sustained because people are being deceived, or because they sacrifice their freedom for small gains and benefits. To underline this point, Tolstoy inserts a long quote from the *Anti-One,* followed by various central arguments that are, in essence, attempts to paraphrase la Boétie and demonstrate his relevance to contemporary political dynamics:

> One would have thought that just the working people, who derive no kind of profit from the violence done them, would at last see through the deception in which they are entangled, and having seen the fraud, would free themselves from it in the simplest and easiest way: by ceasing to take part in the violence which can only be perpetrated upon them thanks to their participation in it.[36]

La Boétie also plays a central role in Gandhi's thought, primarily via the influence of Tolstoy. Gandhi incessantly stressed how 'deeply impressed' and 'overwhelmed' he was by Tolstoy. Thoreau, likewise,

---

[35] Weil, 'Méditation sur l'obéissance et la liberté', pp. 128–33; Gustav Landauer, *Die Revolution* (Frankfurt: Rutten and Loening, 1907); de Ligt, *The Conquest of Violence,* pp. 104–6.

[36] Leo Tolstoy, *The Law of Violence and the Law of Love* (London: Unicorn Press, 1959), pp. 38–40. See also *Tolstoy's Writings on Civil Disobedience and Non-Violence* (London: Peter Owen, 1967).

was acknowledged as an important source.[37] Not surprisingly, Gandhi ended up with a distinctive la Boétiean approach to popular dissent. He theorised from the perspective of the masses and viewed social dynamics through the eyes of the ruled, rather than the rulers. Gandhi too argued that power is dependent upon popular consent:

> I believe, and everybody must grant, that no Government can exist for a single moment without the co-operation of the people, willing or forced, and if people suddenly withdraw their co-operation in every detail, the Government will come to a stand-still.[38]

Various romantic voices resonate in Gandhi's and Tolstoy's reformulation of the *Anti-One*. But neither of them is a romantic in the strict sense of the term. Romanticism as a self-conscious and coherent cultural movement disintegrated by the middle of the nineteenth century, some would even say it ended with the death of Hegel in 1831.[39] Yet, romantic ideas endured far beyond the historical epoque that is associated with them. Tolstoy's prime medium of expression, the novel, embodies the romantic suspicion towards scientific objectivity. It celebrates diversity, life's emotional and individualistic features. Many of Gandhi's more subtle arguments are constructed around a frontal assault at the core of mainstream Western thought, the concept of instrumental rationality. For both Tolstoy and Gandhi opposition to rationalism amounted to a return of the sacred, a prominent romantic theme. Tolstoy could only overcome the decay of his time, nihilism, through an affirmation of Christian faith and morality.[40] Likewise, Gandhi's political philosophy is rooted in a strong moral framework. All of his writings, he stresses, have a spiritual end.[41]

The two most distinctly romantic elements in Tolstoy and Gandhi are the belief in an autonomous Self and the refusal to cooperate with a state that violates the dignity and rights of its subject. Both express a strong belief in an individualistic form of human agency. Tolstoy was constantly drawn back and forth between engaging with society

---

[37] Mohandas Gandhi, *The Story of My Experiments With Truth*, tr. M. Desai (Boston: Beacon Press, 1959/1927–1929), pp. 90, 137/8, 160; *Hind Swaraj or Indian Home Rule*, tr. M. Desai (Ahmedabad: Navajivan, 1984/1938), p. 105.

[38] Gandhi, *Satyagraha*, tr. V.G. Desai (Ahmedabad: Navajivan, 1958), p. 157.

[39] Robert A. Caponigri, *A History of Western Philosophy*, vol. III (Notre Dame: University of Notre Dame Press, 1963–71), p. 471.

[40] Tolstoy, *The Law of Violence*, esp. pp. 15–17, 21–4.

[41] Gandhi, *The Story of my Experiments with Truth*, p. 272. Among the ones who explicitly acknowledge the romantic dimensions of Gandhi's thought is Partha Chatterjee, *Nationalist Thought and the Colonial World* (London: Zed Books, 1986), pp. 97–8.

and renouncing it. Symptomatic of this are the final days of his life, when he decided, at the age of 82, to withdraw for good from society. He secretly left his family just to perish of pneumonia, a few days later, at the railway station of Astapovo: tragic and dramatic, the typical death of a romantic hero. The same romantic oscillation between social being and outcast is present in Gandhi's life. His activism and practice of self-reliance constantly subverted the power of the state. Indeed, Gandhi's very life, mythologised as it has become, represents the ideal autonomous subject: a skinny Indian lawyer who, transformed into a romantic hero, dared to stand up and defy the entire British Empire.

Gandhi's writings on human agency and dissent were primarily intended to promote social change. The vortex of this approach was satyagraha, a term coined in 1906, in the early days of Gandhi's involvement with the struggle that Indian immigrant workers waged against the South African regime. Satyagraha encapsulates a great variety of methods, including strikes, demonstrations, refusal to serve the state, or non-payment of fines and taxes. In this political context, the romantic hero, the satyagrahi, does not simply withdraw to Walden Pond. 'He' is willing to 'sacrifice his property and even his family', and 'suffers unto death' to fight for justice and a better world.[42] Satyagraha demands, Gandhi argues, total dedication from an activist. Sacrifice of the self is indispensable for a successful campaign of non-cooperation. Besides adhering to the principle of *ahimsa*, of non-violence as an ethical principle, this practice demands from a satyagrahi to renounce all possessions, live in poverty, and take the vow of *brachmacharya*, of chastity. Gandhi's romantic hero must be willing to endure abuse, live in deprivation, fast as a sign of protest, or, as Thoreau had already advocated, freely submit to imprisonment:

> Our triumph consists in thousands being led to the prisons like lambs to the slaughter house. If the lambs of the world had been willingly led, they would have long ago saved themselves from the butcher's knife. . . The greater our innocence, the greater our strength and the swifter our victory.[43]

There are pragmatic political reasons for these rather extreme posi-

---

[42] Gandhi, *Satyagraha*, pp. 67, 314.
[43] Gandhi, *Satyagraha*, p. 172. For further discussions see Joan V. Bondurant, *Conquest of Violence: The Gandhian Philosophy of Conflict* (Berkeley: University of California Press, 1967), pp. 35–104 and Raghavan Narasimhan Iyer, *The Moral and Political Thought of Mahatma Gandhi* (New York: Oxford University Press, 1973), pp. 251–344.

tions on personal sacrifice and self-reliance. A true satyagrahi could hardly be coopted or bribed by a government. 'He' is always ready to make any sacrifice necessary to push non-cooperation to its limits. Furthermore, a sustained effort of non-violent resistance, conducted by self-sacrificing satyagrahis, has a profound psychological effect. It is a conversation with the consciousness of the opponent. It evokes pity, Gandhian tactic implies, which may convert the opponent and thus lead to accommodation.

The shift from radical individualism to collective action marked the beginning of a coherent and increasingly global tradition of popular dissent. The fact that authors of the stature of Tolstoy or Gandhi advocated this move was instrumental for its dissemination. Gandhi, in particular, added a truly global dimension to the theory and practice of popular dissent. He provided unprecedented political momentum to a notion of human agency that before had existed primarily on a rhetorical level. His thoughts and deeds informed countless civil disobedience campaigns. Independently of whether or not we agree with them, our perceptions of popular dissent have been influenced substantially by the ideas and practices that ensued from Gandhi's application of la Boétian rhetoric.

With the move towards collective action, the notion of human agency became intertwined with political activism. Tolstoy lectured workers on exploitation, encouraged peasants to stop obeying their landlords, and advised conscripts to refuse military service – and all this against the backdrop of the la Boétian idea that suffering is caused by one's own enslavement, that if one desires it, one can be free.[44] Gandhi's entire life consisted of activism. His political engagement began when he was a lawyer in South Africa. Appalled by various race related discriminations against Indian immigrants, Gandhi became increasingly active in acts of social non-cooperation. Between 1906 and 1914 he led countless satyagrahi campaigns, including refusals of registration, strikes, protest marches and fasts. Back in his native India, Gandhi and his increasingly numerous followers used the same political techniques to fight British colonial rule. Mass civil disobedience became a powerful tool in the struggle for independence.

Gandhi's activism demonstrated that the idea of withdrawing consent is actually applicable in practice. He was able to establish the

[44] Tolstoy, *The Law of Violence*, pp. 37–42, 55–9, 98–9.

dialectical link between intellectuals and the masses that Gramsci so convincingly portrayed as the key to successful resistance.[45] Representative for Gandhi's various campaigns of non-cooperation is the famous salt march of 1930. The production of salt, an indispensable product for every Indian, was a government monopoly and levied with exorbitant taxes. As a protest against this practice, Gandhi and some eighty fellow satyagrahis embarked upon a 240 mile walk to the Gujarat coast, where they intended to extract their own salt from the sea. The immediate objective of this symbolic and carefully planned public defiance was the annulment of the salt tax. On a more fundamental level, the salt march was intended to undermine the legality of the colonial government as such. The satyagrahis tried to attract as much public attention as possible. They walked through many villages, where they paused, informed the people of their cause, and encouraged them to defy the law and manufacture their own salt. In some towns their appearance drew as many as 30,000 eager listeners. The satyagrahis also incited village headmen to resign and stop cooperating with the colonial authorities, an appeal that had considerable success. Although the British salt monopoly was never threatened, the salt march had a dramatic impact. It was the prelude of a powerful nationwide campaign of mass civil disobedience. By mid 1930, Judith Brown argues, civil disobedience posed a severe challenge to British colonial rule in India.[46] Knowledge of the Gandhian technique of resistance had spread and non-cooperation was practised in every province. Throughout the one-year-long campaign an estimated 60,000 people were arrested and many more participated in one way or another in acts of non-cooperation, for example by boycotting foreign cloth.[47]

The campaign that followed the salt march was one of the first cases of carefully planned and coordinated mass civil disobedience, a successful manifestation of massive popular dissent. Although the campaign did not uproot the British colonial empire, it demonstrated that the notion of withdrawing consent could no longer be dismissed as a mere utopian dream. La Boétie's rhetorical arguments had spread

[45] Antonio Gramsci, *Selections from the Prison Notebooks*, tr. Q. Hoare and G.N. Smith (New York: International Publishers, 1985/1929–1935), pp. 5–24, 334.
[46] Judith Brown, *Gandhi and Civil Disobedience* (Cambridge: Cambridge University Press, 1977), p. 123.
[47] Ibid., p. 124.

beyond national boundaries and made the transition from theory to practice – but with what consequences?

To implement the la Boétiean idea of withdrawing consent in practice, Gandhi had to reduce complex arguments about human agency to a few parsimonious propositions that deal with the power of people to raise against domination. Undoubtedly, this strategy has a number of distinct advantages. A simple slogan, like 'people power', 'long live the revolution', or 'we are the people' can provide a movement of popular dissent with a sense of unity and with the momentum necessary to unleash its potential of resistance. Such an activist promotion of human agency is a double-edged sword. It may gather forces of dissent, but not without engendering problems at both theoretical and practical levels. Gandhi's political engagement demonstrates why. Pushed to the extreme, his celebration of human agency may lead, paradoxically, to an annihilation of the subject. Much like some describe the changing nature of Romanticism in general,[48] Gandhi's activism relocated human agency from rebellious individualism to an almost functionalist position that reduced the role of individuals to the logic of societal totality. During Gandhi's salt march, for example, it was always assumed that everyone would agree with the direction and desirability of the particular change that was intended. Minorities within the protesting population were largely irrelevant. All that mattered were the masses and the uniform function that was superimposed on often diversely motivated individuals.

Neo-romanticism had moved full circle and returned to the determinism it initially reacted against. Gandhi's conception of mass dissent is a far cry from Thoreau's warning that 'there is but little virtue in the action of masses of men'.[49] For Gandhi the protesting population is a coherent and homogeneous element which, almost like the subject in Hegel's philosophy of history, becomes conscious of itself and dialectically proceeds to unify humanity. This approach implies that a great number of individuals can reach a consensus about what kind of action is desirable for what purpose.

One could, of course, problematise other aspects of Gandhi's ideas and practices too. One could draw attention to the masculine values of an activist who abandons wife and children to fight for freedom

---

[48] Nader Saiedi, *The Birth of Social Theory* (Lanham, Md: University Press of America, 1993), pp. 64–98.
[49] Thoreau, 'Civil Disobedience', p. 229.

and justice. One could rethink the moral celebration of self-denial and sacrifice. It was precisely in these apparently unegoistic actions that Nietzsche detected a will for power, a thirst for triumph, a desire to subjugate.[50] Or one could further scrutinise the image of moral right-eousness that is entailed in the fusion of religion and activism. Gandhian morality ignores that there is value in truth, and that it is always the moral ones themselves who define the parameters of morality. A Nietzschean position would, instead, recognise untruth as a condition of life and explore issues of inclusion and exclusion by investigating the constituted nature of all moral claims.[51]

Deconstructing Gandhi is not my task here. It is far more important, at least at this stage of the inquiry, to recognise how Gandhi and other writer-activists discussed in this chapter have laid the foundations for a coherent and still relevant tradition of popular dissent. It is at this moment, during the Romantic period and its aftermath, that the la Boétiean tradition transformed itself from an obscure and localised radicalism into political practices that spread beyond national borders and could no longer be ignored or circumvented. The stunning success of Gandhi's non-violent activism, in particular, illustrated the practical and increasingly globalised dimensions of la Boétie's rhetorical claim that 'if one concedes nothing to [the tyrants], if one refuses to obey them, then without fighting, without striking, they become naked and defeated and are no more'.[52]

Summary

This chapter has continued a genealogical inquiry into the framing of human agency during the modern period. The focus has now been with observing how the theory and practice of popular dissent evolved from the end of the Renaissance to the nineteenth century.

The humanist discourse that had replaced the medieval world-view clearly survived the death of Renaissance 'man'. Humanism, which placed the subject at the centre of history, successfully dealt with various onslaughts. It constantly changed appearance and focus and

---

[50] Friedrich Nietzsche, *Zur Genealogie der Moral* (Frankfurt: Insel Taschenbuch, 1991/1887), pp. 9–47.
[51] Friedrich Nietzsche, *Jenseits von Gut und Böse* (Stuttgart: Philipp Reclam, 1988/1886), pp. 8–10; *Zur Genealogie der Moral*, pp. 19–20.
[52] Étienne de la Boétie, 'Discours de la Servitude Volontaire', in P. Bonnefon (ed.), *Oeuvres Complètes* (Genève: Slatkine Reprints, 1967/1552), p. 148.

gradually turned into the vortex of Western thought. The tradition of dissent that was influenced by la Boétie's work became entangled in these superseding humanist interpretations. After having achieved prominence in radical Huguenot circles during the Reformation, the *Anti-One* returned to the realm of anonymity. La Boétie's notion of human agency was overpowered by the scientific revolution that dominated the subsequent two centuries. The sceptical Humanism of the Renaissance gave way to an Enlightenment celebration of reason and science. While this secular objectivism ensured the final transition from the medieval to the modern world, it also annihilated the agent. Or so at least resonate some of the dominant (but not only) intellectual trends of the period. In a universe that was perceived to function according to a set of predetermined and scientifically assessable principles, the notion of human agency became largely irrelevant. The world was still interpreted in a humanist way, but the central position that 'man' occupied was primarily one of rational observer, rather than agent.

Romanticism reacted against the rationalism and determinism of mainstream Enlightenment thought. It reintroduced the subject as agent by shifting the focus from the realm of detached objectivity to the one of emotion, passion and individual autonomy. Aesthetics became central. While the Enlightenment had grounded its worldview in science and reason, Romanticism constructed it around the notion of an autonomous Self. This meant, above all, that history was again open to be shaped by human agency. The *Anti-One* re-emerged in the wake of this discursive shift. Its popularity surged in the context of the labour unrest that dominated France in the 1830s. It became an object of scholarly attention, was reprinted numerous times and gradually spread beyond French national borders.

Thoreau was among the authors who popularised the notion of radical resistance and provided it with political momentum in various parts of the world. With or without directly drawing on la Boétie's work, he rearticulated its conceptual core – the proposition that any rule is ultimately dependent upon popular consent – and embedded it in a romantic framework. Thoreau's main focus, however, rested with issues of individual autonomy, rather than the promotion of collective dissent. He strove for the highest romantic aspiration, a Self that is autonomous and has priority over everything else. The embodiment of this canonical version of Romanticism is the bold hero who successfully defies all forces around 'him' and withdraws altogether from the state, which is perceived to be the main obstacle to freedom and self-fulfilment. The ensuing practice of anarchical individualism may have lacked an element of direct political engagement, but it provided a crucial theoretical stepping stone for the creation of a coherent tradition of popular dissent.

Romantic dissent achieved global political momentum and started to transgress national boundaries when Tolstoy and Gandhi implemented la Boétie's and Thoreau's theoretical claims. They shifted foci from individual to collective action and from rejecting society to engaging with it. Human agency once more acquired new dimensions. Popular dissent became a mass phenomenon of far-reaching and global political significance. Gandhi's various civil disobedience campaigns in South Africa and India, for instance, were instrumental in demonstrating the practical relevance of la Boétie's rhetorical links between power and consent. The worldwide attention Gandhi received not only helped to establish a coherent tradition of popular dissent, but also influenced considerably how interactions between domination and resistance are perceived in today's transversally operating world.

3   Global legacies of popular dissent

> It seems that we are born half-way between the beginning and the
> end of the world. We grow in open revolt almost as furiously against
> what draws us onward as against what holds us back.[1]

The previous two chapters have traced the modern idea of popular
dissent back to its Renaissance origins and then observed its radicalis-
ation and transversal dissemination during the romantic period. The
inquiry has focused on interpretations of Étienne de la Boétie's *Anti-
One*, a sixteenth-century treatise that was presented not as an authentic starting point, but as a text whose broad conceptual wake has
influenced the emergence of a tradition of popular dissent. The present chapter observes what happened when the legacy of this tradition
entered the twentieth century.

During the twentieth century practices of popular dissent surged
and became increasingly global in nature and scope. There is no way
a survey could possibly do justice to the complexity of these phenomena and the various perceptions of human agency that they espouse.
An analysis can, however, evoke some of the main themes that have
come to play a crucial role in our understanding of dissent. For this
purpose I investigate practices of direct action, a specifically la Boétiean form of resistance that is employed when the official channels for
political action, such as elections, referenda, petitions or lobbying do
not exist or are considered inadequate for the resolution of the conflict
in question. Direct action aims to empower those who do not have
access to conventional forms of political influence. It seeks to open up

---

[1] René Char, 'Redness of the Dawnbreakers', in *The Dawn Breakers*, tr. M. Worton
(Newcastle upon Tyne: Bloodaxe Books, 1992), pp. 148–9.

possibilities for social change that are absent within the context of the established legal system.[2]

Direct action entered the twentieth century through a number of authors who have interpreted and expanded Gandhian practices of resistance. After analysing two of its early advocates, Clarence Marsh Case and Richard B. Gregg, the inquiry will focus on the work of Martin Luther King Jr and Gene Sharp to reveal the images of human agency that are implied in their approach to popular dissent. The investigation remains genealogical insofar as it seeks to draw attention to the constitution of meaning by focusing on a relatively unfamiliar representation of dissent, direct action, to then reveal how more familiar images of popular resistance have emerged out of it. They are images of heroic rebellion, of social change through great events. To be more precise, the common image that underlies many contemporary forms of dissent reflects a legacy of thought that emerged from interactions between romantic attachments to an autonomous Self and an Enlightenment quest for certainty in an age of turmoil and constant flux. The resulting fusion of reason and free will upholds and freezes one specific image of dissent to the detriment of others. The present chapter takes the first step towards demonstrating how this image has shaped and delineated not only our understanding of human agency but also its practical applicability.

While the legacy of modern thought provides dissident practices with a number of strong continuities, their dynamic is characterised by equally striking discontinuities. Processes of globalisation, in particular the advent of new communicative capabilities, have fundamentally transformed the nature of dissent and its ability to shape socio-political dynamics. In a world that is strongly influenced by global media networks, an act of dissent has the potential to reach a much wider audience than in previous epochs. The dissemination of a dissident message no longer occurs gradually, but transgresses, almost instantaneously, various spatial and political boundaries. A brief reading of Paul Virilio's and Jean Baudrillard's work on globalisation serves to evoke the far-reaching consequences that issue from these fundamental transformations – consequences that the later parts of this book will then scrutinise in more detail.

---

[2] For a summary of the literature on direct action see Doug Bond, 'Nonviolent Direct Action and the Diffusion of Power', in P. Wehr, H. Burgess and G. Burgess (eds.), *Justice Without Violence* (Boulder, Col.: Lynne Rienner, 1994).

Framing radical resistance: the modernization of direct action

First to the continuities that link early modern with contemporary manifestations of dissent. By the beginning of the twentieth century the la Boétiean legacy had left the realm of obscurity. Through the writings and activism of Thoreau, Tolstoy and Gandhi the ideas first expressed in the *Anti-One* became absorbed by large audiences and formed the theoretical vortex of an important and meanwhile truly global tradition of dissent. One could now recognise the practical significance of la Boétie's rhetorical claim that any form of rule is dependent upon popular consent and that even the most ruthless dictatorship crumbles if this consent is withdrawn. Paradoxical about this evolution is the fact that while the *Anti-One*'s arguments were now discussed and applied on a global scale, the actual text that provided much of the initial intellectual momentum became blurred, effaced and all but vanished from the memory of most who either feared or thrived upon its ideas. Some authors, such as Tolstoy or Sharp, still go back and extensively engage the original sixteenth-century text, others are aware of it via references from secondary sources, but for many who manoeuvre within the context of its ideas, the *Anti-One* is at best an obscure essay from a far distant dark age. What one must do, then, is locate the shadows of the *Anti-One*, the spaces that are left by the disappearance not only of the author, but also of the text.

Gandhi has played a monumental role in directing the shadows of the *Anti-One* from the nineteenth to the twentieth century. His writings and activism provided much of the conceptual foundation for the literature on non-violent direct action.[3] The previous chapter analysed how Gandhi transformed la Boétiean rhetoric into a practice of popular dissent that contained direct political implications and was practised in South Africa, India and several other parts of the world. Various authors then built upon this insight and developed radical approaches to direct action. But what happened to la Boétiean ideas in this process. What was taken on board? What was left out or added

---

[3] The actual term direct action is somewhat contentious and dates back to Georges Sorel, who employed it in the context of revolutionary syndicalism during the early days of this century. See Georges Sorel, *Réflexions sur la Violence* (Paris: Marcel Rivière, 1972/1908).

on? And how do these changes reflect contemporary perceptions of human agency?

Gandhi's work was characterised by a profound distrust towards Western ideas and practices, including imperialism, market economics, scientific reasoning and instrumental rationality. He criticised not only aspects of European culture and politics, but also the modern values upon which they are based. It is in the various processes of modernisation that Gandhi detected, according to Partha Chatterjee, the prime reason for India's oppression and its submissive acceptance of voluntary servitude.[4]

Gandhi's sceptical attitude was largely brushed aside as his ideas gave rise to a systematic approach to direct action. His anti-modern core and his romantic idealism were dropped in a quest to establish a grand theory of modern non-violent resistance, a globally applicable assessment of human agency.

Clarence Marsh Case and Richard B. Gregg, two Americans writing during the 1920s and 1930s, played an important role in directing the Gandhian legacy on a modern course. The writings of Case, a sociologist, initiated the transformation of Gandhian strategy into a grand theory that aims at providing an objective measuring device with which one could assess, plan and predict a great variety of non-violent protests. Case followed Gandhi in claiming that the persuasive power of direct action works by way of producing a change of mental attitude in the mind of those against whom the action is directed.[5] Case, however, adds an element of coercion to this position. He argues that the withdrawal of popular consent can force an opponent to act against 'his' initial will or judgement. In a labour strike, for example, non-violent protest actions interfere with the dynamics between employer and worker. The employer against whom pressure is being exerted has basically two choices. 'He' can suffer the interruption of the productive activities caused by the strike or accommodate those who have withdrawn the supply of their labour. Either option is unappealing and the result of an act of coercion – not one that involves violence, but nevertheless an act of coercion.[6]

[4] Partha Chatterjee, *Nationalist Thought and the Colonial World* (London: Zed Books, 1986), pp. 85–130.
[5] Clarence Marsh Case, *Nonviolent Coercion: A Study in Methods of Social Pressure* (New York: Century, 1923), p. 397–414.
[6] Ibid., pp. 401–2.

Case almost literally restates la Boétie's core concept of voluntary servitude. But the argument is no longer a rhetorical defence of human agency. The assessment of popular dissent is now embedded in a search for objective, stable and universal foundations around which the turbulent contemporary world can revolve:

> One and the same principle underlies all these various manifestations [the strike, the boycott, and non-coöperation], and that is a strategic recognition of the fundamental and indispensable importance of *coöperation* in every form and phase of associated life. More vital even than this is its recognition that this coöperation is necessarily more or less *voluntary* in every social situation and process, not excepting the grossest forms of exploitation, oppression, and tyranny. In the last analysis the victims always gild their own chains, even where they do not help to forge them.[7]

Richard B. Gregg built upon Case's work and further systematised the study and practice of Gandhian non-violent resistance. Gregg, an American lawyer, was involved in settling major labour disputes during the 1920s. He considered the choice of non-violent over violent methods of social change not so much a moral, but primarily a strategic matter, a decision for the more sound and efficient form of struggle. For this purpose Gregg appropriated the methods through which traditional German military tacticians, especially von Clausewitz and von Caemmerer, portray war as a constant process of reciprocal actions. Extending their line of thought, Gregg emphasised the similarities between strategies of non-violent resistance and strategies of war, namely, 'to demoralise the opponent, to break his will, to destroy his confidence, enthusiasm and hope'.[8] Yet, instead of using violence to counter violence, which would only drain the resisters' energy and reassure the attacker about the adequacy of the chosen method of repression, Gregg outlines in detail why non-violence would provide a more effective form of resistance.

Non-violent action is, in Gregg's view, a manipulative activity, a psychological weapon, an intervention that causes emotional and moral perturbations which in turn can trigger processes of social change. It is based upon an understanding of balance and how to disturb it. Non-violent resistance, Gregg argues, is comparable to jiu-jitsu. Like its physical equivalent, the Japanese wrestling practice,

---

[7] Ibid., p. 401.
[8] Richard B. Gregg, *The Power of Nonviolence* (Philadelphia: J.B. Lippincott, 1934), p. 89.

100

moral jiu-jitsu employs the very strength and weight of the opponent to counter an attack. Collective non-violent resistance, if pursued in a determined, fearless and consistent way, will throw the attacker off balance and open up possibilities for social change that resistance through physical strength never could.[9]

Much of the conceptual framework that informs present practices of direct action was established by the time Case and Gregg had systematised and modernised Gandhi's ideas. A few decades later, in the 1950s and 1960s, Martin Luther King further consolidated this form of popular dissent and once more demonstrated its practical relevance. King clearly operated within the la Boétien legacy. He drew extensively upon the writings of Thoreau, Gandhi, Case and Gregg. Not surprisingly, the concept of voluntary servitude is again the starting point. King claims that 'he who passively accepts evil is as much involved in it as he who helps to perpetrate it. He who accepts evil without protesting against it is really coöperating with it'.[10] The refusal to cooperate, by contrast, unleashes forms of dissent that can break chains of domination. Direct action is able to succeed in this enterprise because it interferes with and paralyses the very power structures against which it is directed.[11] A passage from King's famous 'Letter from Birmingham Jail', initially scribbled into the margins of an old newspaper, reveals how the idea of non-violent action is to force a community to confront an issue it has refused to deal with. 'We know through painful experience', King says, 'that freedom is never voluntarily given by the oppressor; it must be demanded by the oppressed'.[12]

King was, of course, best known for the practical application of his ideas. As a young Baptist minister in the southern part of the United States, he played a crucial role in what became famous as the Montgomery bus boycott. These events were triggered when, in 1955, a Black female passenger was arrested for having refused to vacate her seat in the front section of a local bus, a section reserved for whites. Henceforth, King and a number of other Black community leaders organised a boycott against the bus company. Although the immediate aim of the Montgomery boycott was to repeal segregationist

[9] Ibid., pp. 43, 41–54.
[10] Martin Luther King, *Stride Toward Freedom: The Montgomery Story* (San Francisco: Harper, 1986/1958), pp. 51, 84–5, 91.
[11] Martin Luther King, *Why We Can't Wait* (New York: Penguin, 1964), p. 39.
[12] Ibid., pp. 79–80.

seating arrangements on buses, it reached much further. King recalls that 'I came to see that what we were really doing was withdrawing our coöperation from an evil system, rather than merely withdrawing our economic support from the bus company'.[13] The success of the boycott was astonishing. For a whole year, 17,500 Black Americans who previously relied on two daily bus rides, systematically boycotted all public transport. This sustained practice of non-cooperation attracted nationwide attention. It did not uproot the existing political system or eradicate racial discrimination, but it led to an increased discussion of civil liberties and a Supreme Court decision that declared segregational seating on interstate buses illegal.

Direct action as a global strategy of mass protest

Martin Luther King Jr was an influential prelude, both in theory and practice, to the widespread re-emergence of non-cooperation in North America and Western Europe during the 1960s and 1970s. The revival of the idea of withdrawing consent is linked to at least two interconnected events, the increasing opposition against the United States' involvement in the Vietnam War, as well as the larger malaise and cultural transformation which occurred in the wake of the events associated with the student rebellion of May 1968. This malaise was due, at least partly, to what Joan Bondurant at the time described as a fundamental weakness of liberal democracy, namely its failure to 'provide techniques of action for those critical occasions when the machinery of democratic government no longer functions to resolve large-scale, overt conflict'.[14] The legacy of the *Anti-One*, designed to push beyond the parameters of institutional boundaries, was ideally suited to address these perceived shortcomings.

Various authors began to search for forms of dissent that could challenge the existing socio-political order. In an insightful and influential analysis, April Carter presented direct action as a practice of resistance that is waged not only to bring about reform within the established constitutional framework, but also to 'repudiate the entire political system'.[15] Other authors pushed the spatial boundaries of popular

---

[13] King, *Stride Toward Freedom*, p. 51.
[14] Joan V. Bondurant, *Conquest of Violence: The Gandhian Philosophy of Conflict* (Berkeley: University of California Press, 1967), p. x.
[15] April Carter, *Direct Action and Liberal Democracy* (London: Routledge and Kegan Paul, 1973), p. 3, 139–59.

dissent. George Lakey paid attention to acts of non-cooperation that took place in various non-western contexts. Lakey also illustrated, once more, how the practice of direct action is built upon la Boétie's concept of voluntary servitude. Freedom is never given, he argued. People must claim it themselves: 'Mass civil disobedience, tax-refusal, boycott of elections, and draft resistance help people to unlearn their submissiveness'.[16] It is not my intention here to provide a coherent and complete account of the various approaches to direct action and civil disobedience that have emerged since the late 1960s. Such a synthesis could never do justice to the complexities of the issues involved. I will, instead, seek to reveal some of the underlying assumptions of contemporary practices of dissent by focusing on a representative contribution.

Gene Sharp's *The Politics of Nonviolent Action*, which appeared in 1973, has played an important role in shaping the theory and practice of direct action. Particularly among activists, Sharp is recognised as 'one of the most important theorists', even as the 'patron theorist'.[17] His approach revolves around a parsimonious theory of power that was lifted, quite literally, right out of the *Anti-One*. Power, which Sharp loosely defines as 'the capacity to control the behaviour of others', is perceived as something located in the dualistic interactions between ruler and ruled, command and obedience.[18] A government's range of command is said to be dependent upon the degree of cooperation and submission that the ruler can obtain from his subjects. By advancing such a la Boétien position Sharp seeks to counter the determinism of structural and functional scholarship. He rejects arguments that present power as given, static and self-perpetuating. This is to say that power is neither vested in governments nor emanating from the exercise of physical threats and violence. For Sharp power is something that comes from below. It is located in the people and in societal dynamics. In advancing such a position, Sharp is among the

---

[16] George Lakey, *Strategy for a Living Revolution* (New York: Grossman Publishers, 1973), p. 127.
[17] Brian Martin, 'Gene Sharp's Theory of Power', *Journal of Peace Research*, 26, 2, 1989, 213–14; Kate McGuinness, 'Gene Sharp's Theory of Power: A Feminist Critique of Consent', *Journal of Peace Research*, 30, 1, 1993, 102; Peter Ackerman and Christopher Kruegler, *Strategic Nonviolent Conflict: The Dynamics of People Power in the Twentieth Century* (Westport, Conn: Praeger, 1994), pp. 213–14.
[18] Gene Sharp, *The Politics of Nonviolent Action*, Vol. I (Boston: Porter Sargent, 1973), pp. 7–16. See also *The Role of Power in Nonviolent Struggle* (Cambridge, Mass.: The Albert Einstein Institution, 1990), pp. 2–3.

few contemporary authors who still reach back to the *Anti-One*. La Boétie is given the same importance as Machiavelli or the social contract theories of Rousseau and Hobbes. Sharp also draws extensively upon various authors that operate in the broad conceptual wake of the *Anti-One*, including Thoreau, Tolstoy, Gandhi, Case, Gregg and King.

Sharp's reliance on la Boétie is as one-sided as it is extensive. Comparable to interpretations of the *Anti-One* during previous centuries, Sharp downplays la Boétie's subtle arguments about the engineering of popular consent. Instead, he singles out and explores fully the *Anti-One*'s rhetorical claims about the links between power and consent.

> The most important single quality of any government, without which it would not exist, must be the obedience and submission of its subjects. Obedience is at the heart of political power.[19] [. . . .] The rulers of governments and political systems are not omnipotent, nor do they posses self-generating power. All dominating elites and rulers depend for their sources of power upon the cooperation of the population and of the institutions of the society they would rule.[20]

Sharp's next step is also taken literally from the *Anti-One*. He rehearses the argument that if consent is given by the people and necessary to rule, it can also be withdrawn. And the most effective way of withdrawing it, Sharp argues, is non-violent direct action. It is a way of waging, rather than eliminating conflict. 'It involves the matching of forces and the waging of "battles", requires wise strategy and tactics, and demands of its "soldiers" courage, discipline, and sacrifice'.[21]

Non-violent mass protests have been conducted in most parts of the world. Indeed, Sharp and like-minded authors have demonstrated convincingly how direct action has been applied, often successfully, in virtually every cultural context. Examples include the suffragette campaign in England, the resistance of the German Ruhr population against French and Belgian occupation forces during the 1920s, the Indian independence movement, the civil rights campaign in the United States, the popular resistance against the 1962 coup by French generals in Algeria, the Greenham Common Camp and other protests against nuclear armament, the velvet revolutions of Eastern Europe,

---

[19] Sharp, *The Politics of Nonviolent Action*, vol. I, p. 16.
[20] Sharp, *The Role of Power in Nonviolent Struggle*, p. 3.
[21] Sharp, *The Politics of Nonviolent Action*, vol. I, pp. 4, 67.

and manifestations of people power in Third World autocracies (such as against Marcos in the Philippines, Chun Doo Hwan in Korea or Noriega in Panama).[22]

How exactly have we come to understand these influential dissident practices? What image of human agency do they reflect? Sharp's approach is, once more, quite illustrative. There are two striking features in his understanding of direct action. The first one is the continued influence of romantic values, particularly a strong belief in autonomy and human agency. Sharp relies on a position that endows the subject with an almost unlimited ability to shape the world. He has confidence in people's ability to recognise and defy domination. He speaks of popular empowerment that makes it possible 'to end social oppression by direct popular efforts which turn helpless victims into masters of their own destinies'.[23]

Sharp's trust in the autonomy of human action is then supplemented with an Enlightenment desire for order and certainty. Much of the research that has been conducted by Sharp and like-minded theorists has turned away from Gandhi's critique of instrumental rationality and embarked, instead, on more scientific processes of ordering and classifying. Factual evidence was gathered in an attempt to discover underlying patterns of dissent. The prime objective became the establishment of a systematic model for the global assessment of popular dissent. Thomas Schelling writes in the preface to Sharp's influential trilogy:

> The original idea was to subject the entire theory of nonviolent political action, together with a full history of its practice in all parts of the world since the time of Christ, to the same cool, detailed scrutiny that military strategy and tactics are supposed to invite.[24]

In the ensuing attempt to construct a grand theory of popular dissent, Sharp precisely defines how mechanisms of change operate and

---

[22] See, for instance, Ackerman and Kruegler, *Strategic Nonviolent Conflict*; Judith Brown, *Gandhi and Civil Disobedience* (Cambridge: Cambridge University Press, 1977); Barbara Epstein, *Political Protest and Cultural Revolution: Nonviolent Direct Action in the 1970s and 1980s* (Berkeley: University of California Press, 1991); R.S. Powers and W.B. Vogele (eds.), *Protest, Power and Change: An Encyclopaedia of Nonviolent Action from ACT-UP to Women's Suffrage* (New York: Garland Publishing, 1997); Adam Roberts, *Civil Resistance in the East European and Soviet Revolutions* (Cambridge: The Albert Einstein Institution, 1991); Paul Routledge, *Terrains of Resistance: Nonviolent Social Movements and the Contestation of Place in India* (Westport: Conn.: Praeger, 1993).
[23] Gene Sharp, *Social Power and Political Freedom* (Boston: Porter Sargent, 1980), p. 376.
[24] Thomas Schelling in Sharp, *The Politics of Nonviolent Action*, vol. I, p. xix.

carefully lists almost two hundred different ways of waging non-violent conflict. They are divided into three main categories, non-cooperation, intervention and protest/persuasion. Sharp then enumerates the specific mechanisms of change through which these acts of dissent operate, such as conversion, accommodation, non-violent coercion and disintegration. The examples he lists to illustrate the range of his theoretical model include speeches, marches, protest emigration, strikes, election boycotts, conscientious objections, refusals to pay taxes, hunger strikes, lockouts, walkouts, quickie walkouts, sit-downs, sit-ins, teach-ins, stand-ins, ride-ins, wade-ins, mill-ins, stall-ins, speak-ins, sick-ins and pray-ins.[25] Everything needs to have its proper place. Nothing ought to remain outside, Horkheimer and Adorno once observed, 'because the mere idea of outsideness is the actual source of fear'.[26] But, of course, the very act of classifying creates even more ambivalence by relegating everything that does not fit into a sphere of otherness.[27]

Presented as radical dissent against all forms of authority, Sharp's approach to direct action expresses at the same time a widespread modern urge for certainty and control, the desire to ground our existence in an external source – if not in God, then in something else that could take over his stabilising position. For Sharp and many like-minded authors this something else is the confidence of being able to discover the essence of domination and resistance, the underlying factors that determine social dynamics.

Substituting God: modernity and the quest for certainty

Significant about Sharp's and other la Boétiean approaches to direct action are not the details of their propositions, but the consequences that issue from them – that is, the image of human agency that they espouse and the manner in which this image shapes the actual functioning of dissent in concrete political circumstances. Not surprisingly, direct actions turned out to be practices of dissent that are both radically subversive and, at the same time, reflective of the values that

[25] Sharp, *The Politics of Nonviolent Action*, vol. II, pp. 109–445.
[26] Max Horkheimer and Theodor W. Adorno, *Dialektik der Aufklärung* (Frankfurt: Fischer Taschenbuch, 1991/1944), p. 22.
[27] See Zygmunt Bauman, *Modernity and Ambivalence* (Oxford: Polity, 1991), p. 3.

underlie the modern forms of domination they seek to oppose. The la Boétiean tradition of dissent remained confined within the discursive boundaries of various modern and humanist discourses that have superseded each other from the Renaissance until today.

Recognising the modern dimensions of contemporary dissident practices is crucial if one wants to probe their limits and, perhaps, glance beyond them. A brief theoretical review of the linkages between modernity and dissent is thus necessary before moving to the task of scrutinising how transversal dissent operates in concrete socio-political contexts. Locating the boundaries of modernity is, however, no easy task. Modernity itself is virtually impossible to define. It is an elusive set of complexities that defies single meanings.

Modernity has no clear beginning and end. While the roots of this period reach back somewhere to the early days of Renaissance Humanism, scholars today are engaging in relentless disputes about whether we find ourselves in a late modern age or whether we have already taken the first steps into a beyond, some kind of postmodernity. I tend to side with the former. This has consequences. The recognition that we have not yet transgressed modernity means that we cannot look at it from the outside. A self-critical look at modern discursive practices can never be detached from the eye of the viewer. It is more like a look in a mirror – an incomplete image of reflections and distortions, a mixture of vanity and self-doubt. But if we are to explore and stretch the dimensions of human agency in the late modern age we must nevertheless grapple with the contours of life reflected in the mirror, even if we know that they will always remain distorted images.

Instead of looking at modernity as a historical period or a set of institutions, I follow Foucault's advice and treat it primarily as an attitude, 'a way of thinking and feeling', 'a mode of relating to contemporary reality'.[28] Modernity, then, is the broad common theme that runs through a set of diverse discursive practices which, superseding and intersecting with each other, have come to constitute our collective consciousness.

The dominant frame of contemporary consciousness today, including manifestations of popular dissent, ensued to a considerable extent from the tension between Romanticism and the Enlightenment. Sharp's approach to direct action perfectly epitomises this fusion.

---

[28] Michel Foucault, 'What is Enlightenment', tr. C. Porter in P. Rabinow (ed.), *The Foucault Reader* (New York: Pantheon Books, 1984), p. 39.

What has been retained from the romantic ideal is the autonomy of the Self, the quest for independence and self-determination, the belief that the subject can shape history. This form of modern idealism was then supplemented with the scientific heritage of the Enlightenment, the desire to systematise, to search for rational foundations and certainty in a world of turmoil and constant flux.

The romantic element of our contemporary consciousness is epitomised in Hegel. What makes modernity different in Hegel's view is its attempt at self-understanding, the desire to establish normativity out of itself rather than by way of borrowing from or rejecting the ideas of a surpassed epoch. The keystone of this process of self-grounding is the principle of subjectivity, which, at least in Habermas' reading of Hegel, is linked to a perception of freedom that recognises an individual's autonomy and responsibilities in the realms of action and reflection.[29] The Enlightenment's contribution was to provide this subjectivity-oriented approach with stable and scientific foundations. Jean Baudelaire, in a much-cited passage, draws attention to the recurring quest for certainty in a world of turbulence and chaos. While describing modernity as 'the transient, the fleeting, the contingent', Baudelaire points towards the constant attempts to discover underlying patterns behind these ephemeral features. He describes the recurring quest for essences as a desire to 'extract the eternal out of the transient'.[30] With the fusion of romantic idealism and Enlightenment rationalism, Humanism reached its peak, at least in theory. The subject now possesses both the privilege of free will and the capacity to assess 'his' environment in a detached and objective way.

Within such modern attempts to fuse subjectivity and science there is ample room for discussion and diversity, more than in any preceding period. Indeed, Hegel considers the right of criticism as one of modernity's key characteristics.[31] The breathing space necessary for criticism was provided by the emergence of a bourgeois public sphere in eighteenth- and nineteenth-century Europe.[32] Passionate debates have thus been waged about all aspects of modern life. Virtually every

---

[29] Jürgen Habermas, *Der philosophische Diskurs der Moderne* (Frankfurt: Suhrkamp, 1985), pp. 13–30, 34–58.
[30] Jean Baudelaire, 'Le Peintre de la Vie Moderne', *Oeuvres Complètes* (Paris: Gallimard, 1961), p. 1163.
[31] Habermas, *Der Philosophische Diskurs der Moderne*, p. 27.
[32] See Jürgen Habermas, *Strukturwandel der Öffentlichkeit* (Frankfurt: Suhrkamp, 1990/1962).

opinion, every thought, every theory is attacked, refuted or at least submitted to intense and sustained scrutiny. The debate about human agency is one of these various sites of contestation. There are, as mentioned before, many narratives of modern dissent, accounts that tell different stories about resistance and potentials for social change.

But while the waging of fierce intellectual debates emerged as a key feature of modernity, the range of these debates is not as boundless as it appears at first sight. William Connolly leads us right to the core of this paradoxical issue. He emphasises that modern debates all have a distinctive character. They are all well framed, and the contours of this framing process, Connolly emphasises, have to a large extent been drawn by the recurring unwillingness to deal with the death of God.[33] The refusal to accept the contingency of foundations has been a constant modern theme ever since la Boétie and his fellow Renaissance humanists disenchanted the world and placed 'man' at its centre. When the old theocentric world crumbled, when the one and only commonly accepted point of reference vanished, the death of God became the key dilemma around which modern debates were waged. Yet, instead of accepting the absence of stable foundations and dealing with the new burden of responsibility, many prominent modern approaches embarked upon desperate evasive attempts to find replacements for the fallen God.[34]

The first three chapters have demonstrated how this quest has taken different shapes in various stages of the modern project. For Renaissance humanists it centred around a sceptical and rhetorical belief in human agency and the virtue of 'men'. During the Enlightenment it was trust in science and universal reason. For romantics it was the belief in a deified Self, and for Marxists, one could add, it consisted of faith in history's teleological dimension. The search for essences has remained one of the prominent themes in the twentieth century, a period haunted by rapid change and devastating global conflicts. The contemporary quest for foundational authority manifests itself primarily in a desire to control, to take charge of the world. Jean-François Lyotard portrays this tendency as an attempt to ground and legitimise knowledge in reference to a grand narrative, a universalising

---

[33] See William E. Connolly, *Political Theory and Modernity* (Ithaca: Cornell University Press, 1993/1988).
[34] Ibid., p. 13.

framework that aims at emancipating the individual by mastering the conditions of life.[35]

Modernity is not the only bounded set of discourses. Every discourse has limits, revolves around a set of underlying assumptions, advances propositions that banish others to conceptual exiles. Neither can modernity be reduced to the recurring desire to repress ambiguity. Of course not. But the search for certainty is an important and widely applied modern theme.

Many assumptions that underlie the la Boétiean legacy of dissent perfectly illustrate this modern tendency to repress ambiguity. Sharp's approach to direct action reveals the continuities of modern life. His theory of non-violent direct action epitomises the modern desire for control, the compulsion to systematise and categorise the world, such that all its various features can be understood and held accountable to one generally accepted frame of reference.

Time, space and speed in a transversal world

Before scrutinising the consequences of this persistent modern theme, it is important to recognise that contemporary practices of dissent are not only characterised by continuity. While embedding deeply entrenched modern values, dissident practices today have taken on an entirely new dynamic. They transgress conventional political boundaries to the point that the distinctions between the local, the national and the global have become increasingly blurred. The implications of these transformations for our understanding of dissent are far-reaching and will be discussed in more detail later in the book. At this stage a brief theoretical exposé must suffice to draw attention to the centrality of the issue.

The globalisation of political space is a theme that resonates strongly in the work of two French authors, Paul Virilio and Jean Baudrillard. Both have written provocative and often controversial texts about various effects of globalisation, particularly the rapidly changing nature and impact of mass media and means of communication. They show how these transformations have rearranged the relationship between time and space, and thus fundamentally altered contemporary social dynamics.

---

[35] Jean-François Lyotard, *La Condition Postmoderne: Rapport sur le Savoir* (Paris: Les Editions de Minuit, 1979), pp. 7–9.

Virilio points out that the contraction of distances has become a strategic reality. The corresponding negation of space carries with it incalculable economic and political consequences.[36] He claims that we are currently witnessing a revolution in global relations, comparable to the fundamental impact of changing mass transportation in the nineteenth century and means of telecommunication in the twentieth. We are undergoing a sea change in social dynamics. This change revolves around the use and regulation of speed. Speed is the relationship between various phenomena, notably space and time. Space has become annihilated, Virilio claims, and time has taken over as the criterion around which global dynamics revolve. The instantaneous character of communication and mass media have annihilated duration and locality. The 'now' of the emission is privileged to the detriment of the 'here', the space where things take place.[37] What matters are no longer the three spatial dimensions of height, depth, and width, but above all a fourth one, time. Or, rather, what matters is the present, for our notion of 'real time' has been transformed into a universal fetish, a situation in which local and chronological time has given way to world time, to speed, which regulates our political, social and economic interactions.[38]

Various consequences arise from this. Virilio predicts that the globe will no longer primarily be divided spatially into north and south, but temporally into two forms of speed, absolute and relative. The 'haves' and 'have-nots' are then sorted out between those who live in the hyperreal shrunken world of instant communication, cyberdynamics and electronic money transactions – and those, more disadvantaged than ever, who live in the real space of local villages, cut off from the temporal forces that drive politics and economics.[39] Virilio also believes that the prevalence of speed has led to the disappearance of consciousness in the form of direct perceptions of our existence. Cinematography and televised images, for example, are only technically transmitted optical illusions, and not the representations of 'reality' they are often taken to be.[40] It is in this domain that Baudrillard takes up the argument and pushes it a step further.

---

[36] Paul Virilio, *Vitesse et Politique* (Paris: Éditions Galilée, 1977), p. 131.
[37] Paul Virilio, *La Vitesse de Libération* (Paris: Éditions Galilée, 1995), pp. 21–34.
[38] Ibid., pp. 23, 89.
[39] Jean-Baptiste Marongiu, 'Excès de Vitesse', *Libération*, 21 September 1995, p. xi.
[40] Paul Virilio, *Esthétique de la Disparition* (Paris: Éditions Galilée, 1989/1980), pp. 56–7, 117.

For Baudrillard the present world is hyperreal, a model of something real that has no origin in reality. The distinctions between reality and virtuality, political practice and simulation are blurred to the extent that they are no longer recognisable. Indeed, these distinctions have been effaced altogether, Baudrillard claims, owing mostly to the impact of mass media. Our media culture has annihilated reality in stages, such that in the end its simulating image 'bears no relation to any reality whatever: it is its own pure simulacrum'.[41] Television, the unproblematic transmission of the hyperreal, has conditioned our mind such that we have lost the ability to penetrate beneath the manifest levels of surface. It has changed fundamentally social dynamics in the late twentieth century, where politics has disappeared in a void and is reduced to a trace that only operates on the level of virtuality, somewhere between our mental television screens and public opinion polls.[42]

It is not my intention to endorse all of Virilio's and Baudrillard's positions. Many of their arguments are problematic, even though they draw attention to undeniable contemporary phenomena. For instance, their analyses deal primarily with aspects of Western culture. Although this culture has spread throughout the globe, an undifferentiated universal assessment of its dynamics suppresses important local differences. It fails to appreciate the fragmentations and contradictions, the practices of dissent that arise precisely as a reaction against processes of homogenisation. Problematic as well is the claim, especially pronounced in Baudrillard, that current cultural trends have robbed us of the ability to appreciate reality. Many authors have criticised this position as a form of metaphysical idealism, a naive desire to return to some pre-mass media authenticity.[43] There cannot be unmediated access to reality, authentic awareness of our existence. Representations of the 'real', even before the advent of mass media, were inevitably intertwined with social images embedded in language. The advent of speed has not fundamentally changed, but only intensified this aspect of social dynamics.

---

[41] Jean Baudrillard, 'The Precession of Simulacra', *Simulations*, tr. P. Foss, P. Patton, P. Beitchman (New York: Semiotext(e), 1983), p. 11.

[42] Baudrillard, 'The Ecstasy of Communication', in Hal Foster (ed.), *Postmodern Culture*, tr. J. Johnston (London: Pluto Press, 1985); pp. 126–34; 'Les ilotes et les élites', *Libération*, 4 September 1995, p. 4.

[43] Linda Hutcheon, *The Politics of Postmodernism* (London: Routledge), pp. 33–4; John Docker, *Postmodernism and Popular Culture* (Cambridge: Cambridge University Press, 1994), pp. 104–8.

What does the changing relationship between time and space entail for our understanding of transversal dissent? Do human actions still matter in a world where the exchange of virtual capital through computerised networks plunges the global economy, at random so its seems, into up and down spirals that sweep across traditional boundaries of identity and sovereignty? And, even if we suppose that actions matter, can we understand them at a time when political and social consciousness gushes out of five-second sound-bites and corresponding hyperreal images that flicker over our television screens?

Virilio and Baudrillard are highly pessimistic about the prospects of dissent in the contemporary world. One of the main themes in Virilio's latest book revolves around the environmental pollution of not only our atmosphere and hydrosphere, but also our planet's time–space relationship. This 'dromospheric pollution', he claims, eludes all democratic controls and will soon precipitate a yet unknown fatal event, 'the accident of all accidents, or, in other words, the [global] circulation of the generalised accident'.[44] Baudrillard's apocalyptic vision looks slightly different. For him, human agency has been annihilated because the link between 'realities' and 'referents' no longer exists. And since we have no more reality, theory can no longer be dissent against it.[45] The task of the theorist is then reduced to revealing the elusive nature of contemporary life.

One can acknowledge the phenomena that Virilio and Baudrillard describe without accepting the overall conclusions they have reached from their analyses. Yes, the blurring of distinctions between global and local, national and international, has altered the interaction between domination and resistance today. If 'real space' has become absorbed into the domains of speed and simulation, as Virilio and Baudrillard claim, then dynamics of dissent do not primarily, or at least not only, take place in their immediate spatial environment. Dissent operates as least as much in the virtuality of speed, the instantaneity of globalised communication.

This phenomenon, however, does not annihilate possibilities of engaging in acts of dissent. Speed may well have erased space to the benefit of some kind of globalised instantaneity. Yet, hyperreal images

[44] Virilio, *La Vitesse de Libération*, pp. 90 and 35, 47, 83–4, 98–9.
[45] Or so at least interpret Barry Smart, *Postmodernity* (London: Routledge: 1993), pp. 122–3; and Wolfgang Welsch, *Ästhetisches Denken* (Stuttgart: Reclam, 1993), pp. 208–11.

racing daily over our television screens nevertheless take part in a struggle over 'real time'. Independently of how instantaneous, distorted and simulated they are, these images influence our perceptions of the world and thus also our responses to the issues in question. To accept the logic of speed, then, is not to render 'real time' obsolete, but to acknowledge multiple and overlapping spatial and temporal spheres within which political practices are constantly formed and reformed.

The prevalence of speed in contemporary global politics provides increasing opportunities to interfere with various political processes. Acts of dissent now have the potential to transcend their immediate spatial context and enter domains that lie beyond national boundaries. But how has the nature of dissent itself changed in the wake of these transformations. And how can we – those who seek to understand the political dynamics of a globalised world – conceptualise the complex transversal processes that make up the interactions between domination and resistance today?

Summary

The first three chapters have narrated the development of a tradition of dissent that has emerged in the broad conceptual wake of a six-teenth-century humanist text, Étienne de la Boétie's *Anti-One*. La Boétiean ideas acquired political relevance as they were diffused, directly or indirectly, by such authors as Thoreau, Tolstoy, Gandhi, King and Sharp. The ensuing legacy of popular dissent is part of our cultural heritage. Knowledge of it has travelled across national boundaries and influenced countless practices of popular dissent in all parts of the world. Examples include Gandhian civil disobedience campaigns in South Africa and India; the civil rights movement in the United States; the velvet revolutions in East-Central Europe; the uprising against dictatorial regimes in South Korea, Burma, Panama or the Philippines; activist interventions by Amnesty International and Greenpeace; or countless other instances where common people rose up to defy and challenge the power of the existing political order.

The la Boétiean tradition of dissent is, of course, not the only modern practice of popular resistance. Its story about human agency is only one among many, a diverse and disputed narrative of modern dissent. Analysing its legacy, even if done carefully, cannot possibly reflect the extremely wide-ranging modern scholarship conducted on

114

human agency and social change. Yet, the particular way in which la Boétie's intellectual legacy evolved can tell us much about the outer limits that modern discursive practices have imposed on the apparently limitless range of debates about human agency.

Prevalent modern images of dissent are framed by a widespread unwillingness to accept the responsibilities that arose from what Nietzsche called the death of God, the loss of certainty which had existed in a theocentric world before Renaissance humanists elevated 'man' to be the measure of all things. Recurring attempts to find replacements for the fallen God, to discover essences that could provide a stable world-view, have left a lasting mark on contemporary perceptions of human agency.

The present chapter has drawn attention to this phenomenon by analysing the body of literature that deals with direct action, forms of popular dissent that seek to challenge not only practices of governance, but also existing political and legal structures. Although radical on many accounts, direct action is bound by limits too—limits that have been drawn not by the confinement to a certain political order, but by the underlying assumptions that characterise the fight against repression. Grand theories of popular dissent have been established in a quest for certainty and systematic knowledge. Scholars have searched for underlying patterns that could explain, once and for all, the functioning of direct action in diverse historical and cultural settings. What has emerged from these efforts is a universalised narrative that upholds one specific image of dissent and thus excludes possibilities of seeing domination and resistance in different ways. 'How this world suffers', René Char would say, 'from being crushed between the four walls of a book in order to become the world of men!'[46]

While operating within a long and bounded tradition of modern thought, contemporary practices of dissent have also undergone fundamental transformations. Their impact is no longer limited to local dynamics. Dissent today operates in various transversal grey-zones – political spaces that lie somewhere between the local, the national and the international.

Two main sets of questions arise from the way in which continuities and discontinuties have shaped the theory and practice of popular dissent. These questions necessitate a fundamental rethinking of what dissent is and how we can understand the role it plays in global polit-

---

[46] Char, 'Redness of the Dawnbreakers', pp. 144–5.

ics. First: if a long tradition of conceptualising human agency in essentialist terms has promoted specific images of dissent to the detriment of others, we must ask what consequences emerge from this practice. What specific images of dissent have actually been frozen in time and space? What are its features, its grins and grimaces? And what are the political implications that issue from this framing process? Second: if processes of globalisation have led to a fundamental transformation of political dynamics we must ask whether or not our old perceptions of dissent and human agency can remain valid. Is the la Boétiean tradition, which conceptualises human agency through a spatial and ahistoric understanding of the relationship between ruler and ruled, still adequate to understand dissident practices at a time when conventional boundaries of sovereignty and identity are becoming increasingly blurred?

Part II: Reading and rereading transversal struggles

But now, for one minute, let it be as it might have been.[1]

Part I of this book has analysed the theory and practice of popular dissent. The purpose of this genealogical inquiry was to illustrate, through an example, how modern dissent has been framed, and how this framing process has delineated contemporary understandings of human agency. I argued that conventional perceptions of popular dissent are characterised by a recurring inability to come to terms with the death of God. Among the most noteworthy manifestations of this refusal to accept the contingent character of foundations are grand theories of dissent, approaches that search for ahistoric and universal patterns of social change.

Part II investigates whether or not this long-standing perception of dissent remains adequate in a world that has undergone fundamental transformation. Processes of globalisation, I argue, have led to a situation in which ahistoric and spatial modes of representation are no longer able to capture the increasingly transversal nature of dissent. Rather than searching for an essence of dissent and relying on several separate levels of analysis, I advance a discursive approach that focuses on transversal dynamics and on the constituted dimensions of dissident practices. Two parallel shifts are necessary for this purpose. The first one is of a methodological and epistemological nature. It entails moving away from grand theories towards an approach that recognises the contingency of foundations, that deals with, rather than

---

[1] Fyodor Dostoevsky, *The Brothers Karamazov*, tr. R. Pevear and L. Volokhonsky (London: Everyman's Library, 1997), p. 766.

circumvents, the death of God. The second shift is of a focal nature and suggests that the key to understanding social change does not lie in great events, such as mass demonstrations, but in the slow and cross-territorial transformation of values that precedes them.

Accepting the death of God means that one can no longer theorise dissent in ahistoric and universal terms. Meaningful answers to questions of dissent and social change can only be gained by analysing the interaction between domination and resistance in a specific historical and geographic context. A concrete case study is thus required for an adequate theoretical inquiry into aspects of human agency. It is with this recognition in mind that the investigation now turns to the political situation in East Germany during the 1980s.

The fall of the Berlin Wall in November 1989 is for many commentators not only a turning point in European history, but also a key event in global politics, perhaps even the defining moment of the late twentieth century.[2] It signified the end of the Cold War and the transition to a new phase in international politics. The sudden and stunning collapse of entrenched political structures also led to a crisis in international relations theory. None of the existing approaches to global politics was able to anticipate, let alone predict, the momentous transformations that took place when the Iron Curtain crumbled and the Soviet-led alliance system fell apart. For Martin Hollis and Steve Smith this failure calls for a fundamental re-examination of the role that human agency plays in global politics. The dominant structural theories of international relations, they point out, focused on explaining the continuity and stability of the bipolar system. Such a perspective not only eschewed questions of transformation, but also offered little opportunity to theorise agency. 'The Collapse of the Cold War system', by contrast, 'seems to depend largely on calculating agents'.[3] How, then, are we to rethink agency in light of the momentous events that took place in East-Central Europe in the late 1980s? Who actually were the agents in question and how can their actions be conceptualised?

For many international relations scholars the fall of the Berlin Wall was an event that could be understood by focusing on how the actions

---

[2] For example, David W. Ziegler, *War, Peace, and International Politics* (New York: HarperCollins, 1993), p. 70.
[3] Martin Hollis and Steve Smith, 'Two stories about structure and agency', *Review of International Studies*, 20, 3, 1994, 241.

of politicians, diplomats and generals – the traditional state-bound bearers of agency – were carried out against the contextual constraints of Cold War politics. From such a perspective the focus rested, in Thomas Risse's words, 'on the relationship between structural conditions (e.g., the decline of Soviet power) on the one hand, and the policies of individual decision makers (e.g., Mikhail Gorbachev, Ronald Reagan, George Bush) on the other'.[4] Such state-centric and spatial modes of representation, I argue, cannot adequately account for the events of 1989. Statesmen were not the only bearers of agency. Superpower politics was not the only structural force at work.

The fall of the Berlin Wall is an inherently transversal phenomenon – one in which various discursive dynamics and various forms of agency were operating in a multitude of interconnected spheres, including terrains of dissent that ranged from street protest to the publication of underground literary magazines. The constant presence of global mass media networks accounted for the fact that during the revolution of 1989 the local became instantaneously global. And it is in the context of the ensuing trans-territorial dynamics that aspects of dissent and agency must be understood. This understanding, however, cannot emerge from searching for and upholding a correct interpretation of the events. Neither can it be limited to a specific level of analysis. Rather, the inquiry must revolve around multiple readings of the events in question – rereadings that explore the complex, transversal and often fragmented dynamics that led to the events of 1989.

[4] Thomas Risse, 'The Cold War's Endgame and German Unification', *International Security*, 21, 1997, p. 160.

4 From essentialist to discursive conceptions of power

Great, glowing vault
with the
outward- and away-
burrowing black-constellation swarm:

into the silicified forehead of a ram
I burn this image, between
the horns, therein,
in the singing of the coils, the
marrow of the curdled
heartseas swells.

What
doesn't he
butt against?

The world is gone, I have to carry you.[1]

How to understand popular dissent, the power unleashed by protesting masses, the build-up of rage, resentment, passion and might,
spilling into the streets, this 'outward- and away-burrowing black-
constellation swarm'? How to problematise the prevalent image of
human agency, this image of heroic rebellion, burnt between the horns
of our dissident drive, into the forehead of contemporary consciousness? How to listen to the more subtle singeing of the coils, the
spiralling entanglement of domination and resistance?

The present chapter grapples with these questions by dealing with

---

[1] Paul Celan, 'Great, glowing vault', *Breathturn*, tr. P. Joris (Los Angeles: Sun and Moon Press, 1995), p. 233.

the issue that lies at the centre of human agency, the concept of power. Two readings of the East German case serve to explore questions of power and social change. The first reading focuses on a key feature of the revolution of 1989, the massive acts of popular dissent that attracted worldwide media attention. These events represent one of the most common perceptions of contemporary human agency, an image of protesting masses that is, indeed, burnt into the forehead of contemporary consciousness. The la Boétiean tradition deals precisely with such practices of dissent. It explains their functioning through a parsimonious theory of power that revolves around the assumption that any form of rule is ultimately dependent upon popular consent. Since this consent can be withdrawn, it is argued, massive efforts of popular resistance can topple even the most ruthless dictatorship.

A second reading of the East German revolution problematises this essentialist understanding of power relations. A closer look suggests that power relations are far too complex to be assessed by a grand theoretical model that revolves around a spatially delineated understanding of the interaction between rulers and ruled.

Dissent in East Germany took on various transversal dimensions, for it challenged state sovereignty and transgressed the political and spatial givenness of international relations. The ensuing cross-territorial dynamics, I suggest, can be understood more adequately through Michel Foucault's theoretical propositions. Power, from this perspective, is not reducible to an essence. Neither is it stable nor can be assessed through a grand theoretical model. Power, Foucault argues, is a complex and constantly changing relational force that depends largely on its interaction with the production and diffusion of knowledge. Drawing on this Foucauldian position I then introduce what will become the theoretical core of the subsequent chapters: a concept of power and dissent which relies on an understanding of discursive practices that operate within and across various political territories.

Voice and exit: popular dissent as cross-territorial transgression

The scenes of common citizens walking through the Berlin Wall represent a common image of dissent, an image of protesting masses, of thousands of people taking to the street and rising against the dark forces of a repressive regime. In the case of East Germany, the success of such resistance was spectacular by any measure. Within a few weeks of popular rage, Erich Honecker's notorious regime fell apart, a seemingly invincible iron fortress suddenly lay in ruins. Of course, one could have anticipated some form of social change once the Soviet Union, East Germany's key ally and protector, started to embark on an internal reform process. But nobody was prepared for the force and momentum that developed in the streets of East Germany during the autumn of 1989.

The present section scrutinises the revolutionary events from the perspective of mass protest movements. How important were they? What form of power did they unleash? What image of human agency did they embody?

Popular dissent undoubtedly played an important role in triggering radical processes of social change. Jürgen Habermas, for example, notes that 'the presence of large masses gathering in squares and mobilising on the streets managed, astonishingly, to disempower a regime that was armed to the teeth'.[2] But Habermas, and many others, emphasise that the force of street demonstration must be seen in its reinforcing combination with the impact created by the increasing number of East Germans that were leaving for the West. Albert O. Hirschmann, who termed these two protest forms 'voice' and 'exit', argues that their common force gradually eroded the foundations of the existing regime.[3] Both of these dissident practices were transversal in nature – they transgressed various political boundaries and challenged the notion of national sovereignty. A brief elucidation:[4]

---

[2] Jürgen Habermas, 'The Rectifying Revolution and the Need for New Thinking on the Left', *New Left Review*, 183, 1990, 7.

[3] Albert O. Hirschmann, 'Exit, Voice, and the Fate of the German Democratic Republic', *World Politics*, 45, January 1993, pp. 173–202.

[4] Needless to say, the interaction of domination and resistance in East Germany is a highly complex issue that I cannot possibly represent adequately in this short summary. Countless German language material has appeared about the revolution of 1989, as, for example, Hannes Bahrmann and Christoph Links, *Wir sind das Volk: Die DDR zwischen 7. Oktober und 17. Dezember 1989* (Berlin: Aufbau-Verlag, 1990); Bärbel Bohley et al., *40 Jahre DDR. . .und die Bürger melden sich zu Wort* (Frankfurt: Büchergilde Gutenberg, 1989); R. Deppe, H. Dubiel and U. Rödel, *Demokratischer Umbruch in Osteuropa* (Frankfurt: Suhrkamp, 1991); Ralf Dahrendorf, *Betrachtungen über die Revolution in Europa* (Stuttgart: Deutsche Verlags-Anstalt, 1990); Gert-Joachim Glaeßner, *Der schwierige Weg zur Demokratie: Vom Ende der DDR zur Deutschen Einheit* (Opladen: Westdeutscher Verlag, 1991); Christiane Lemke, *Die Ursachen des Umbruchs 1989* (Opladen: Westdeutscher Verlag, 1991); K. Löw (ed.), *Ursachen und Verlauf der deutschen Revolution von 1989* (Berlin: Duncker & Humblot, 1991); Marlies Menge, *'Ohne uns läuft nichts mehr': Die Revolution in der DDR* (Stuttgart: Deutsche Verlags-Anstalt, 1990). For analyses in English see, for example, Timothy Garton Ash, *We the*

The practice of exit refers to massive waves of East Germans leaving for the West despite the government's desperate attempt to enforce a closed border policy. Mass migration occurred primarily through two channels. Starting in August 1989, East German citizens used the extraterritorial status of diplomatic missions in the communist bloc to claim refugee status. Soon, the West German representations in East Berlin, Prague, Budapest and Warsaw had to be closed because they were overcrowded with thousands of East Germans determined to leave their country. An agreement between Berlin and Bonn at the end of September allowed for transport of these refugees by special train – via East German territory – to the West. When news of this evacuation spread, the regime desperately tried to prevent its citizens leaving the country. But the spatial logic of national sovereignty was no longer operative. Bodies transgressed boundaries with ease. In a matter of days, the diplomatic representations were packed anew and special trains brought again 7,600 refugees to West Germany. These spectacular transversal dynamics attracted worldwide media attention and robbed the regime of what little bit of legitimacy it had left. Even more damaging was Budapest's resolution to dismantle the 'iron curtain'. On 11 September, Hungary unilaterally decided to open its borders to Austria. Within three days, 15,000 East Germans (who could easily travel to Hungary) walked through the iron curtain and then settled in West Germany. This was only the beginning of the exit wave. Illegal border crossings, for which several East Germans had been shot during the preceding decades, became a mass movement by the fall of 1989.[5] Transversal dissent had begun to challenge the spatial givenness of Cold War politics.

Meanwhile, opposition activities within East Germany became more organised. Between July and September, various illegal grassroots opposition movements emerged, such as *Neues Forum, Demokratischer Aufbruch* and *Demokratie Jetzt*. Popular demonstrations now appeared at various places. For example, each Monday, after the traditional Protestant service at Leipzig's *Nikolaikirche*, people gathered outside the church to demand reforms. Their number continually increased

<hr/>

People: The Revolution of 1989 (London: Granta/Penguin, 1990); Mark R. Thompson, 'Why and How East Germans Rebelled,' in *Theory and Society*, 25 2, April 1996, pp. 263–99; and the special issue of *New German Critique*, 64, winter 1994.
[5] For statistical details on the exit wave see Thomas Ammer, 'Stichwort: Flucht aus der DDR', in *Deutschland-Archiv*, 22, November 1989, p. 1207; and Hartmut Wendt, 'Die deutsch-deutschen Wanderungen', in *Deutschland-Archiv*, 24, April 1991, p. 390.

week after week. On 2 October, 25,000 of them were violently dispersed by the police.

During the celebration of East Germany's fortieth anniversary, on 7 October, Erich Honecker made one last attempt to redress the balance. But his categorical refusal to acknowledge the need for change only increased the pressure from below. Street protests became a normal feature in virtually every city in the country. The Monday demonstration in Leipzig was by now a weekly event of mass protest; 70,000 people participated on 9 October and 120,000 a week later. Meanwhile, the transversal exit wave continued to grow. Thousands of East Germans kept leaving their country every day. The young age of the emigrants and the resulting loss of future leadership and labour potential constituted an almost insurmountable obstacle for the regime's attempt to impose order. The human drain created chaotic situations throughout the country. Many spheres, such as industry, the service sector, public transportation and hospitals either totally collapsed or functioned only with great difficulty. Exit had torn holes in the East German society, to the extent that even the anachronistic leadership could no longer ignore the volatility of the situation. In a series of highly unusual public declarations, the government acknowledged the threat that transversal exit waves constituted for the socialist order. On 12 October, the Politburo avowed on the front page of the official party organ that 'socialism needs everybody, . . .we cannot remain indifferent if people break away from our East Germany'.[6]

The continuously increasing pressure from below triggered a power struggle within the Politburo. On 18 October, Honecker, the long-time autocrat, and two of his closest and oldest allies, Günter Mittag and Joachim Hermann, were forced to resign. Yet, the new government, headed by another long-time Honecker confidant, Egon Krenz, could not calm the situation with the announced reforms. Too little, too late was the general consensus in the population. Demonstrations became again more frequent and dramatically increased in size. Calls for more democracy, free elections and mobility rights could be heard all over East Germany. 'We are the people' echoed day after day, hundreds of thousands of times, through the streets of Leipzig, Dresden, East Berlin, Karl-Marx-Stadt, Potsdam and many other cities. Leipzig alone witnessed several demonstrations attended by more than 200,000 people. On 4 November, over a million people took to the streets in

---

[6] *Neues Deutschland*, 12 October 1989, p. 1.

East Berlin. The day after, an almost equal number of protesters gathered in Leipzig.

The massive street protests transgressed the spatial givenness of German politics at least as much as the exit waves, which were, at the same time, tearing holes in the Iron Curtain. As pictures of mass demonstrations were televised around the globe, the nature of protest took on various transversal dimensions. It transcended the immediate territoriality of the protest actions and became entangled in the temporal and non-spatial logic of speed.

The local became instantaneously global. The global, in turn, started to shape local dynamics. Hundred of thousands of protesting citizens, shouting 'we are the people', monopolised television screens around the world for weeks during the autumn of 1989. These images were not without effect. Various foreign governments put pressure on East Germany's leadership. The Soviet Union decided not to support Honecker's struggle to retain power. Maybe most importantly, the spectacular televised images returned, via West German television, to the East German population and thus led to a self-triggering and spiralling dynamic of popular dissent. Through easily available Western media sources East German citizens witnessed day by day how mass emigration and large-scale street protests further undermined the legitimacy of their government. This transversal informational dynamic gave many people the necessary courage to join the continuously growing crowds in the streets. The virtuality of global media also provided direct incentives for East Germans to take the risk of participating in the exit wave. For instance, West German television coverage revealed to East Germans how their copatriots who sought refuge in diplomatic representations were brought by special trains to the West, or how barbed-wire installations were removed from the Austro-Hungarian border.[7]

By early November 1989, the transversal dynamics that took hold of dissident forces in East Germany had clearly undermined not only the legitimacy of the government, but also the very spatial givenness of Cold War international relations. Media coverage of protests was

---

[7] For further analyses of the transversal role that foreign media sources played in the revolution of 1989 see P.C. Hall (ed.), *Fernseh-Kritik: Revolutionäre Öffentlichkeit: Das Fernsehen und die Demokratisierung im Osten* (Mainz: v. Hase & Koehler, 1990); Kurt Hesse, *Westmedien in der DDR* (Cologn: Wissenschaft und Politik, 1988); and W. Claus (ed.), *Medien-Wende, Wende-Medien? Dokumentation des Wanders im DDR-Journalismus* (Berlin: Vistas, 1991).

by now a regular global television event. Meanwhile, the lack of man- and women-power that resulted from the exit wave, which continued at a rate of about 10,000 East Germans a day, further paralysed the country. Personal accounts, published later by high-ranking party officials, reveal how decisive these illegal transgressions of state boundaries were in triggering processes of social change. Two import- ant members of the Politburo, Egon Krenz and Günter Schabowski, acknowledge that mass emigration had a tremendous impact on them and other leading figures involved in the decision-making process. Members of the government believed that they could under no cir- cumstances survive extended mass emigration, that exit created a situ- ation against which the regime was absolutely helpless.[8]

Soon the mounting pressure claimed its next victims. More key fig- ures were forced to 'retire', including Margot Honecker, Harry Tisch, Kurt Hager and Erich Mielke. On 7 November the entire government stepped down. The day after, the Politburo followed suit. Then, on the evening of 9 November 1989, came the beginning of the end, the *coup de grâce* to the old order: Schabowski, in his capacity as spoke- sperson of the government, declared a new travel policy, rather inad- vertently, as one commentator notes, 'as an afterthought at the last minute, in response to a parting journalistic question'.[9] The effects were nevertheless dramatic and historic: with immediate effect, all East German citizens were free to travel abroad without prior permis- sion from state authorities. The spatial order of Cold War politics had crumbled. The same night, sensational pictures were seen all over the world: thousands of people climbing over, dismantling and simply walking through the meanwhile anachronistic Berlin Wall in front of puzzled and helpless East German guards. In the days to come, hun- dreds of thousands of East Germans squeezed through the Iron Cur- tain to take a glimpse at the West, a possibility that had been incon- ceivable to them for decades.

From then on it took little time for what remained of the authoritar- ian regime to vanish into the annals of European history. Emigration increased even more and demonstrations did not cease until all rem- nants of the old order were gone. Placing Hans Modrow, a reform-

---

[8] Egon Krenz, *Wenn Mauern Fallen* (Wien: Paul Neff Verlag, 1990), p. 13, 29, 61, 161–8; Günter Schabowski, *Das Politbüro: Ende eines Mythos* (Reinbeck: Rowohlt, 1990), pp. 62, 90, 305; and *Der Absturz* (Berlin: Rowohlt, 1991), pp. 118, 256, 305.
[9] Melvin J. Lasky, *Voices in a Revolution: The Collapse of East German Communism* (New Brunswick: Transaction Publishers, 1992), p. 111.

oriented communist, at the head of the government did not postpone the fall. In December, Egon Krenz resigned from all his functions. On 18 March 1990, the first free parliamentary elections took place in East Germany. On 3 October of the same year Germany was formally unified. Spatial transgression had led to political transformation. One of the most repressive regimes of Central and Eastern Europe seemed to have crumbled like a house of cards under the pressure from below.

Probing consent based conceptions of power

The image of human agency that these spectacular transversal events evoke are not only reflective of the media-infused contemporary consciousness. They are also part of a much deeper entrenched modern perception of political resistance, of revolutionary masses overthrowing their tyrannical rulers. Marxist activism has substantially contributed to the prevalence of this image. And so have other traditions, including the one that has evolved in the conceptual wake of la Boétie's notion of voluntary servitude. Its intellectual legacy has given rise to grand theories of dissent that revolve around the assumption that power is dependent upon popular consent. The withdrawal of this consent, through practices of resistance as in the above voice and exit example, can topple even the most ruthless forms of oppression. Or so at least goes the la Boétiean argument.

Consent-oriented understandings of power have left a lasting mark on contemporary political ideas and social practices. Barry Hindess, for instance, divides modern conceptions of power into two main approaches. One focuses on the capacity to act. The other understands power not only as a capacity, but also as a right to act, 'with both right and capacity being seen as to rest on the consent of those over whom the power is exercised'.[10] The la Boétiean model clearly epitomises this latter view, a view that has been, according to Hindess, 'at the centre of Western political and social thought throughout the modern period'.[11]

But are consent-based models of power really adequate to understand a transversal revolutionary event like the collapse of the Berlin Wall? Can a grand theory of dissent capture such a complex set of

---

[10] Barry Hindess, *Discourses of Power: From Hobbes to Foucault* (Oxford: Blackwell, 1996), p. 1.
[11] Ibid, p. 10.

127

transgressions and the processes of social change that issued from them? Michel Foucault, arguably one of the most influential contributors to discussions on power, offers help.

A comparison between Foucault and the la Boétiean tradition highlights some of the issues that are at stake in conceptualising power relations that are operative in transversal political dynamics. Both approaches rely on a similar relational view of power, at least at first sight. The la Boétiean notion of withdrawing popular consent is based on the premise that power dynamics operate in the interactive relationship between ruler and ruled. If people draw upon this power source they can fundamentally alter existing political structures and practices. Thus, by engaging in street demonstration and protest migration, as the East Germans did, common citizens are said to be interfering directly with power relations. Foucault shares some of these theoretical assumptions. He defines the exercise of power, somewhat like la Boétie, as 'a mode of action upon the actions of others', which indicates that his object of analysis is not power itself, but power relations.[12] Foucault does not deny that institutions are crucial embodiments of power. Indeed, they are often the place where power is inscribed and crystallised. Yet, the fundamental point of anchorage of power relations, Foucault claims, is always located outside institutions, deeply entrenched within the social nexus. Hence, instead of looking at power from the vantage point of institutions, one must analyse institutions from the standpoint of power relations.[13]

The shared concern with how power functions relationally leads Foucault and la Boétie away from what most modern theorists (and international relations scholars in particular) have constituted as the key focus of power analyses: the state. From a relational perspective, the state is only one among many sites of power, a superstructural site that operates primarily on the grounds of other, already existing power networks.[14] Foucault and la Boétie also diverge from the common tendency to define power primarily as a negative, restraining and repressive force. Both imbue power with an important positive and enabling component. In the la Boétiean tradition, it is the ability

[12] Michel Foucault, 'The Subject and Power', in H. Dreyfus and P. Rabinow (eds.), *Michel Foucault: Beyond Structuralism and Hermeneutics* (New York: Harvester Wheatsheaf, 1982), pp. 219, 221.

[13] Ibid., p. 222.

[14] Michel Foucault, 'Truth and Power', in C. Gordon (ed.), *Power/Knowledge: Selected Interviews and Other Writings*, (New York: Pantheon Books, 1980/1972), p. 122.

to overcome domination through the withdrawal of popular consent. With Foucault things are more complicated. His earlier so-called archaeological phase clearly privileges systemic and discursive restraints over the individual's capacity to employ power for emancipatory objectives.[15] His later work, however, revolves around a more affirmative core, one that sees power not just as a negative and repressive force, but at least as much as something enabling, an opportunity, an instrument of resistance.[16]

This is where similarities between Foucault and the la Boétiean tradition end. Foucault may well rely on a relational and enabling view of power, he may even endorse the la Boétiean claim that 'power stems from below'.[17] But Foucault strongly opposes global and ahistoric models of power relations that focus on dualistic interactions between oppressor and oppressed:

> [T]here is no binary and all-encompassing opposition between rulers and ruled at the root of power relations, and serving as a general matrix – no such duality extending from the top down and reacting on more and more limited groups to the very depths of the social body. One must suppose rather that the manifold relationships of force that take shape and come into play in the machinery of production, in families, limited groups, and institutions, are the basis for wide-ranging effects of cleavages that run through the social body as whole.[18]

Foucault clearly rejects the essentialist assumptions around which grand theories of dissent revolve. By characterising power not as an interaction between ruler and ruled, but as a complex, stratified, interwoven, multi-dimensional and, above all, transversal phenomenon, he undermines the most fundamental theoretical foundation of the entire la Boétiean tradition of dissent. In particular, he dismantles the notion of voluntary servitude, the parsimonious claim that any form of government, no matter how ruthless and oppressive, is dependent upon popular consent. Foucault argues that consent may well serve to sustain power, so may violence. Yet, neither consent nor violence form the basic nature of power. 'The crucial problem of power,' for Foucault,

---

[15] See especially Michel Foucault, *L'Archéologie du Savoir* (Paris: Gallimard, 1969).
[16] Michel Foucault, *La Volonté de Savoir*, vol I of *L'Histoire de la Sexualité* (Paris: Edition Gallimard, 1976), p. 133.
[17] Ibid., p. 124.
[18] Ibid., p. 124, as translated by R. Hurley in Foucault, *The History of Sexuality* (London: Penguin Books, 1978), p. 94.

'is not that of voluntary servitude, . . .but the recalcitrance of the will and the intransigence of freedom.'[19] Power does not work directly from people to people in a spatially delineated and consent-oriented manner. Power is a strategic situation, far too complex and idiosyncratic to be assessed through a grand theory, let alone a parsimonious one. Power relations are always part of a social network. They need to be assessed in their unique spatio-temporal setting.

The contextual dynamics of transversal politics

Is Foucault's hostility towards essentialist conceptions of power warranted? Is his stratified notion of power relations more adequate to understand contemporary global politics? A second reading of the East German revolution now explores these questions. This time the focus lies with locating some of the unique, multiple and overlapping power relations that Foucault so extensively theorised.

The fall of the Berlin Wall is a set of inherently transversal events. The first section of this chapter has already demonstrated how voice and exit forms of dissent were characterised by cross-territorial dynamics that linked East German politics with a variety of other political spheres. But dissident practices were, of course, not the only forms of agency that contributed to the revolution of 1989. Neither was dissent operating in a void. Various political and societal contexts mediated the manner in which dissident practices came to play a role in the disintegration of the East German regime. These contextual dynamics too were of a transversal nature. For the sake of intelligibility, I denote them, at least for now, in state-centric terms (as national, intra-national, and inter-national), if only to emphasise with how much ease political dynamics transgressed the boundaries of the established domestic and international political order.

Power relations at the international level undoubtedly played a crucial role in the East German revolution. Social dynamics within East Germany during the late 1980s were intrinsically linked to Cold War politics and the overall crisis of the Soviet-led alliance system. Indeed, many analysts argue that changes in Moscow's foreign policy constituted an important, if not the key factor in the German revolution of

---

[19] Foucault, 'The Subject and Power', pp. 219–22.

1989.[20] The survival of Honecker's authoritarian regime was directly linked to its incorporation into the globalised structures of Cold War politics. East Germany's importance for the Soviet-led alliance system was a crucial component of domestic power relations. This remained so as long as the international system was dominated by ideological schism and a bipolar power structure. However, the situation radically changed in the mid 1980s, when Mikhail Gorbachev started to restructure Soviet foreign policy. The principle of 'new thinking' now recognised explicitly that each nation has the right to determine its own policies.[21] This meant that the East German regime could no longer count on Moscow's financial and military support for the suppression of domestic popular resistance. The gradual decay of the Soviet Union and the resulting dissolution of the Cold War system fundamentally altered power relationships within East Germany. These factors permitted domestic social dynamics to take a course that was far less circumscribed by Soviet geopolitical and ideological interest.

Intranational dynamics constituted another sphere in which complex and stratified power relationships operated much like Foucault's theoretical model suggests. The ethnic bonds and fierce ideological competition between the two politically distinct German States intrinsically and interactively linked their political and social dynamics. Many aspects of resistance in East Germany must be understood in the context of such transversal intra-German dynamics. For example, the massive emigration waves would not have been able to emerge without West Germany's economic attraction and its constitutionally entrenched policy of granting citizenship to East German refugees. Ulrich Beck appropriately captures this intranational power dimension by pointing out that 'Poland minus communism is still Poland. But East Germany minus communism is the Federal Republic of Germany'.[22]

The domestic level displays perhaps the most complex picture of

---

[20] For example, Dahrendorf, *Betrachtungen über die Revolution*, p. 17; Deppe, Dubiel and Rödel, *Demokratischer Umbruch*, p. 10; and Glaeßner, *Der schwierige Weg zur Demokratie*, p. 25.

[21] Mikhail Gorbachev, *Perestroika: Die zweite russische Revolution*, tr. Gruppe U. Mihr (München: Droemer Knaur, 1987), pp. 230–3.

[22] Ulrich Beck, 'Opposition in Deutschland', in B. Giesen and C. Leggewie (ed.), *Experiment Vereinigung: Ein sozialer Grossversuch* (Berlin: Rotbuch Verlag, 1991), pp. 24–5.

power relationships. An account of the struggle for control over the Politburo and its implication for the fall of East Germany could alone fill volumes. For instance, the regime's commanding structure of the 1980s could be considered tripartite, consisting of Erich Honecker, Günter Mittag and Erich Mielke. Yet, Honecker had occupied the key role for such a long time that the system's functioning was to a considerable extent dependent upon his personality, on what Max Weber once called a charismatic source of power. Thus, when Honecker fell seriously ill in 1989, the Politburo was paralysed and unable to respond to the mounting pressure from the population.

Domestic power relationships were also conditioned by the system of privileges in which East Germany's authoritarian commanding structure was embedded. Privileges were not only available to the members of the Politburo, who had access to a great array of Western consumer goods and lived in well-equipped and secluded 'fortresses', first in Pankow and, from 1960 on, in Wandlitz, north of Berlin. Rather, the reward principle reached a much greater circle of citizens. For example, the notorious *Stasi*, the Ministry of State Security, employed a range of methods to draw people into the machinery of the oppressive state system. Besides its 85,000 full-time employees, it is estimated that approximately 10 per cent of the population was in one way or another involved with this institution that functioned as an omnipresent surveillance system.[23] These informants, combined with the *nomenclatura*, the police, the army, fire-fighters, justices, teachers, post-office employees and all their families and friends and many more, comprised a substantial web of people who were in some manner intertwined with the ruling apparatus. Informants were paid according to the usefulness of the material they provided. Non-cooperation with the authorities, by contrast, could easily result in highly consequential financial, political and other disadvantages for the respective individuals and their families. This system of reward and punishment existed at all societal levels and in all geographical

---

[23] Ursula Jaekel, '40 Jahre Staatssicherheit – Ziele, Tätigkeit, Auswirkungen', in K. Löw, *Ursachen und Verlauf der deutschen Revolution*, pp. 140, 145; Tilmann Moser, *Besuche bei Brüdern und Schwestern* (Frankfurt: Suhrkamp, 1992), p. 56. Revelations about the *Stasi* are among the most intensively discussed aspects of the East German system. See, for example, Rainer Eppelmann, *Wendewege* (Bonn: Bouvier Verlag, 1992); Erich Loest, *Die Stasi war mein Eckermann oder: mein Leben mit der Wanze* (Göttingen: Steidel Verlag, 1991); Hans Joachim Schädlich (ed.), *Aktenkundig* (Berlin: Rowohlt Verlag, 1992); Christina Wilkening, *Staate im Staate: Auskünfte ehemaliger Stasi-Mitarbeiter* (Berlin: Aufbau, 1990).

areas of the country. It created various systems and sub-systems of power relations that helped to sustain an authoritarian societal structure. This is why some analysts, such as Artur Meier, portray the collapse of the East German regime primarily as the obsolescence of a system of positive and negative privileges.[24]

One could easily argue with this or that aspect of the above interpretations of social dynamics in East Germany. One could elaborate on them or draw attention to countless other transversal spheres where power dynamics operated. To engage with the details of these debates is outside the objective of this book and better left to specialists in German politics – a status to which I lay no claim. My explorations are meant, above all, as a theoretical rethinking of dissent and human agency – and from this vantage-point the message is clear: power relations and power structures that influenced the collapse of the East German regime were far too complex and transversal to be assessed through a parsimonious and spatially delineate theoretical model.

Foucault's notion of power is more adequate than la Boétie's to understand the complexities and transversal dynamics that made up the events in East Germany. Power relations operate in multiple terrains and can be assessed meaningfully only in a specific historical and cultural setting. No grand theory can ever capture the essence of power relations. My brief rereading of the various contexts within which the revolutionary events of 1989 were embedded confirms Foucault's claim that power, capitalised or not, concentrated or diffused, does not exist at a universal level.[25] But this is not to say that power as such does not exist. In fact, Foucault explicitly operates within the Nietzschean premise that nothing exists outside power, that 'there cannot be a society without power relations'.[26] There will always be forms of domination and attempts to break free from them. 'To demand of strength,' Nietzsche says, 'that it should not express itself as strength, that it should *not* be a desire to overcome, a desire to throw down, a desire to become master, a thirst for enemies and resistances and triumphs, is just as absurd as to demand of weakness

---

[24] Artur Meier , 'Abschied von der sozialistischen Ständegesellschaft', *Aus Politik und Zeitgeschichte*, 16–17, April 1990, pp. 3–14.
[25] Foucault, 'The Subject and Power', p. 219.
[26] Ibid., p. 223.

that it should express itself as strength.'[27] Despite this omnipresence
of relations of domination and resistance – or, rather, because of it –
one cannot speak of power and human agency in global and ahistoric
terms. A theory of power, Foucault argues convincingly, is unable to
provide the basis for analytical work, for it assumes a prior objectification of the very power dynamics the theory is trying to assess.[28]

Towards a discursive understanding of power relations

Since a systematic theory cannot capture the intricate functioning of
power, one must explore different ways of understanding the frameworks within which domination, resistance and social change take
place. One must search for more subtle foundations that could, maybe,
provide momentary ground for understanding how human agency
functions in a transversal context. But how is one to embark upon this
intricate task? Foucault continues to provide useful guidance, at least
up to a certain point. He approaches power by adding an extra step
to understanding it. Power, he argues, is not simply the relationship
between individuals or groups, a type of force that one person exerts
on another. It works in a more intricate, more indirect way:

> [W]hat defines a relationship of power is that it is a mode of action
> which does not act directly and immediately on others. Instead it
> acts upon their actions: an action upon an action, on existing actions
> or on those which may arise in the present or the future. . .[T]he exer-
> cise of power. . .is a total structure of actions brought to bear upon
> possible actions.[29]

Power is a complex strategic situation, something that shapes and
frames the boundaries within which actions can be carried out. Such
a definition inevitably raises a number of questions. What mediates
the exercise of power? What is the space that lies between actions, this
mesh of social forces through which actions frame the actions of
others? One mediating factor is the relationship between power and
knowledge. Foucault, drawing once more on Nietzsche, argues that
knowledge and power are intrinsically linked. There are no power

---

[27] Friedrich Nietzsche, *On the Genealogy of Morals*, tr. W. Kaufmann and R.J. Hollingdale
(New York: Vintage Books, 1989/1887), § 13, p. 45.
[28] Foucault, 'The Subject and Power', p. 209.
[29] Ibid., p. 220.

relations which do not constitute corresponding fields of knowledge. And there are no forms of knowledge that do not presuppose and at the same time constitute relations of power.[30]

Power is not a stable and steady force, something that exists on its own. There is no essence to power, for its exercise is dependent upon forms of knowledge that imbue certain actions with power. This is to say that the manner in which we view and frame power also influences how it functions in practice.

'It is within discourse,' Foucault claims, 'that power and knowledge articulate each other.'[31] Discourses are subtle mechanisms that frame our thinking process. They determine the limits of what can be thought, talked and written in a normal and rational way. In every society the production of discourses is controlled, selected, organised and diffused by certain procedures. This process creates systems of exclusion in which one group of discourses is elevated to a hegemonic status while others are condemned to exile. Discourses give rise to social rules that decide which statements most people recognise as valid, as debatable or as undoubtedly false. They guide the selection process that ascertains which propositions from previous periods or foreign cultures are retained, imported, valued, and which are forgotten or neglected.[32] Although these boundaries change, at times gradually, at times abruptly, they maintain a certain unity across time, a unity that dominates and transgresses individual authors, texts or social practices.

Not everything is discourse, but everything is in discourse. Things exist independently of discourses, but we can only assess them through the lenses of discourse, through the practices of knowing, perceiving and sensing which we have acquired over time. Nietzsche:

> That mountain there! That cloud there! What is 'real' in that? Subtract the phantasm and every human *contribution* from it, my sober friends! If you *can*! If you can forget your descent, your past, your training – all of your humanity and animality. There is no 'reality' for us – not for you either, my sober friends. . .[33]

---

[30] Michel Foucault, *Surveiller et Punir: Naissance de la Prison* (Paris: Gallimard, 1975), p. 32.

[31] Foucault, *La Volonté de Savoir*, p. 133.

[32] See Michel Foucault, 'Politics and the Study of Discourse', in G. Burchell *et al.* (eds.), *The Foucault Effect: Studies in Governmentality* (London: Harvester Wheatsheaf, 1991), pp. 59–60; *L'Archéologie du Savoir*; and *L'Ordre du Discours* (Paris: Gallimard, 1971).

[33] Nietzsche, *The Gay Science*, tr. W. Kaufmann (New York: Vintage Books, 1974/1882), § 57, p. 121.

Nietzsche's point, of course, is not that mountains and clouds do not exist as such. To claim such would be absurd. Mountains and clouds exist no matter what we think about them. And so do more tangible social practices. But they are not 'real' by some objective standard. Their appearance, meaning and significance is part of human experiences, part of a specific way of life. A Nietzschean position emphasises that discourses render social practices intelligible and rational – and by doing so mask the ways in which they have been constituted and framed. Systems of domination gradually become accepted as normal and silently penetrate every aspect of society. They cling to the most remote corners of our mind, for 'all things that live long are gradually so saturated with reason that their emergence out of unreason thereby becomes improbable'.[34]

Discourses are more than just masking agents. They provide us with frameworks to view the world, and by doing so influence its course. Discourses express ways of life that actively shape social practices. But more is needed to demonstrate how the concept of discourse can be of use to illuminate transversal dissident practices. More is needed to outline a positive notion of human agency that is not based on stable foundations. This section has merely located the terrains that are to be explored. It is now up to the following chapters to introduce, step by step, the arguments and evidence necessary to develop and sustain a discursive understanding of transversal dissent and its ability to exert human agency.

Summary

This chapter has started to prepare the ground for the articulation of a more subtle, alternative conception of human agency. The focus has been with rethinking power, an issue that is central to an adequate understanding of the role that human agency plays in global politics.

A theoretical engagement with Michel Foucault and a rereading of the events in East Germany has demonstrated that power dynamics are far too complicated to be assessed through a parsimonious grand theory. The idea, espoused by the la Boétiean tradition of dissent, that power is located in the interactive relationship between ruler and ruled, proved too simplistic and too spatially delineated to assess the

---

[34] Nietzsche, *Morgenröte* (Frankfurt: Insel Taschenbuch, 1983/1881), § 1, p. 17.

complex and transversal events that toppled the authoritarian regime in 1989. The events that led to the fall of the Berlin Wall were above all a series of transversal dynamics – an intertwined array of actions and contextual restraints that operated across the territorial givenness of East German and international politics. Exit and voice forms of protest easily transgressed the spatial boundaries of geopolitically perceived necessity – the former through physical crossings of the Iron Curtain, the latter through a mass-media-induced fusion of the local and the global. The contextual dynamics within which these transgressions were carried out was equally transversal. Power relations penetrated virtually all societal aspects, to the point that no theory could ever hope to capture the stratified, interwoven and cross-territorial manner in which power operated in practice.

Acknowledging the complexities of power is not unproblematic for a re-articulation of human agency. Many commentators have criticised Foucault for putting us in a situation in which we can do nothing but express bewilderment at an overwhelming world around us – a world in which the potential for human agency no longer seems to exist. Nancy Hartsock, for example, dismisses such a Foucauldian world as one in which systems move, not people, in which the subject becomes obliterated or reduced to an impotent passive object. She claims that in defining power as omnipresent, as ever expanding and penetrating all aspects of society, 'Foucault has made it very difficult to locate domination.'[35] Resistance, then, becomes virtually impossible.

But Foucault can be read in more than just one way. His later work, in particular, offers ground for more optimistic interpretations. Indeed, Foucault explicitly points out that acknowledging the omnipresence of power is not to say that it is a fatality which cannot be overcome.[36] 'Where there is power', he says, 'there is resistance.'[37] Paul Patton, extending this line of thought, convincingly argues that Foucault can be read in ways that 'offer a surrogate for hope'.[38] By distinguishing between power, power over and domination, Patton shows that Foucault espouses a conception of human being. Even though this conception is 'thin', it can 'be filled out in a manner which

[35] Nancy Hartsock, 'Foucault on Power: A Theory for Women?', in Linda J. Nicholson (ed.), *Feminism/Postmodernism* (New York: Routledge, 1990), esp. pp. 168–70.
[36] Foucault, 'The Subject and Power', p. 223.
[37] Foucault, *La Volonté de Savoir*, p. 125.
[38] Paul Patton, 'Foucault's Subject of Power', *Political Science Newsletter*, 6, 1994, p. 61.

explains both resistance to domination and the possibility of transforming existing economies of power'.[39]

Patton's reading of Foucault demonstrates how one can accept the inevitability of power and still articulate a concept of human agency, even develop concrete strategies of resistance. The present chapter has taken the first step in this direction by proposing a shift away from grand theories of popular dissent towards a transversal and discursive understanding of power. This shift is not meant to replace concrete practices of resistance, but to supplement them with a more subtle understanding of the effects that they produce. Power, from this perspective, is not something fixed and stable, but a complex and constantly changing relational situation that is intrinsically linked to the production and diffusion of knowledge.

Accepting that there is no essence to power requires coming to terms with the death of God. In a world that no longer revolves around stable foundations, human beings must take responsibility for their own thoughts and actions. We must recognise the contingent character of foundations, the absence of an overarching world-view that unifies humanity, provides certainty and stability. 'The world is gone, I have to carry you', Celan said at the beginning of this chapter. The prospect is frightening, to say the least. Nietzsche already knew how daring a task it is, having to affirm from denial, having to create out of negation: 'Who can feel with me what it means to feel with every shred of one's being that the weight of all things must be defined anew?'[40] The following chapters engage in such a Nietzschean rethinking, but in a much less ambitious way. They do not aspire to define anew the weight of human agency. Far from such a presumptuous ambition be their task. They merely attempt to ground an understanding of transversal dissent in nothingness.

---

[39] Ibid., p. 66.
[40] Nietzsche cited in Erich Heller, 'Rilke and Nietzsche', in I. Howe (ed.), *The Idea of the Modern in Literature and the Arts* (New York: Horizon Press, 1967), p. 270.

First interlude Confronting incommensurability

> [The problem] is precisely this gesture of totalized reasoning, which subsumes, or pretends to be able to subsume, everything into *one* concept, *one* theory, *one* position. The resulting philosophical 'master discourse' then turns into an intellectual domination by the Same, the One – a form of domination in which there is no room for the views of the Other, the Heterogeneous.[1]

Before embarking on more rereadings of the transversal dynamics that led to the collapse of the Berlin Wall it is necessary to pause for a moment and reflect upon some of the central theoretical dilemmas that have arisen with a rethinking of human agency in global politics. What precisely is entailed in accepting the death of God? What does it mean to take over, rather than deflect responsibility? If one abandons the desire to understand the world in its totality, how can one deal with the ensuing proliferation of diverse and often incommensurable positions? Can we still articulate dissent, can we assert any kind of normative claim, without relying on stable foundations? Can we retain hope for articulating a viable but non-essentialist concept of human agency? And how can Foucauldian notions of power and discourse possibly offer help? Are they not, as some suggest, merely faddish concepts, destined to wax and wane with fleeting intellectual trends of the postmodern and poststructural kind?

---

[1] Elisabeth List, *Die Präsenz des Anderen: Theorie und Geschlechterpolitik* (Frankfurt: Suhrkamp, 1993), p. 11.

This Interlude grapples with some of these dilemmas by engaging the literature on postmodernism. It does so not to provide a coherent account of this complex body of knowledge, but to underline the need to embrace difference and confront incommensurability. Accepting the contingent character of foundations does not necessarily result in a nihilist void, a relativist abyss that renders dissent or critique impossible. Indeed, any approach that fails to take postmodern epistemological warnings seriously runs the risk of objectifying systems of exclusion by imposing inevitable cultural prejudices upon an idiosyncratic array of social phenomena.

Only by confronting incommensurability, by accepting its epistemological and methodological consequences, can one adequately work through the complex and often paradoxical aspects of transversal struggles. Searching for this difficult path is our best hope for retaining a viable notion of human agency.

Postmodernism, or life after the death of God

Accepting the death of God is necessary for an adequate understanding of dissent and human agency in global politics. Prevalent approaches to popular dissent have, by and large, failed to take this crucial step. They have often engaged in ahistoric and universal endeavours to discover recurring patterns of social change. Such grand theories of dissent run the risk of objectifying and entrenching forms of domination. They lead to what Adorno called 'identity thinking', a practice of reflection that ignores the desire for control and the will to power entailed in all thought forms. They subsume the particular under the general, force subjective and idiosyncratic identities into one unitary system of thought, one universal point of reference, one truth that silences all others.[2]

A postmodern position embraces difference and emphasises that an understanding of human agency and dissent need not, and must not, resort to a universal and essentialist standpoint. Indeed, Foucault links the very notion of a progressive politics to an acceptance of difference and ensuing attempts to explore possibilities of transformation.[3] But

---

[2] Theodor W. Adorno, *Negative Dialektik* (Frankfurt: Suhrkamp, 1992/1966), pp. 15–86.
[3] Michel Foucault, 'Politics and the Study of Discourse', in G. Burchell *et al.* (eds.), *The Foucault Effect: Studies in Governmentality* (London: Harvester Wheatsheaf, 1991), p. 70.

what precisely does a postmodern position entail besides the acceptance of difference?

The postmodern has become a stretched, widely used and highly controversial term. It first achieved prominence in literary criticism and architecture, but eventually spread into virtually all realms, penetrating such fields as architecture, art, music, sociology, geography, philosophy and, with some delay, the study of international politics. What the postmodern actually means is highly disputed and dependent on links with equally ambiguous concepts, such as modernism and modernity. The increasing sense of confusion in the proliferation of the postmodern leads Gianni Vattimo to note that this term is so omnipresent and faddish that it has become almost obligatory to distance oneself from it.[4] But Vattimo, and many others, nevertheless hold on. He, alongside such diverse authors as Jean-François Lyotard, Jean Baudrillard, David Harvey and Fredric Jameson, view the postmodern as both a changing attitude and a fundamentally novel historical condition. They focus on cultural transformations that have taken place in the Western world and assume, as Andreas Huyssen summarises, that we are witnessing 'a noticeable shift in sensibility, practices and discourse formations which distinguishes a postmodern set of assumptions, experiences and propositions from that of a preceding period'.[5] Such shifts are recognised in various features, including the rapid evolution and spread of mass media, computers and other communicative features, which have created a 'transparent society' (Vattimo), an 'ecstasy of communication' (Baudrillard); a fundamental rearrangement of the relationship between time and space (Harvey); a post-industrial phase whose main feature is knowledge production (Lyotard); or the advance of new technologies and a consumer democracy which provides capitalism with an inherently new cultural logic (Jameson).

The postmodern should be viewed in a more precise and limited

---

[4] Gianni Vattimo, *The Transparent Society*, tr. D. Webb (Baltimore: The Johns Hopkins University Press, 1992), p. 1.

[5] Andreas Huyssen, 'Mapping the Postmodern', *New German Critique*, 33, 1984, p. 8. Jean Baudrillard, *Simulations*, tr. P. Foss, P. Patton and P. Beitchman (New York: Semiotext(e), 1983) and 'The Ecstasy of Communication', in Hal Foster (ed.), *Postmodern Culture*, tr. J. Johnston (London: Pluto Press, 1985); Fredric Jameson, 'Postmodernism or the Cultural Logic of Late Capitalism', in *New Left Review*, 146, 1984; David Harvey, *The Condition of Postmodernity* (Cambridge: Blackwell, 1989); Jean-François Lyotard, *La Condition Postmoderne* (Paris: Les Editions de Minuit, 1979).

way, such that a clear distinction is drawn between postmodernism (an attitude, an approach to studying social phenomena) and post-modernity (a new historical epoque).[6] The former position is compelling, while the latter appears premature. This is not to say that the above-mentioned so-called postmodern phenomena do not exist. Indeed, later chapters will deal with them in detail. Yet, there is not enough evidence to suggest that these features have ushered in a fundamentally new historical period, one that has superseded modernity and deserves the label 'post'. Among the authors who advance such cautious positions are Paul de Man and Michel Foucault, for whom modernity is already such a vague and dubious historical term, that postmodernity becomes nothing but a parody of the notion of modernity.[7] Even Lyotard, in a departure from earlier terminology, now prefers to 'rewrite modernity'. The very concept of postmodernity, he points out, represents an effort in historical periodisation, an obsession with ordering that is typically modern.[8]

The term postmodernism is a more useful analytical tool than post-modernity for it does not imply the end of a historical epoque called modernity, but merely draws attention to the need for rethinking the concepts and categories through which this epoque has been constituted. Compelling for such a conceptualisation are the aspects of Lyot-ard's work that differentiate between the modern and the postmodern by defining the former as any science that legitimates itself in reference to a grand narrative, while employing the latter term to express an incredulity towards this totalising form of knowledge.[9] The refusal to orient oneself in relation to one 'master discourse' applies, of course, to all aspects of life. Umberto Eco, for instance, defines the postmodern, analogous to the argument presented in chapter 4, as 'the orientation of anyone who has learned the lessons of Foucault, i.e., that power is not something unitary that exists outside us'.[10] Vattimo's

---

[6] For elaborations of this distinction see Linda Hutcheon, *The Politics of Postmodernism* (London: Routledge, 1989); and Barry Smart, *Postmodernity* (London: Routledge, 1993).

[7] Paul de Man, *The Resistance to Theory* (Minneapolis: University of Minnesota Press, 1986), p. 120; Michel Foucault, 'Space, Knowledge, and Power', tr. C. Hubert in P. Rabinow (ed.), *The Foucault Reader* (New York: Pantheon Books, 1984), pp. 248–9; Foucault in Smart, *Postmodernity*, p. 5.

[8] Jean-François Lyotard, 'Rewriting Modernity', in *The Inhuman: Reflections on Time*, tr. G. Bennington and R. Bowlby (Stanford: Stanford University Press, 1991/1988), pp. 24–35.

[9] Lyotard, *La Condition Postmoderne*, p. 7.

[10] Eco cited in Hutcheon, *The Politics of Postmodernism*, p. 3.

postmodernism rejects the idea of a single, unilinear notion of history, one that progresses towards an end, a telos. He considers history as 'images of the past projected from different points of view'.[11] Conceptualising the postmodern along these lines of celebrating difference, Wolfgang Welsch argues, goes beyond merely rejecting and superseding modernity. It is a transition into a true form of plurality that includes past epoques and modern ideas.[12]

Postmodernism can thus be considered, at least at this point, as a methodological and epistemological position, which revolves around the issue of what knowledge is, how it is constructed, and how it relates to language and power. Epistemology here is not, as it was in pre-Kantean philosophy, a privileged form of insight into the human mind. The postmodern notion of episteme rejects the existence of truth beyond power, a privileged site of knowledge. It draws attention to the constituted and multiple dimensions of social practices. Postmodernists search for solutions outside the teleological and rational imperatives of Enlightenment notions of universal emancipation. Given the acceptance of epistemological fragmentation, it is almost self-evident that this search is characterised more by diversity than by a single and coherent set of positions and assumptions about life.

If there is a unifying point in postmodernism then it is precisely the acceptance of difference, the refusal to uphold one position as the correct and desirable one. 'The postmodern begins,' Welsch says, 'where totality ends.'[13] Its vision is the vision of plurality, a positive attempt to secure and explore multiple dimensions of the processes that legitimise and ground social practices. Once the end of totalitarian thought is accepted, it becomes, of course, very difficult to talk about the postmodern without descending into clichés or doing grave injustice to individual authors who explore various terrains of difference. Jane Flax recognised this difficulty and admits that by speaking about postmodernism one already runs 'the risk of violating some of its central values – heterogeneity, multiplicity, and difference'.[14] With this sense of terminological caution in mind, the present analysis engages

<hr/>

[11] Vattimo, *The Transparent Society*, p. 3.
[12] Wolfgang Welsch, 'Postmoderne: Genealogie und Bedeutung eines umstrittenen Begriffes', in P. Kemper (ed.), *Postmoderne oder der Kampf um die Zukunft* (Frankfurt: Fischer Taschenbuch, 1988), pp. 31–2. See also William E. Connolly, *The Ethos of Pluralization* (Minneapolis: University of Minnesota Press, 1995).
[13] Welsch, 'Postmoderne', pp. 29–30.
[14] Jane Flax, *Thinking Fragments: Psychoanalysis, Feminism, and Postmodernism in the Contemporary West* (Berkeley: University of California Press, 1990), p. 188.

in epistemological and methodological issues deemed postmodern, but does so by and large without relying upon this stretched and abused term.

The actual term postmodernism may vanish together with current intellectual fads. The substantial issues that it brought to the forefront, however, are here to stay. They underline, and this is particularly relevant for a rethinking of dissent and human agency in global politics, the need to take on board Nietzsche's advice and deal with, rather than deflect the death of God. The central importance of this task explains why authors who have otherwise not much in common generally recognise Nietzsche as the conceptual turning point from the modern to the postmodern.[15] This is because Nietzsche has shown that ever since the Renaissance, when the certainty of the theocentric order gave way to a less secure humanist world-view, many influential thinkers have searched for alternative foundations to anchor their understanding of the world. They include the early humanist elevation of 'man' to be the measure of all things, the Enlightenment trust in reason and science, the romantic deification of the Self, and the contemporary combination of the latter two into a positivist understanding of social change that focuses on grand theoretical models of dissent. Such modern compulsions to anchor the world in stable foundations are not only futile, but also dangerous, for they impose one image of reality to the detriment of others.

Instead of continuously trying to fill the void left by the fallen God, I argue for a methodological approach that no longer searches for alternative Archimedean foundations. The complex and increasingly intertwined social dynamics of contemporary life require more than ever that one accepts ambiguities and deals with the inevitably contingent character of foundations. One must try to approach issues of transversal struggles and human agency by relying on various forms of insight and on multiple levels of analysis, even if they seem at times incompatible.

Confronting incommensurability is often equated with a fall into a nihilist abyss. Not so. Welsch convincingly argues that a celebration of difference neither lacks potentials for resistance nor degenerates into some form of relativism. Rather, postmodern dissent is an active, positive and compelling way of safeguarding plurality, of resisting

---

[15] Welsch, 'Postmoderne', p. 12; Jürgen Habermas, *Der philosophische Diskurs der Moderne* (Frankfurt: Suhrkamp, 1985), pp. 104–29.

uniformity and totalitarian tendencies in such diverse realms as language, technology, aesthetics and politics.[16] But the practical relevance of such a postmodern approach to power, dissent and human agency is far easier asserted than demonstrated. The latter task, daunting as it may be, constitutes the main challenge for what follows.

[16] Wolfgang Welsch, 'Für eine postmoderne Ästhetik des Widerstands', in *Ästhetisches Denken* (Stuttgart: Reclam, 1993), p. 166.

5   Of 'men', 'women' and discursive domination

As her tutor you have the duty to keep her in ignorance.[1]

Grand theories of popular dissent cannot capture the intricate functioning of cross-territorial power relations. So demonstrated a reading of the East German revolution in chapter 4. Power must be understood in discursive and transversal terms. But what happens if one ignores the complex, constituted and constantly shifting aspects of power, if one continues to rely on grand theories and refuses to accept the death of God, the contingent character of foundations? Resulting essentialist and positivist approaches, I suggested, uphold a specific image of dissent, one that becomes frozen in time and space – an image that forecloses alternative views and thereby runs the risk of entrenching some forms of domination.

The present chapter sustains these claims by demonstrating how prevalent images and practices of popular dissent, even if they transgress political boundaries, are often unable to deal with subtle discursive forms of domination. To acknowledge this problematic aspect of dissent is to take one more step in the shift away from grand theories towards an articulation of human agency that is not anchored in stable foundations, but revolves around a discursive understanding of power relations. This is no easy task, for the power contained in discourses is slippery and difficult to detect. Discursive forms of domination rarely appear as what they are. Only seldom, if ever, William Connolly notes, 'does a policy of repression or marginalisation simply

---

[1] Tom Stoppard, *Arcadia* (London: Faber and Faber: 1993), p. 11.

146

present itself as such'.[2] Indeed, it is precisely this ability to mask and normalise domination that makes discursive systems of exclusion more powerful and lasting than their overt counterparts, like military regimes or dictatorships.

The power contained in discourses becomes particularly evident if one examines the interaction between popular dissent and patriarchy, discursively embedded identity constructs which support gender hierarchies. For this purpose, the analysis now scrutinises the prevalent image of popular dissent as epitomised by the la Boétien tradition. Such an inquiry soon reveals a consistent masculinist trait at the core of the theory and practice of popular dissent. Embedded in an essentialist notion of human agency, this gendered core accounts for the fact that for all its transversal dimensions and for all its spectacular oppositions to dictatorships, the la Boétien tradition has had little success in uprooting discursive forms of domination. Indeed, it further strengthened a model of dissent based on the image of a male revolutionary riding toward freedom while ignoring and even entrenching the patriarchal social order that made this heroic fight possible.

A rereading of the East German situation, this time from a gender sensitive perspective, serves to probe the extent to which such masculinist images of dissent may still be prevalent today. What role did women play in the protests of 1989, and what did change for them as a result of the subsequent redrawing of Cold War political boundaries? Were women able to exert human agency during this important transition period? And what do the answers to these questions entail for our understanding of dissent and global politics?

Problematising sex and gender

Before probing the East German revolution for gender specific traits it is necessary to draw attention to the complexities that are entailed in this task. There are heated debates in feminist theory about the meaning and significance of such concepts as 'gender', 'sex', 'masculinity', and 'femininity'. Indeed, the very terms 'men' and 'women' – seemingly incontestable and unproblematic categories – are being scrutinised from various angles.

---

[2] William E. Connolly, *Identity/Difference: Democratic Negotiations of Political Paradox* (Ithaca: Cornell University Press, 1991), p. 159.

Consider the concept of patriarchy, which Kathy Ferguson loosely defines as 'a set of institutions and practices that asserts and enforces the power of men as a group over women as a group'.[3] These institutions and practices are not stable or rooted in some essence. They are always in a state of flux. The functioning of patriarchy constantly changes, for it is itself a discursive construct and, as Jean Elshtain points out, dependent upon a reinforcing ideology that penetrates all levels of society.[4] This discursive order renders natural and rational the specific characteristics and role assignments that have been attributed to men and women. But outside this order there are no compelling reasons to link, for example, people with male bodies and masculine values or people with female bodies and feminine values. These links and the corresponding social division of labour are not biologically conditioned. They are discursively assigned and only appear natural because they have been objectified through a regime of truth. Even in the context of these narrow role assignments, people have fragmented and hyphenated identities. These mobile subjectivities, as Ferguson calls them, are ambiguous and unstable. They move across and along axes of power which are themselves in motion.[5]

One could draw attention to a whole range of consequences that arise from the subjectivity, fluidity and constituted nature of gendered role assignments. Such is not the task of this chapter. Its main purpose lies in observing the relatively consistent overall discursive regime within which men and women interact as social groups. This means that one must pay less attention to the subjective and constantly shifting criteria by which people are identified as belonging to either of these groups. Rosi Braidotti advances convincing arguments in favour of such an approach by scrutinising the interaction between sex (a biological category) and gender (a performative norm, a social practice). Too much focus on the discursive construct of gender, Braidotti believes, detracts from more imminent political problems, such as masculine domination and structurally asymmetrical power relationships between men and women. Instead of theorising gender,

[3] Kathy Ferguson, *The Man Question: Visions of Subjectivity in Feminist Theory* (Berkeley: University of California Press, 1993), p. 185.
[4] Jean Bethke Elshtain, *Public Man, Private Woman* (Princeton: Princeton University Press, 1981), p. 215.
[5] Ferguson, *The Man Question*, p. 154.

148

Braidotti proposes to focus on 'sexual difference'.[6] This is, of course, not unproblematic.

Judith Butler strongly criticises a sexual difference approach for its alleged essentialist understanding of gender relations, its uncritical acceptance of the categories 'men' and 'women'. She argues that sexual difference is always marked and formed by discursive practices. It is normative, a subtle form of power, a Foucauldian 'regulatory practice that produces the bodies it governs'.[7] Braidotti counters. She tries to valorise sexual difference in an attempt to oppose what she believes is a hasty dismissal of this concept 'in the name of a polemical form of "anti-essentialism", or of a utopian longing for a position "beyond gender"'.[8] Braidotti even claims that the very attempt to distinguish between sex and gender re-essentialises sex, for it reduces women's oppression to either materialism or language, nature or culture, body or mind.[9]

Much of the heated debate between essentialist and discursive approaches to relations between the sexes is a vicissitude of the English language. Or so at least believes Braidotti.[10] The English language allows for a clear terminological distinction between sex and gender. This linguistic situation forces people to position themselves on either side of these artificially drawn boundaries. But sex and gender are not mutually exclusive categories, they are intrinsically linked with each other. In many non-English contexts, Braidotti points out, a discussion of gender makes no epistemological or political sense, for there are no linguistic tools to distinguish this concept from sex.[11]

The German word *Geschlecht* is a case in point. It denotes both sex and gender. By defining sexuality in both biological and discursive manners, this term semantically recognises that the boundaries between them are fluid and artificial. This sets the stage for very different forms of feminist theorising. Consider the intensive discussions

---

[6] See Rosi Braidotti, with Judith Butler, 'Feminism by Any Other Name', in *Differences: A Journal of Feminist Cultural Studies*, 6, 2+3, 1994, 27–61; and 'The Politics of Ontological Difference', in T. Brennan (ed.), *Between Feminism and Psychoanalysis* (London: Routledge, 1989), pp. 89–105.

[7] Judith Butler, *Bodies That Matter: On the Discursive Limits of 'Sex'* (New York: Routledge, 1993), p. 1.

[8] Braidotti, 'Feminism by Any Other Name', p. 48.

[9] Ibid., pp. 46–7.

[10] Ibid., pp. 37–8.

[11] Ibid., p. 38.

that were triggered by translations of Butler's work into German.[12] Due to the broad meaning of the word *Geschlecht*, the actual English terms sex and gender were often used to capture some of Butler's complex arguments. The ensuing discussions, to simplify things a bit, led to a radical deconstruction of the very concept *Geschlecht*.[13] Many German feminists express strong reservations about the resulting tendency to emphasise the performativity and discursive construction not only of gender, but also of sex. They point towards the idealistic dangers of such a position and reassert, much like Braidotti does, the need to theorise the linguistic, social and political dimensions that are entailed in issues of sexual difference.[14] Similar trends are visible in France too. Luce Irigaray, for example, stresses that the human species is divided into two sexes which assure production and reproduction. Hence, she claims, equality must be attained not through a process of gender neutralisation, but through an acceptance of difference – anything else would be disastrous for humanity.[15]

A sexual difference approach is useful, at least up to a certain point. For now, then, the analysis will leave aside some of the complexities entailed in the conceptual tension between sex and gender. This means that the focus lies less with how women and men are differently constituted in different historical periods. Instead, the examination concentrates on how, in the context of these constantly changing identity constructs, patriarchy has remained a relatively constant social and political practice. To adopt such an analytical perspective is not to deny the complexities that are entailed in the entanglement of gender and politics. The point is, rather, to recognise that as a discursive form of exclusion patriarchy is strikingly persistent, even if there are occasional interferences that defy the logic of existing gender stereotypes and their corresponding political practices. Only once the broad boundaries of these discursive consistencies are identified, can

---

[12] Most notably Judith Butler, *Das Unbehagen der Geschlechter* (Frankfurt, 1991), tr. of *Gender Trouble: Feminism and the Subversion of Identity* (New York: Routledge, 1990).

[13] Christina Thürmer-Rohr, 'Zur Dekonstruktion der Kategorie Geschlecht', in *FRAZ: Frauezitig*, 1, 1995, 22–5.

[14] See, for example, Frigga Haug, 'Anmerkung zur Diskussion um die Kategorie 'Geschlecht'', *Das Argument*, No. 202, 35/6, November/December 1993, 899–900; Hilde Landweer and Mechthild Rumpf, 'Einleitung' to *Kritik der Kategorie 'Geschlecht'*, special issue of *Feministische Studien*, 2, 2, November 1993, 3–9; Christina Thürmer-Rohr, 'Denken der Differenz: Feminismus und Postmoderne', in *beiträge zur feministischen theorie und praxis*, 18, 39, 1995, 87–97.

[15] Luce Irigaray, *Je, tu, nous: pour une culture de la différence* (Paris: Grasset, 1990), pp. 10–11.

one investigate diverging patterns and theorise, as subsequent chapters will do, about the possibilities of resistance that emerge from the constituted and fragmented nature of the subject.

The masculinist dimensions of popular dissent

The analysis now returns to the la Boétiean tradition in an attempt to identify the gendered values that may be entailed in prevalent images of transversal popular dissent. If one examines this body of knowledge and its related political practices systematically, one soon discovers a strong presence and striking persistence of masculinist traits. Patriarchal values prevailed with virtually all prominent (male) authors and activists who devoted their lives to the struggle against political oppression. Many of their thoughts and self-sacrificing deeds were characterised by either ignorance of or contempt for the system of exclusion in which women are confined.

The theory and practice of popular dissent has revolved around gendered assumptions ever since its early Renaissance days. La Boétie, for instance, uses the term 'effeminate' to describe the cowardly behaviour of voluntary servitude – situations where people do not have the courage to stand up and request their natural right to freedom. The heroic battle against repression, by contrast, is portrayed in strong masculine terms.[16] The assumption of this text is, clearly, that men and women are meant to fulfil fundamentally different societal roles. This is, of course, not only compatible with prevailing practices at the time, but also characteristic of modernity in general. La Boétie's approach perfectly illustrates what Jean Elshtain, in a study on war, identified as a key discursive construct from Antiquity to today: the societal division into 'just warriors' (male fighters/protectors) and 'beautiful souls' (female victims/non-combatants). This stereotypical imagery has persisted, Elshtain emphasises, despite countless historical incidents that defy its simplistic gender assumptions.[17] In la Boétie's masculine image of the world, Renaissance men, newly unchained from the deified universal order, heroically venture out into the turbulent political realm to fight tyrants of all kind. Women, by contrast, are portrayed – often contrary to factual evidence – as

---

[16] Étienne de la Boétie, *Discours de la Servitude Volontaire*, ed. P. Bonnefon in *Oeuvres Complètes* (Genève: Slatkine Reprints, 1967/1552), esp. pp. 5–6, 16, 22, 65.
[17] Jean Bethke Elshtain, *Women and War* (New York: Basic Books, 1987).

passive onlookers to this unfolding drama. They are viewed as representing 'home and hearth and the humble verities of everyday life'.[18]

Gendered aspects of popular dissent intensified when la Boétie's legacy came of age during the romantic period. Chapter 2 already drew attention to the strong masculinist values entailed in the deification of the Self and the quest for a form of freedom that is not bound by the state. A glimpse beyond romantic writings, into the private lives and opinions of its protagonists, clearly affirms this interpretation. Henry David Thoreau, while describing how he lost all his remaining respect for the state, compared this allegedly timid, pitiful and half-witted institution to 'a lone woman with her silver spoons'.[19] Leo Tolstoy was even more explicit in advancing a societal image that revolves around a division between 'just warriors' and 'beautiful souls'. His political writings clarify what he really thought about 'the nonsense called women's rights'. Women, for him, are inferior to men. They fulfil the function of a breeding stock.[20] Not surprisingly, Tolstoy had no hesitation in storming off to sites of masculine social struggles, to the heroic battlefield of romantic idealism, while leaving his family behind in poverty. His wife Sofia hardly perceived this form of dissent as an advancement of freedom and justice. Her diaries shed a different light on her husband's self-sacrificing devotion to peace and nonviolence. Many entries, written over decades, display her frustration and anger about being reduced to an underappreciated caretaker, mother and secretary.[21]

Romanticism may have salvaged the concept of human agency from an Enlightenment obsession with reason and science, but this resurrection continuously refused to extend the capacity of human agency to women. A glimmer of hope for a more inclusive approach to popular dissent emerged when Gandhi started to popularise the practice of civil disobedience. He strongly criticised the common practice of calling women the weaker sex. 'If by strength is meant moral power,' he claims, 'then women are immeasurably man's superior.' They have

[18] Ibid, p. xiii.
[19] Henry David Thoreau, 'Civil Disobedience', in *Walden and Civil Disobedience* (New York: W.W. Norton, 1966/1848), p. 236.
[20] Tolstoy, cited in A.N. Wilson, *Tolstoy* (London: Hamish Hamilton, 1988), p. 365. See also his 'Letter to N.N. Strakov, 19 March 1870', in *I Cannot Be Silent: Writings on Politics, Art and Religion* (Bristol: Bristol Press, 1989), pp. 40–2.
[21] *The Diaries of Sofia Tolstoya*, tr. C. Porter (London: Jonathan Cape, 1985).

greater intuition, courage and powers of endurance. 'If nonviolence is the law of our being, the future is with women.'[22] Elshtain sees in this Gandhian rhetoric a challenge to masculine representations, a calling into question of male identity as warriors and protectors. She finds support for this position in the disproportionately high representation of women in pacifist movements.[23]

A gender sensitive reading of Gandhi and popular dissent also yields less optimistic results. It reveals that the presence of active women in resistance movements has not necessarily changed the prevalent masculinist image of dissent. Indicative of this tendency is that Gandhi's seemingly progressive rhetoric was not matched by his actions, not even by many of his other writings. His famous civil disobedience campaign against colonial rule in India was by and large a male affair. There was not a single woman among the eighty satyagrahi that participated in the important salt march of 1930. Women assumed a more vocal role during the ensuing nationwide campaign of non-violent resistance.[24] This increasing prominence of women satyagrahis may have shaken the foundations of British Colonial rule, but it in no way challenged the patriarchal character of Indian society. Patriarchy as a discursive system of exclusion proved to be strikingly persistent. Indeed, Gandhi's personal behaviour, like Tolstoy's, embodies the conventional masculinist image of a hero who embraces the vow of chastity and is willing to 'sacrifice his property and even his family' to fight for justice and a better world – a continuously unchallenged male-dominated world that is.[25]

While these behavioural traits are indicative of larger societal trends, the most consequential masculinist dimensions of popular dissent operate not at a personal, but at a discursive level. The underlying patriarchal values of the theory and practice of popular dissent are most strongly rooted in the key concept of voluntary servitude, the idea that any form of rule, even the most despotic one, is ultimately dependent upon consent. Chapter 4 already revealed multifarious problems entailed in consent oriented approaches to power. Feminist

---

[22] Mohandas Gandhi, *Satyagraha* (Ahmedabad: Navajivan Publishing House, 1951), p. 325.
[23] Elshtain, *Women and War*, pp. 139–40.
[24] See Judith Brown, *Gandhi and Civil Disobedience* (Cambridge: Cambridge University Press, 1977), pp. 136, 146.
[25] Gandhi, *Satyagraha*, p. 67.

theorists criticise this body of theory as well, particularly for its inability to recognise and deal with obvious gender biases. Carole Pateman's work has been particularly path-breaking in this regard.

Pateman draws attention to various reasons why, even within the institutions of a liberal democratic state, genuine consent is hardly the ground upon which social dynamics, and especially gender relations, are operating. In the context of a discursively entrenched patriarchal social order, women are not constituted as full-fledged members of civil society. The discursive construction of sexual difference, of what it means to be a man or a women, is such that the position of women in civil society is not based on consent, but, rather, on an exchange of obedience for protection.[26] Other feminists, such as Nancy Hirschmann, reiterate that voluntarist perceptions of obligation reflect a societal gender bias that actually denies women the opportunity to give (or withdraw) consent.[27] One could easily object to the categorical nature of this statement, for there is sufficient evidence – from the behaviour of individual medieval nuns to the women's movements of the twentieth century – that demonstrates how individual women have successfully withdrawn consent and challenged the existing patriarchal order. But such instances of public defiance are exceptions. They cannot serve as models that show how to address and rectify the inequalities that are perpetuated through discursively fortified patriarchal systems of exclusion. Indeed, because many obligations women have are not voluntary, consent-oriented perceptions of social dynamics may actually entrench the patriarchal status quo. This is why Hirschmann stresses that the gender-biased social order will remain intact as long as the underlying structures of obligation remain embedded in masculinist world-views.[28]

Many women cannot follow Tolstoy and Gandhi's lead, leave their children and everything else behind to then ride heroically towards freedom. Withdrawing consent does not work as easily for most women. In many situations, mass protest is not an option for them because the patriarchal order is entrenched at the level of societal values – and these values have assigned radically different social tasks

---

[26] This is, of course, a grossly simplified representation of Carole Pateman's arguments. See in particular her *The Sexual Contract* (Stanford: Stanford University Press, 1988) and 'Women and Consent', in *Political Theory*, 8, 2, May 1980, 149–68.

[27] Nancy J. Hirschmann, 'Freedom, Recognition, and Obligation: A Feminist Approach to Political Theory', *American Political Science Review*, 83, 4, December 1989, p. 1228.

[28] Ibid., p. 1229.

and responsibilities to women than to men. The suggestion that servitude is voluntary, and that any system of domination would crumble immediately if only its subjects would withdraw consent, fails to understand the complexities of the discursive system of domination in which women are confined. Kate McGuiness, for instance, argues convincingly that Gene Sharp's consent-based theory of power fails to assess adequately the power dynamics that are operative in gender relations. Basing her analysis on Pateman's critique of contract theory, McGuiness shows that Sharp's notion of popular dissent cannot offer a way of resisting patriarchal forms of oppression.[29]

How can a tradition of dissent that is so intensively concerned with fighting oppression overlook a system of exclusion as fundamental and persistent as patriarchy? How could this neglect permeate the work of authors as diverse as la Boétie, Thoreau, Tolstoy and Gandhi – authors who are known for their selfless dedication to the cause of non-violence and social justice? What does this neglect tell us about the potential and limits of transversal dissent today? And what does it entail for our understanding of human agency in global politics?

Writing his-story: the power of framing the past

The inability to see beyond masculinist images of the world is, of course, not unique to the theory and practice of popular dissent, but characteristic of modernity in general. The advent of globalisation and the increasing importance of transversal dissent have not changed this. Patriarchy remains a widespread, consistent and deeply entrenched discursive practice.

To recognise the subtle power contained in discursive practices it is necessary to take a step back and observe forms of repression that are less obvious than those targeted by the prevalent theory and practice of popular dissent. Overt forms of domination, such as the long-standing male control of politics, are undoubtedly important aspects of patriarchy. Yet, the most entrenched systems of exclusion operate on more subtle discursive levels, beyond what is usually seen or known.

Discursive forms of domination are powerful precisely because they do not operate at manifest levels, but penetrate spheres of life which

---

[29] See Kate McGuiness, 'Gene Sharp's Theory of Power: A Feminist Critique of Consent', *Journal of Peace Research*, 30, 1, 1993, 101–15.

are considered objective and value free. Consider the links between patriarchy and science. Nietzsche had already detected a will to power in science, an arbitrary attempt to control nature, to impose order and stability upon a chaotic world. The objective of science, then, 'is not "to know", but to schematise, – to impose upon chaos as much regularity and form as our practical needs require'.[30] Feminist theorists focus more specifically on the ways in which the Enlightenment idea of epistemological objectivism – knowledge independent of a subject – is often intrinsically linked with an androcentric world-view.[31] Donna Haraway, for example, analyses the scholarship on primatology and shows how scientific discourses interweave fact and fiction. Looking at such aspects as research design or data interpretation, she suggests that this interweaving produces clear Western and sexualised values.[32]

A comparable discursive system of exclusion is at work in the writing of history. Historical events cannot be represented in an objective and value free way. History is a narrative, a story about a particular vision of the past, one that selects, weighs and displays events. It separates what is deemed memorable from perspectives that are considered incorrect or irrelevant. 'History is a construct', Margaret Atwood's fictional characters tell us convincingly. 'Any point of entry is possible and all choices are arbitrary.'[33] But this is not to say that every story about the past is equally relevant, that there is no foundation from where one could look at events and epoques gone. What must be acknowledged, however, is that power relations interfere with the writing of history, that the narrator cannot be erased from the narration. Recognising this Nietzschean will to power makes the writing of history a political act.

Modern history, scrutinised from a gender sensitive perspective, is primarily a story of men narrated by men. Things past are presented, selected and ordered according to criteria that men considered worthwhile to be remembered. Women and their views are largely absent from this account. They are marginalised at best, obliterated at worst.

---

[30] Friedrich Nietzsche, *The Will to Power*, tr. W. Kaufmann and R.J. Hollingdale (New York: Vintage Books, 1968), § 515, p. 278.
[31] See Sandra Harding, *The Science Question in Feminism* (Ithaca: Cornell University Press, 1986).
[32] Donna J. Haraway, *Primate Visions: Gender, Race, and Nature in the World of Modern Science* (New York: Routledge, 1989) and *Simians, Cyborgs, and Women: The Reinvention of Nature* (New York: Routledge, 1991).
[33] Margaret Atwood, *The Robber Bride* (London: Virago Press, 1994), p. 4.

'Women have no history', Huguette Bouchardeau says.[34] But how does discursive power precisely come into play in this gendered representation of the past? What consequences, besides filtering our knowledge of the past, are entailed in women's obliteration from history?

A masculinist perception of history annihilates many aspects of women's agency. It imposes a patriarchal vision upon social dynamics and then objectifies this form of domination. Gayatri Spivak is one of many authors who point towards the grave consequences of historiographical systems of exclusion. Looking at colonial and post-colonial contexts, she argues that despite female participation in insurgency movements, the annihilation of women's voices from the representation of things past has led to persistent practices of subjugation.[35]

The power of discursive practices becomes most apparent when one observes development patterns over a long time-span. Gerda Lerner examines how patriarchy functioned and evolved throughout the Middle Ages and modernity. She argues convincingly that grave consequences arose from men's ability to frame history, to define what is a political issue and what is not.[36] Men had access to education. They wrote history, transmitted knowledge and built upon their insight, generation after generation. Because women were often denied access to education, they were also deprived of passing on their knowledge to subsequent generations of women. In making this claim, Lerner implicitly refutes Simone de Beauvoir's position that women's powerlessness is to be explained by the passive role that they have fulfilled historically.[37] Lerner, by contrast, argues that there was no lack of outspoken women who advanced insightful critiques of patriarchy. She draws attention to Hildegard von Bingen and Christine de Pizan who, writing in the twelfth and fifteenth century respectively, advanced powerful feminist criticisms of biblical texts.[38] But this critique was largely in vain. As a result of their marginalisation from religious and philosophical thought, critical authors like von Bingen and de Pizan could, in the long run, neither influence patriarchal

---

[34] Huguette Bouchardeau, *Pas d'histoire les femmes* (Paris: Syros, 1977).

[35] Gayatri Chakravorty Spivak, 'Can the Subaltern Speak?', in C. Nelson and L. Grossberg (eds.), *Marxism and the Interpretation of Culture* (Chicago: University of Illinois Press, 1988), p. 287.

[36] Gerda Lerner, *The Creation of Feminist Consciousness: From the Middle Ages to Eighteen-Seventy* (New York: Oxford University Press, 1993), p. 10.

[37] Simone de Beauvoir, *Le deuxième Sexe* (Paris: Gallimard, 1976/1949).

[38] Lerner, *The Creation of Feminist Consciousness*, pp. 138–166.

practices nor further the creation of a feminist consciousness. Traces of their work were largely erased by the overwhelming mass of masculine historiographers.

Women never knew what other women before them wrote. As opposed to men, they could not build upon previous knowledge, but had to invest their time, energy and talent simply to reinvent the same insight century after century. The importance of this point warrants quoting Lerner at length:

> Men created written history and benefited from the transmittal of knowledge from one generation to the other, so that each great thinker could stand 'on the shoulders of giants', thereby advancing thought over that of previous generations with maximum efficiency. Women were denied knowledge of their history, and thus each woman had to argue as though no women before her had ever thought or written. Women had to use their energy to reinvent the wheel, over and over again, generation after generation. Men argued with the giants that preceded them; women argued against the oppressive weight of millennia of patriarchal thought, which denied them authority, even humanity, and when they had to argue they argued with the 'great men' of the past, deprived of the empowerment, strength and knowledge women of the past could have offered them.[39]

Although men and women are hardly the stable sites of identity and meaning that Lerner's analysis implies, the insight she advances opens up various opportunities to scrutinise the discursive dimensions of transversal dissident practices. But before embarking in this direction, a word of caution is warranted. Because Lerner feels compelled to anchor her arguments in an essentialist standpoint, she enters a highly contentious theoretical terrain. She claims that because women have theorised from a marginalised position and derived knowledge from essential social interactions, rather than books, the knowledge that they acquired was 'more nearly correct and adequate than was the knowledge of men'.[40] Such standpoint positions rely on the problematic belief that there is authentic insight and that feminist scholarship requires a resort to essences and universals to anchor an argument. The emancipatory practices that emerge from the search for authenticity may well lead to a repositioning of some actors (they may, for example, bring more women from the outside to the inside), but they

---

[39] Ibid., p. 166.
[40] Ibid., p. 11.

entrench at the same time the underlying systems of domination that prevent a truly inclusive politics. As Braidotti puts it, 'the point is to overcome the dialectics of domination, not to turn the previous slaves into new masters. . .Just slotting women in, without changing the rules of the game, would indeed be a mere reification of existing social conditions of inequality.'[41] Lerner's historical argument must thus be taken on board with a sense of epistemological caution.

An act seemingly as simple as writing history proved to be one of the most powerful discursive weapons to defend patriarchy and prevent women from organising collectively against it. To look at how this system of domination persists despite the occurrence of radical social change on other fronts, one needs to observe how major historical events affect women and men differently. Valuable lessons for understanding transversal dissent and its role in global politics can be derived from such a scrutiny.

Various feminists who have dealt with discursively entrenched and concealed forms of domination have argued that historical periods which are usually considered liberating and progressive often had the opposite effect on women. Joan Kelly-Gadol was one of the first authors to question conventional methods of periodisation by drawing attention to women's historical experiences. Her analysis focuses on the Renaissance, which, as outlined in chapter one, is usually credited with having ushered in modernity and liberated humanity from the darkness of the Middle Ages. But despite the rhetoric of utopianism and radical egalitarianism, of which la Boétie's work is representative, this period influenced the lives of men and women in fundamentally different ways. By scrutinising changing forms of courtly love, Kelly-Gadol shows that while men were able to explore new horizons, women as a group, especially among higher urban classes, experienced a sharp reduction of social and personal options.[42]

It would, of course, be too simplistic to equate all 'progressive' historical epochs with an automatic regression for women. Things are more complex. But there is enough evidence to demonstrate that courtly love during the Italian Renaissance is by far no exception. The Enlightenment's attempt to liberate the human mind from superstition

---

[41] Braidotti, 'Feminism by Any Other Name', p. 39.
[42] Joan Kelly-Gadol, 'Did Women Have a Renaissance?', in R. Bridenthal and C. Koonz (eds.), *Becoming Visible: Women in European History* (Boston: Houghton Mifflin, 1977), pp. 137–64.

worsened in some ways the situation for women. The French Revolution, for example, may have brought more fraternity for bourgeois men, but it certainly did not entail more liberty and equality for women. The subsequent Napoleonic code of civil law only fortified the subjugation of women in the realms of marriage, sexual behaviour and education.[43] Similar dynamics occurred in 1848, when women actively participated in the uprising against the re-established monarchy just to witness afterwards how the introduction of universal male suffrage further entrenched gender-related discriminations in the spheres of political and social rights.[44]

Progress as regress? Women and transversal social change

The theoretical and historical perspectives introduced above challenge not only the progressive nature of conventionally recognised processes of social change, but also our very understanding of dissent and human agency. The analysis now engages in one more rereading of the East German revolution in an attempt to take this problematisation a step further and verify its adequacy in the context of a concrete and contemporary transversal struggle.

Was the collapse of the Berlin Wall and the ensuing, much heralded German *Wende*, this turning point from the Cold War to a new world order, really as revolutionary as proclaimed? What role did women play in the transversal dissident movement, and how has the subsequent redrawing of political boundaries affected their position in German society?

The continuously growing body of literature that scrutinises national unification from a gender sensitive perspectives is undoubtedly among the most revealing and compelling contributions to the rethinking of contemporary German politics. But as of yet there has not been a consensus on how to interpret the events of 1989 and their aftermath. Most pronounced are perhaps the differences that have emerged between feminists situated in the eastern and western parts of unified Germany. Disagreements between them epitomise the

---

[43] Marilyn J. Boxer and Jean H. Quataert, 'Restoring Women to History', in *Connecting Spheres: Women in the Western World, 1500 to the Present* (New York: Oxford University Press, 1987), p. 6; and Ruth Graham, 'Loaves and Liberty: Women in the French Revolution', in Bridenthal and Koonz, *Becoming Visible*, pp. 236–54.
[44] Lerner, *The Creation of Feminist Consciousness*, p. 278.

situatedness of the critic, although it must be noted that existing differences may be more reflective of certain mind-sets, rather than the territories with which they have become identified.

West German feminists have been particularly critical of the processes that led to German unity. The tone is, by and large, one of disillusionment. The expectation that the onset of radical social change would also improve the position of women in society has not materialised. Less than two years after the fall of the Berlin Wall, Jutta Gysi and Gunnar Winkler noted that much of the optimism and hope had evaporated.[45] In many respects the situation for women in the eastern part of Germany had worsened, rather than improved. The analysis will later draw attention to the details of this phenomenon. May it suffice, at least at this stage, to note that while many groups profited from a redrawing of Cold War boundaries, women in the East were, according to many commentators, 'the losers of German unity'.[46] This victimisation has been explained in various ways. Particularly influential are analytical approaches that focus on the alleged absence of feminist consciousness in East Germany and on the entrenchment of patriarchal values that occurred with the imposition of a relatively masculinist West German system on the East.[47]

Many women in the eastern part of Germany strongly disagree with such interpretations. They are concerned about the conceptual consequences that issue from the strong dominance of discussions by western authors. 'Western feminist research,' they warn, 'has the power to define the theoretical questions and shape the discourse about the meaning of the transformation.'[48] For instance, many eastern feminists criticise approaches that take the analysis of patriarchal structures as a methodological starting point. Such a focus, they argue, falsely portrays East German women as mere passive objects, helpless victims of patriarchal recolonialisation. It is a fallback into the old

---

[45] Jutta Gysi and Gunnar Winkler, 'Zur Situation von Frauen in den fünf neuen Bundesländern', in A. Lissner *et al., Frauenlexikon* (Freiburg: Herder, 1991), p. 1194.

[46] Ulrike Diedrich, 'Umbruch und Anpassung', in B. Bütow and H. Stecker (eds.), *Eigen-Artige Ostfrauen: Frauenemanzipation in der DDR und den neuen Bundesländern* (Bielefeld: Kleine Verlag, 1994), p.124; Bettina Musall, 'Viele dachten, die spinnen', in *Der Spiegel*, 18 March 1991, pp. 68–84.

[47] For a review of these various positions see Myra Marx Ferree, 'German Unification and Feminist Identity,' in Joan W. Scott, Cora Kaplan and Debra Keates (eds.), *Transitions, Environments, Translations: Feminisms in International Politics* (New York: Routledge, 1997), pp. 46–55.

[48] Eva Maleck-Lewy, 'The East German Women's Movement After Unification', in Scott, Kaplan and Keates, *Transitions, Environments, Translations*, p. 126.

stereotypical image of dominant men/subordinate women. Instead, feminists from the eastern part of Germany point towards the active participation of women in the protest movement of 1989. They stress that after unification many women did not automatically return to the patriarchal domain of home and hearth, but, instead, embarked on active and often innovative attempts to search for alternative employment opportunities.[49]

These and other disputes about feminist interpretations of social change are in some ways central to the task of understanding the gendered dimension of the East German revolution. They illustrate the situatedness of knowledge and thus underline the need to read the events of 1989 in their multiple dimensions. Some of these dimensions will be examined in the account that follows, but to provide a detailed analysis of them would be beyond the scope of this chapter. For now, then, the focus will primarily lie with scrutinising the persistent discursive power of patriarchy, knowing well that this is only one way of approaching the gendered dimensions of social change. The main goal, then, is to understand why, despite an active and relatively effective participation of women in the revolution of 1989, the outcome of German unification has generally been disappointing for women. Such a focus recognises women as active agents, but, at the same time, pays attention to the discursive contexts that frame the possibilities of women's agency.

Women played an unusually prominent role in the transversal protest movement of 1989. The gender-balance of the movement in its early days defies the above-described conventional division between male fighters/protectors and female victims/non-combatants. Rather than confining themselves to the private sphere, many women took on leading dissident roles. The activism of Bärbel Bohley, for instance, has earned her the unofficial title of 'mother of the revolution'. Throughout the autumn of 1989, the protest movement had a strong and consistent female component. Women constituted almost half of the official members of the most influential protest organisations, *Neues Forum*. Some interpreters think that female participation in popular dissent was motivated less by concerns related to women's issues,

---

[49] See chapters in Bütow and Stecker, *EigenArtige Ostfrauen*, especially Birgit Bütow, 'Frauenforschung in Ost und West vor der Aufgabe der Neu- und Umorientierung?', pp. 315–23; and Katrin Rohnstock, 'Frauen sind selbständig – Widerstandsstrategien gegen Arbeitslosigkeit', pp. 175–80.

than by various political reasons that were shared across the sexes.[50] But due to the substantial presence of women in protest moments and dissident organisations, feminist issues were discussed and voiced in various forums. In fact, among the various countries that went through a transition from communism to capitalism, East Germany was the only one in which explicit feminist organisations sought and to a large extent won the right to represent women's interests in shaping the process of transformation.[51] Eva Maleck-Lewy, a co-founder of the influential East German Independent Women's Association (UFV), speaks of the 'glorious heyday of the East German women's movement', of a period (between the autumn of 1989 and the summer of 1990) when highly motivated women activists had a direct impact on decision-making procedures and were appointed to important posts at various levels of government.[52] Some of the progressive practices and institutions that exist today, she says, have their origin in this euphoric period: the foundation for an independent women's moment was laid, women's centres and shelters were opened, magazines founded, identities transformed and important equal opportunity legislation passed. But feminist activism had its limits too.

From a gender perspective, the first signs of patriarchal resistance started to emerge towards the end of 1989. When, in December, the slogans at demonstrations shifted from 'we are the people' to 'we are *a* people', masculinist elements intensified together with this re-emerging form of German nationalism. Look at the Monday demonstrations in Leipzig, which had turned into a key symbol of popular resistance against the regime. Dorothy Rosenberg noted that the atmosphere at these demonstrations became increasingly male, aggressive and nationalistic. Female demonstrators gradually withdrew after women had been booed off the speakers' platform week after week.[53] Similar processes of alienation occurred during the so-called round table discussions, which emerged all over East Germany. Round tables were meant to provide an opportunity for various groups to be heard and to exert influence on the reform process. They were established

---

[50] Francesca Weil, 'Frauen unter diktatorischer Herrschaf', in Bütow and Stecker, *Eigen-Artige Ostfrauen*, p. 60.

[51] Myra Marx Ferree, ' "The Time of Chaos was the Best:" Feminist Mobilization and Demobilization in East Germany, *Gender and Society*, 8, 4, December 1994, p. 601.

[52] Maleck-Lewy, 'The East German Women's Movement After Unification', p. 123.

[53] Dorothy J. Rosenberg, 'Shock Therapy: GDR Women in Transition from a Socialist Welfare State to a Social Market Economy', *Signs*, 17, 1, 1991, p. 140.

at all levels, from the local factory to the national forum, and many of them included representatives from women's organisations. But while women were highly successful in their quest for inclusion, the struggle for voice proved to be more difficult. Kathrin Rohnstock, a member of the feminist group *Lila Offensive*, speaks with great disillusionment about her participation in the central round table in Berlin. This influential forum may have produced two key 'gender plans' for the post-revolutionary period, but Rohnstock resented the masculinist tone of the discussions: very little reflection and problematisation; authoritarian and intimidating leadership; emphasis on unemotional formulation of strategic objectives. The effect of this discussion style did not lead to a politics of inclusion, Rohnstock felt, but was suffocating and marginalising for women.[54]

The gender dimension of the protest movement had clearly changed by the spring of 1990. Women were gradually pushed from the centre to the margins of decision-making procedures. In the national election of March 1990, most seats in the parliament were won by affiliates associated with the West German Conservative Christian Democratic Union, whose campaign promise revolved around the need for rapid unification. And it is the nature of this unification process, which was formally completed on 3 October 1990, that is generally believed to be responsible for the drastic setback for women. Maleck-Lewy speaks for many feminists in pointing out that the East German women's movement lost its organisational cohesion as well as its importance once the West German political structures and parties took over.[55]

Before analysing various dimensions of this phenomenon it must be noted that the perceived need for rapid unification was never beyond contention. Prominent public figures, usually situated left of centre, were critical about the push towards unity. Many East German intellectuals and dissidents, such as Bärbel Bohley, Christa Wolf, Stefan Heym and Volker Braun, but also influential Western personalities of the likes of Jürgen Habermas, Günter Grass and Wolf Biermann, critiqued the legal and political framework and the hasty implementation of unification.[56] There was also a strong presence of explicit femin-

---

[54] Kathrin Rohnstock in Gisela Erler et al., *Familienpolitik im Umbruch?* (Munich: Deutsches Jugendinstitut, 1990), pp. 62–3.
[55] Maleck-Lewy, 'The East German Women's Movement', p. 123.
[56] See, for example, Wolf Biermann, 'Der grässliche Fatalismus der Geschichte', *Deutsche Akademie für Sprache und Dichtung*, January 1991, pp. 150–1; Günter Grass, *Ein Schnäppchen namens DDR* (Frankfurt: Luchterhand, 1990); Jürgen Habermas, 'Die

ist criticism, which drew attention to the implications that would arise from imposing a relatively masculinist West German system upon the population in the East. What could have been a chance to build a more just, democratic and gender-sensitive Germany, these critics argued, ended in a complete subordination to capricious market-oriented incentives. Indeed, unification did not result from a mutual agreement between two equal and sovereign states. Rather, it was a submission of East Germany's fate to the will (and currency) of West Germany. In this sense, the negotiations and constitutional arrangement that led to German unity are much better characterised by the term *Anschluß* (annexation) than *Wiedervereinigung* (reunification). Unified Germany is exclusively built upon the West German political and constitutional structure, including its name, currency, federal system legal norms, diplomatic corps and military personnel.

One could argue with the interpretation of these and other 'normative deficits of unification', as Jürgen Habermas calls them.[57] Less contentious is the fact that the rapid amalgamation of two states made out of entirely different political, ideological, economic, legal, administrative and school systems (not to speak of behaviour patterns, language, values and expectations) proved to be far more difficult than anticipated by the political leadership. The effects on social stability were devastating. Among the indicators of rising tension in the eastern part of Germany were dramatic increases in the number and intensity of frauds, real estate and currency speculation, bank robberies, neo-fascist youth gangs, racist violence, drug consumption, suicides and road accidents. Some of these problems would have been difficult to avoid given the acute pressure and the complex situation that existed at the time of the collapse of the East German regime. Some commentators thus point out that the East German dissident intellectuals who searched for a third way, a middle ground between communism and capitalism, above all spoke for themselves and were out of touch with what the population desired at the time.[58]

To acknowledge that various pressures existed at the time of East Germany's disintegration is, however, not the same as arguing that

andere Zerstörung der Vernunft', in *Die Zeit*, 17.5.1991 and *Die nachholende Revolution* (Frankfurt: Suhrkamp, 1991).

[57] Jürgen Habermas, 'Die Normativen Defizite der Vereinigung', in *Vergangenheit als Zukunft* (Zürich: Pendo Verlag, 1990), pp. 45–73.

[58] John C. Torpey, *Intellectuals, Socialism and Dissent: The East German Opposition and Its Legacy* (Minneapolis: University of Minnesota Press, 1995), p. x.

the outcome of unification was inevitable or that the particular approach taken was the only one available. Yes, the situation was dramatic and action had to be taken. The East German industry had all but collapsed, and so had much of the social and political cohesion. But even if the challenges were gargantuan, the fact remains that the political leadership took particular decisions about the timing and form of unification. The amalgamation of East and West Germany was cast almost exclusively as a monetary and economic issue, rather than a more widely conceived social and political challenge. Unification was presented as a matter of necessity, rather than choice. And it was negotiated and implemented by experts, rather than through democratic participation.

The choices that were made in the approach to unification were masculinist, if not in intent or nature, then at least in their effect on the constitution of post-Wall German politics. The hasty and economically driven implementation of unification led to a political situation in which various issues related to women were clearly overshadowed by other, seemingly more urgent tasks that needed to be faced. By late 1990 the power had passed, so to speak, from the 'mother of the revolution' (Bärbel Bohley) to the 'fathers of unification' (Helmut Kohl and his East German alliance partner, Lothar de Mazière).

The problematic gendered entry into post-Cold War politics has been analysed in a variety of ways. Perhaps the most influential explanation revolves around the observation that unification occurred through the imposition of the West German political and institutional structure – largely perceived as masculinist in character – upon the East German territory. As a result of this annexation process, the East German citizens who took to the street in the autumn of 1989 were deprived of the opportunity to shape their own political and institutional future. There is a puzzling trans-sexual dimension to this amalgamation process, for it blurs traditional images of masculinity and femininity. It has become common in Germany to represent the East–West dynamics in a gendered way. The dominant West German political system, including its female population, is thus portrayed as explicitly masculine, whereas the annexed territory of East Germany is associated with subordinate feminine positions. This imagery captures the fact that not only East German women, but men also were the losers of unity. They too had to submit themselves to the newly imposed Western order. They too were feminised through the masculinist discourse of unification. Although one can, of course, argue with this or that aspect of such transgressive gender readings, they nevertheless underline what has been argued above: that images of masculinity and femininity do not necessarily correspond to traits that are inherent in male and female bodies. Gendered values are not part of an authentic natural order. Rather, they result from discursive constructions that reproduce patriarchal systems of exclusion. The ensuing socio-political practices assign men and women certain values and tasks – characteristics that are superimposed on, but do not always perfectly correspond with people's bodily attributes.

But not all gendered aspects of unification were transgressive. While the social and political consequences of the rapid transition from central planning to a market-oriented economy affected the entire population in the eastern part of Germany, women suffered disproportionately. A case in point is the unemployment rate, which soared after unification. In March of 1991, 55 per cent of all unemployed were women. The following year this figure was as high as 68 per cent, in some areas even 77 per cent. Some women were unusually hard hit. Unemployment among women over fifty five, for example, was three times higher than for men of the same age.[59] Others particularly affected were single mothers and academics. In 1995, 48 per cent of all young mothers were unemployed, compared with 12 per cent in 1991.[60] Women were also the main losers of the process that restructured East German academia. They were not only the first ones to lose their positions, but also the last ones to be taken into account for re-employment. Consider the Humboldt University in Berlin. Of 54 newly advertised professorships, only four were given to women. Before unification, a total of fifteen women occupied tenured positions of this rank.[61] Similar trends became visible in politics too. The number of female representatives in the parliament, for example, decreased from 32.2 per cent under the East German regime to 20.5 per cent in

---

[59] Monika Jaeckel, 'Frauen im Vereinten Deutschland', in R. Süssmut and H. Schubert (eds.), *Bezahlen die Frauen die Wiedervereinigung?* (Munich: Piper, 1992), pp. 22–3; Gisela Helwig, 'Einleitung', to G. Helwig and H.M. Nickel (eds.), *Frauen in Deutschland* (Berlin: Akademie Verlag, 1993), p. 9.

[60] Rick Atkinson, 'Unity Costs Eastern German Women Dear', *Guardian Weekly*, 16 April 1995, p. 19.

[61] Brigitte Young, 'Deutsche Vereinigung: Der Abwicklungsskandal an den ostdeutschen Universitäten und seine Folgen für Frauen', *Feministische Studien*, 2, 1, May 1993, 8, 11.

unified Germany.[62] Figures are even more dramatic in the domain of middle management jobs, where women lost virtually all influence they had before unification.[63]

The increasing exclusion of women from the workplace and from political leadership is neither an exception nor a coincidental by-product of unification. These examples are part of a larger trend that signifies a structural and discursive entrenchment of patriarchy. The voice and exit protests of 1989 may have helped to uproot the East German system of domination, but the people who participated in it were deprived of what the literature on social movements refers to as an independent consolidation phase. Instead of having the opportunity to shape the newly emerging post-revolutionary order, the population in the East was simply absorbed into the already existing West German legal and political structure.

Whether or not an alternative approach to the collapse of communism might have led to a more gender-sensitive new order will always remain speculation. What we do know, however, is that the imposition of the West German political and legal framework had certain effects that were masculinist in character. The new legal order that arrived with the formal unification of Germany abolished a variety of benefits that women had enjoyed under the old East German system. Women were closely integrated into the work force. Just before the revolution of 1989, as many as 91 per cent of working-age women were either in training or pursued an occupation outside the home. This is an unusually high number, especially when compared to the figure of 54 per cent in West Germany.[64] The right to work for women was guaranteed by the East German constitution and the government actively aimed at providing the structural conditions necessary for the exercise of this right. A whole range of institutional arrangements, including extended pregnancy leave and state-subsidised day care centres in virtually every city, provided women with the chance to pursue activities beyond the traditional duties of mothers and house-wives. Wide-ranging reproductive rights existed. A woman had the exclusive authority to decide (and the possibility to implement) the

---

[62] Peggy Watson, 'Osteuropa: Die lautlose Revolution der Geschlechterverhältnisse', in *Das Argument*, No. 202, Vol. 35, No. 6, November/December 1993, pp. 859, 862.
[63] Friederike Maier, 'Frauenerwerbstätigkeit in der DDR and BRD', in Gundrun-Axeli Knapp and Ursula Muller (eds.), *Ein Deutschland – Zwei Patriarchate* (Bielefeld: University of Bielefeld, 1992), pp. 23–35.
[64] Jaeckel, 'Frauen im Vereinten Deutschland', p. 15.

determination of a pregnancy during the first twelve weeks.[65] Many of these and other rights granted to women disappeared with the absorption of East Germany into the constitutional structure of West Germany. Reproductive rights were sharply reduced. The new legal arrangements in unified Germany stopped short of an outright ban on abortion only because of the stern resistance by the oppositional Social Democrats.[66] A large number of day care centres were dismantled and the remaining ones often became too expensive for average women to afford.[67]

To draw attention to the sharp deterioration of the position of women after unification is not to glorify the old East German order. It was not only authoritarian, but also politically and economically bankrupt, perhaps beyond any hope for repair. Even the most vehement feminist critics of unification accept that the East Germany society was strongly influenced by traditional patriarchal values. Despite the officially promulgated principle of equality between the sexes, conventional gender stereotypes and discriminatory practices towards women remained deeply rooted. A gendered division of labour prevailed and leadership styles in all domains were strongly masculinist in character. The higher one moved up the echelons of the East German hierarchy, the lower was the presence of women. Only very few of them occupied influential societal positions.[68]

The redrawing of Cold War geopolitical boundaries, the merger of two gendered systems of exclusion, the East and West German, mutually reinforced existing biases and led to what some feminists believe is a qualitative change in the patriarchal system of domination.[69] Central to this shift is the re-emergence of a market-oriented economy and a strong civil society that is clearly set apart from the private realm. This division, Peggy Watson stresses, is heavily gendered for it is reinforced by a revival of neo-conservative values that place increasing emphasis on the family and the household as the backbone of society. The resulting distribution of rights and duties in the social order is

---

[65] For further details see, for example, Gysi and Winkler, 'Zur Situation der Frauen', pp. 1194–232 and Sabine Berghan, 'Frauenrechte im Vereinigungsprozess', in C. Faber and T. Meyer (eds.), *Unterm neuen Kleid der Freiheit das Korsett der Einheit* (Berlin: Rainer Bohn Verlag, 1992), pp. 64–95.

[66] Rosenberg, 'Shock Therapy', pp. 135–6.

[67] Jaeckel, 'Frauen im Vereinten Deutschland', p. 23.

[68] See Birgit Sauer, 'Weder die Schönen noch die Hässlichen', in Faber and Meyer, *Unterm neuen Kleid der Freiheit*, pp. 110–30;

[69] Watson, 'Osteuropa', p. 860; Young, 'Deutsche Vereinigung', p. 14.

highly consequential: men occupy the powerful central roles in the public sphere while women are relegated back to the private sphere, the family.[70] Various subtle and not so subtle means, such as fiscal and educational policies or the dismantling of day care facilities, ensure the success of this neo-conservative political order.

The separation between private and public spheres and the relegation of women to the latter is, of course, a deeply entrenched patriarchal tradition that has been analysed in detail by many feminist critics. Carol Pateman's above-mentioned work recognises in this separation the transition from traditional paternal forms of patriarchy to a new, specifically modern and fraternal version of the same gendered system of exclusion.[71] If observed from a long-range perspective, the transition in German politics can thus be interpreted, despite a variety of contradictory signs, as one more step in the continuation of a long and consistent discursive practice of domination.

Summary

Discursively entrenched power relations cannot simply be toppled by mass demonstrations or other transversal practices of dissent. A transgression of political boundaries does not necessarily uproot deeply entrenched forms of discursive domination. The present chapter has focused on patriarchy to illustrate this point and to underline the ensuing need to rethink what domination and resistance mean in the context of transversal political struggles.

If a form of resistance, and the image of human agency that it projects, is too deeply embedded in the existing discursive order, it is likely to entrench corresponding systems of exclusion. The la Boétiean theory and practice of popular dissent exemplifies this point. Many of its protagonists have contributed to a strengthening of a revolutionary model that is based on the image of a male hero riding towards freedom while ignoring and even entrenching the patriarchal social order which makes this fight possible.

A rereading of the events that led to the collapse of the Berlin Wall questions some of these stereotypical gendered images of dissent, but confirms the overall power of patriarchal discursive practices. Spec-

---

[70] Watson, 'Osteuropa', pp. 859–74,
[71] Carole Pateman, 'The Fraternal Social Contract', in John Keane (ed.), *Civil Society and the State* (London: Verso, 1988), pp. 102–4.

tacular popular protests against the authoritarian regime, coupled with other factors, triggered processes of fundamental social change. Dissent not only transgressed, but also challenged the spatial and political boundaries of Cold War politics. Yet, a closer look reveals that practices of domination did not crumble equally on all fronts. While the Cold War geopolitical order disintegrated and authoritarian communism gave way to more accountable forms of governance, patriarchal systems of exclusion have persisted, and this despite an unusually widespread and active female participation in the protest movement of 1989. A unification process that consisted of integrating the East German territory into existing West German political structures deprived the people who engaged in mass protest of the opportunity to shape their own political future. Although East German men too had to submit themselves to the newly imposed institutional order, women suffered disproportionately. In many areas, such as employment, political representation and reproductive rights, women in the eastern part of Germany were worse off after than before the collapse of the Berlin Wall. Whether or not other emerging benefits for women will outweigh these setbacks in the long run remains to be seen. At this point a gender-oriented reading of the East German revolution reveals, above all, the striking power of patriarchal discursive practices to mask and protect their corresponding systems of domination.

On a theoretical level, this chapter has underlined the need to approach questions of dissent and human agency not only from a transversal, but also from a discursive perspective. The deeply entrenched nature of discursive power and the resulting normalisation of practices of exclusion draw clear limits to what can be achieved through conventional forms of dissent, even if they transgress the spatial givenness of existing sovereign political territories. The power of discourse forces our minds into submission even when we think we are resisting all forms of external encroachments.

And yet, the recognition that power and discourse are intrinsically linked still leaves us far short of reaching a non-essentialist understanding of human agency in global politics. A discursive approach may well be able to reveal forms of domination, but can it also locate resistance, can it actively account for the occurrence of social change? Is it possible to propose a discursive understanding of power without obliterating the subject or having to abandon the notion of human agency altogether? If power penetrates all aspects of society and is to be seen primarily in a discursive light, can one still carve out terrains of dissent? The next chapter responds to these puzzling questions in the affirmative by demonstrating that a discursive understanding of power can not only explain the persistence of domination, but also account for historical discontinuities.

6   Of great events and what makes them great

> Believe me, friend Hellishnoise: the greatest events – they are not
> our loudest but our stillest hours. Not around the inventors of new
> noise, but around the inventors of new values does the world
> revolve; it revolves *inaudibly*.
>
> Admit it! Whenever your noise and smoke were gone, very little
> had happened. What does it matter if a town became a mummy and
> a statue lies in the mud? And this word I shall add for those who
> overthrow statues: nothing is more foolish than casting salt into the
> sea and statues into the mud.[1]

More than a century after Nietzsche put these words into Zarathustra's mouth, during the summer of 1883 in Sils Maria, overthrowers not far from this Swiss mountain village still believe they have
changed the world by hurling statues into the mud. Of course, the
East German revolution of 1989 was spectacular. It was a key event in
global politics. One of the most authoritarian regimes of East-Central
Europe crumbled as people took to the streets. The scenes of common
citizens climbing over and dismantling the Berlin Wall could not have
been a more sensational, more symbolic termination to the Cold War.
They provided perfect snap-shot pictures that satisfied the short attention span of worldwide television audiences. The corresponding
sound bite, 'we are the people', still resonates throughout the world.
But were these spectacular acts the decisive factors that caused social
change? Was the overthrowing of communist statues really the key to
it all?

The present chapter reads the East German revolution from a

---

[1] Friedrich Nietzsche, *Thus Spoke Zarathustra*, tr. W. Kaufmann in *The Portable Nietzsche*
(New York: Penguin Books, 1982/1954), p. 243.

perspective that focuses not on the demolition of morbid political foundations, but on the slow and transversal transformation of values that preceded it. A shift away from great events entails scrutinising less spectacular daily influences that shape people's lives. It reveals multiple linkages between the local and the global. Theorising these largely inaudible forces from a discursive perspective is a way of actively accounting for the occurrence of social change.

The main theoretical task of this endeavour is to facilitate a discursive understanding of power that not only explains, as the previous chapter did, the continuity of domination, but also accounts for practices of dissent and their influence on processes of societal transformation. Such is, of course, an unduly ambitious task. For now the analysis merely locates the broad grounds where such transformations take place. In doing so, the present chapter builds a stepping stone for the third and last part of this book, which articulates a non-essentialist notion of human agency by exploring discourse-oriented terrains of transversal dissent.

Antonio Gramsci's concept of hegemony is well suited to scrutinise the slow transformation of values that contributed to the collapse of the Berlin Wall. A focus on the discursive struggle for hegemony explains how processes of social change are unleashed when a world-view hostile to the prevalent social order has come to be accepted as legitimate and moral by most of the population. A re-reading of East German politics reveals how such dynamics took place in a transversal context, constantly interweaving domestic social dynamics with discursive forces that operate at global levels. Reading Gramsci in addition to Foucault can overcome the difficulties of locating power. It can counter pessimistic readings of Foucault that interpret his work as an annihilation of human agency. But a fusion of Gramsci and Foucault is not without its problems. The former pays attention to broad hegemonic practices, while the latter focuses on difference and multiplicities.

The key to understanding the complexities of transversal struggles lies precisely in working through such paradoxes, in relying on various forms of insight, even if they are at times incommensurable. With this sense of fragmentation in mind, the present chapter demonstrates how a discursive approach may facilitate a broad understanding of processes of social change that transgress the spatial givenness of global politics. Later chapters then embark on a more finely attuned analysis that theorises possibilities for transversal dissent that arise from the thin and fragmented nature of discursive dynamics.

Transforming values and nurturing dissent in the public sphere

An illustration of transversal struggles through a merger of Foucault's ideas with those of Gramsci requires a few preliminary remarks: Gramsci's approach implies that a movement of dissent can only be victorious and establish a new and stable order if the classes or social groups that conduct the revolutionary struggle enjoy widespread popular support and dominate the institutions of civil society before attempting to seize state power. Without having first won this so-called 'war of position' and achieved hegemonic leadership throughout civil society, a dissident movement is likely to be crushed by the repressive state apparatus. In other words, a movement has a chance of exerting agency only when its ideological alternative to the established order has infiltrated most societal levels and is considered moral and legitimate by a substantial part of the population.[2]

Much of Gramsci's work revolves around the concept of hegemony, the prevalence of a dominant world-view which extends throughout all aspects of a society and encompasses such issues as ideology, morality, culture, language and power. The dissemination of this world-view occurs through subtle and hidden mechanisms which conceal and support the dominance of one social group over others. In this sense, hegemony is a cultural practice before it becomes political.

A focus on the formation of hegemonies can facilitate understanding of the dynamics behind historical discontinuities. Hegemony bears a number of similarities with what Foucault calls a system of exclusion, a subconsciously and discursively diffused set of fundamental assumptions which determines, at a particular time and place, what is right and wrong, moral and immoral, good and evil, true and untrue.[3] Indeed, Gramsci's focus on hegemony and social struggle can supplement Foucault's discursive understanding of power in a way that would provide evidence against a pessimistic reading of this

---

[2] The majority of Gramsci's ideas are contained in notebooks and letters that he wrote between his confinement (1928) and death (1937) in prisons of Fascist Italy. See Antonio Gramsci, *Prison Notebooks*, tr. Q. Hoare and G.N. Smith (New York: International Publishers, 1985/1971). For discussions of his work see Robert Bocock, *Hegemony* (Sussex: Ellis Horwood, 1986); Joseph V. Femia, *Gramsci's Political Thought* (Oxford: Clarendon Press, 1981) and Anne Showstack Sassoon, *Gramsci's Politics* (London: Hutchinson, 1980).

[3] Among the few authors who expanded on the promising links between Gramsci and Foucault is Renate Holub's *Antonio Gramsci: Beyond Marxism and Postmodernism* (London: Routledge, 1992).

approach. Power and discourse would not, as some fear, be every-where and thus nowhere.[4] By theorising the formation of hegemonies and their conditioning of social struggle, a Gramscian addition to Fou-cault's unmasking of power can provide further hints about how rela-tions of domination may be uprooted. This entails, however, a shift of foci from domineering aspects of discursive practices to the subaltern, from whose perspective the concept of hegemony facilitates under-standing of the conditions under which revolutionary societal seg-ments can successfully promote social change.

While Gramsci permits a positive reading of Foucault, Foucault can add important dimensions to Gramsci's understanding of social dynamics, in particular to his attempt at embedding the concept of hegemony in the interaction between civil society and the state. The previous chapter has demonstrated how a rigid separation of private and public sphere may entrench a gendered division of labour. A Fou-cauldian emphasis on discursive practices does not separate the family from civil society, or the local from the global, but, instead, stresses that power relations penetrate virtually all aspects of life. Such a dis-cursive approach recognises an important feminist concern, namely the need for analytical tools that do not objectify the masculinist bor-ders that have been drawn by existing political practices.[5]

Gramsci's distinction between the state and civil society overlaps with Foucault's stratified and transversal notion of discourse. Due, in part, to censorship rules during his imprisonment, Gramsci used a range of different terminologies to theorise this distinction.[6] At its most elementary level, he portrays the state simply as the sphere of coercion that contains such elements as the police, the army, the secret service and the bureaucracy. These are the means of domination and repression at the disposal of the ruling group. Civil society is the sphere where contrasting opinions compete for hegemonic status; in short, the aspects of a society that escape the direct control of the

---

[4] Nancy Hartsock, 'Foucault on Power: A Theory for Women?', in Linda J. Nicholson (ed.), *Feminism/Postmodernism* (New York: Routledge, 1990), pp. 168–70.

[5] See Elisabeth List, *Die Präsenz des Anderen: Theorie und Geschlechterpolitik* (Frankfurt: Suhrkamp, 1993), p. 159.

[6] For detailed discussions see Perry Anderson, 'The Antinomies of Antonio Gramsci', *New Left Review*, 100, 1976–7, 5–78; Bocock, *Hegemony*, pp. 28–37; and Noberto Bobbio, 'Gramsci and the Concept of Civil Society', in J. Keane (ed.), *Civil Society and the State: New European Perspectives* (London: Verso, 1988), pp. 82–92.

state's coercive elements. Gramsci's own words clarify the functions of this distinction:

> What we can do, for the moment, is to fix two major superstructural 'levels': the one that can be called 'civil society', that is the ensemble of organisms commonly called 'private', and that of 'political society' or 'the State'. These two levels correspond on the one hand to the function of 'hegemony' which the dominant group exercises throughout society and on the other hand to that of 'direct domination' or command exercised through the State and the 'juridical' government.[7]

Although the sphere of coercion, embodied in the state, plays an important role in influencing the pace of social change, it is primarily within civil society that hegemony emerges out of conflicting and competing ideas. Thus, when examining the stability of a particular social order, a Gramscian analysis not only focuses on a ruling group's means of domination and coercion, but also on the degree of popular support that the regime acquires through its domination of the non-coercive sphere.

The boundaries between the state and civil society are always in flux. Depending upon the level of direct government control, such institutions as trade unions, the media, religious organisations, schools and universities may either belong to the regime's propaganda and repression apparatus or be part of the pluralistic struggle for hegemony within civil society. The ways in which the boundaries between the state and civil society are drawn are of crucial importance in understanding processes of social change. Before a resistance movement against an authoritarian regime can merge and organise its activities, at least some aspects of civil society must be defended successfully against the encroachment by the state apparatus.

The struggle to carve out a public sphere within an otherwise state-dominated and suffocating authoritarian system is one of the features that explain the underlying dynamics behind the fall of the Berlin Wall in 1989. The East German regime tried everything possible to annihilate civil society. East German leaders, from Ulbricht to Honecker, knew that a certain breathing space from the state is necessary for the emergence of regime-critical opinions and their organised expression in the form of massive popular dissent. Günter

---

[7] Gramsci, *Prison Notebooks*, p. 12.

Schabowski, the former spokesperson of the government, admits that 'repression alone cannot hold together a State. Even Honecker strove to be popular'.[8]

Schabowski's insight reveals why the East German regime not only employed methods of direct control, coercion and intimidation to ensure its survival, but also attempted to erase the public sphere. School curricula and virtually all domestic sources of information (newspapers, journals, radio, television) were under direct and harsh control of the state apparatus. The bourgeois public sphere was officially declared obsolete, and its role was taken over by what Peter Uwe Hohendahl appropriately called a *Parteiöffentlichkeit*, a public sphere of the Party. Form and content of the discussions in this public space were carefully circumscribed by the Communist Party, whose role was to serve as a mediating (read controlling) agent between the state and the mass of citizens.[9]

Despite sustained efforts, the East German regime was unable to annihilate civil society. The regime's efforts were undermined in part by the carving out of a civil society in an otherwise authoritarian system. German social scientists refer to this sphere as an *Ersatzöffentlichkeit*, a replacement for the suppressed public sphere. Various spaces enabled opportunities for dissent to emerge, spread and prepare for the battle against the oppressive state. The Protestant Church, being the only East German mass organisation that was not directly subordinated to the state, provided such a forum for organised dissident activities. Its newspapers were not as harshly censored as the 'normal' media, its photocopying machines were at the disposal of regime-critical writers, and its ministers and representatives were always among the most outspoken critics of the system. When the state attempted to undermine this limited autonomy, the church was usually determined to defend itself. Not surprisingly, most grassroots protest movements initially emerged out of church circles.

One of the church's most influential activities consisted in providing platforms for regular critical discussions and for the expression of popular dissent. For instance, ever since 1983, each Monday evening at five a clock, young Christians met for a peace prayer in Leipzig's

---

[8] Günter Schabowski, *Das Politbüro: Ende eines Mythos* (Reinbeck: Rowohlt, 1990), p. 173. 'Nur mit Repressivität ist der Staat nicht zu machen. Selbst Honecker war bestrebt, populär zu sein.'

[9] Peter Uwe Hohendahl, 'Recasting the Public Sphere', *October 73*, Summer 1995, p. 45.

Nikolaikirche. Initially, this gathering was intended to draw attention to the absurdity of the nuclear arms race. Then it turned into a forum where frustrations about restricted mobility rights were articulated. Chapter 4 has already noted how, in the spring of 1989, the Monday prayers were regularly followed by public protests against the regime. The number of participating citizens continuously grew and by the autumn of that year the Monday demonstrations in Leipzig became a highly symbolic, influential and quasi-institutionalised event of mass dissent.[10]

The fact that this crucial breathing space from encroachment by the state was provided by the Protestant Church has nothing to do with its religious or political aspirations, but is primarily the result of the unusual degree of autonomy that it enjoyed in an otherwise suffocating totalitarian state. The church – and a few other, less prominent forums – facilitated the carving out of a quasi-civil society, an *Ersatzöffentlichkeit*. Within this arduously defended public space, contrasting opinions competed without being directly confined to the dogmatism of the prevalent state ideology.

But the creation of a public sphere, or an ersatz for it, does not by itself prepare the ground for successful outburst of popular dissent. To understand the forces behind social change, we must also examine the struggle for hegemony within civil society, and the manner in which this struggle is linked to transversal dynamics. We must observe whether or not a government or, alternatively, an opposition movement, is able to gain popular support for the particular political and social vision it espouses.

Discursive transgressions, hegemonies, counter-hegemonies

The East German regime enjoyed various degrees of popular support during its existence. But its ability to exert hegemonic leadership decreased year after year. Besides being delegitimised by repressive political practices and disastrous economic policies, a number of more

---

[10] For discussions on the role of the Protestant church see, for example, Detlef Pollack (ed.), *Die Legitimität der Freiheit: Politisch alternative Gruppen in der DDR unter dem Dach der Kirche* (Frankfurt: Peter Lang, 1990); Jörg Swoboda, *Die Revolution der Kerzen: Christen in der Umwältzung der DDR* (Wuppertal/Kassel: Onkenverlag, 1990), and Martin Zagatta, 'Kirche als Ersatzöffentlichkeit', in H. Wehling (ed.), *Politische Kultur in der DDR* (Stuttgart: W. Kohlhammer, 1989).

subtle factors undermined the ruling group's attempt to impose its ideology through domination and indoctrination. A series of transversal discursive factors engendered a gradual emergence of a regime-hostile world-view, which, in turn, created the precondition for the successful revolution of 1989.

Among the most noteworthy influences on the transformation of values in East Germany was the regime's inability to uphold the territorial logic of Cold War politics. East Germany's porous borders to the West assured the constant mental presence of an ideology, an economic system and a way of living that was fundamentally opposed to the official ideological discourse employed by the ruling group to justify its dominance. Ever since *Ostpolitik* replaced the West German Hallstein doctrine, mail exchange between East Germany and the outside world was permitted and 'capitalist' newspapers and magazines were relatively easily available. With the establishment of the *Grundlagenvertrag*, the basic treaty between the two German states signed in 1972, cross-border visits became a normal feature.[11]

Discursive transgressions came to play an inaudible but, in the long run, an increasingly influential political role. A particularly consequential transversal influence on the struggle for hegemony in East Germany must be ascribed to the constant presence of outside audio and media sources. Western radio broadcasts had always been available throughout East Germany and since the 1970s about 90 per cent of the population was able to regularly tune in to West German television.[12]

The presence of outside media sources intrinsically linked local political dynamics with the flow of global politics. Egon Krenz, Honecker's successor, confirmed in retrospect that the availability of Western media sources had a strong influence on daily life in East Germany.[13] The image that these media programs projected rendered the population alert to the enormous economic gap that separated them from their Western European neighbours. Given the long-term deprivation of consumer items, the incentives that an awareness of the West German materialistic society provided for East German cit-

---

[11] For details see Eckehard Jesse, 'Die innerdeutschen Beziehungen under der christlich-liberalen Regierung', in E. Jesse (ed.), *Bundesrepublik Deutschland und Deutsche Demokratische Republik* (Berlin: Colloquium Verlag, 1985), esp. pp. 435–6.

[12] Gunter Holzweissig, *Massenmedien in der DDR* (Berlin: Verlag Gebrüder Holzapfel, 1989), pp. 69–71.

[13] Egon Krenz, *Wenn Mauern Fallen* (Wien: Paul Neff Verlag, 1990), p. 90.

izens could only lead to a strong and widespread dissatisfaction with the present regime. The widely available Western media sources not only deprived East Germany's harsh domestic censorship practices of all their purpose, but also imbued them with a counter-productive effect. Since Western television devoted regular attention to exposing the underside of communist life in East Germany (corruption, bureaucratic despotism, pollution, etc.), the official East German propaganda appeared even farther removed from 'reality' and thus increased the population's distrust of the ruling group. One cannot better express this phenomenon than in the words of Karl Eduard von Schnitzler, the protagonist commentator of East Germany's legendary 'counter-propaganda' television series *Der Schwarze Kanal*: 'One who thinks that it would not be of any harm to listen to antidemocratic television and radio programs or to read Western newspapers, opens his ear to the deadly enemy.'[14]

Discursive transgressions had political effects far beyond the infiltration of explicitly political messages. The penetration of seemingly apolitical ideas and practices influenced the struggle for hegemony at least as much. Among these rapidly spreading features of West European culture, all of them officially denounced by the government as expressions of capitalist decadence and ideological weapons of the bourgeoisie, were phenomena such as rock, beat and punk music, Franz Kafka and Marcel Proust novels, or, even 'worse', literary traditions of an existentialist, avantgardist or poststructuralist nature.[15] These cultural expressions, which will receive more detailed attention in chapter 9, questioned some of the most fundamental tenets of the modern East German political discourse, especially the (Marxist) historicist belief in linear evolution and confidence in liberation through rational, scientific and bureaucratic planning.

The constant presence of transversal discursive factors significantly shaped social dynamics in East Germany. As a result of the infiltration

---

[14] Karl Eduard von Schnitzler, quoted in Holzweissig, *Massenmedien in der DDR*, p. 62. 'Wer der Meinung ist, daß es nicht schaden könne, antidemokratische Fernseh- und Rundfunksender zu hören oder Westzeitungen zu lesen, öffnet sein Ohr dem Todfeind.'

[15] See Susanne Binas and Peter Zocher, 'Eigentlich habe ich Hunger, eigentlich hab ich's satt...', in R. Blanke and R. Erd (eds.), *DDR – Ein Staat vergeht* (Frankfurt: Fischer Tagebuch, 1990), pp. 52–60; and Günter Erbe, 'Moderne, Avantgarde und Postmoderne: Zur neueren Rezeption in der Literaturwissenschaft der DDR', in M. Gerber (ed.), *Studies in GDR Culture and Society*, vol VI (Lanham, M.D.: University Press of America, 1986), pp. 157–72.

and dissemination of 'subversive' values and the regime's inability to counter them, a discourse which was antithetical to the prevalent communist ideology became hegemonic, i.e., was accepted as legitimate and moral by most people. This new hegemony clearly pointed towards the desire and need for some form of social change, and in this sense it was a crucial precondition for the successful revolution against the regime. The spectacular force of popular dissent unfolded during what could be called a window of opportunity. During a few months in late 1989, a great variety of domestic and external circumstances came together and permitted mass protest movements to tear down the old despotic structures. Yet, what facilitated processes of social change was not primarily the spectacular revolutionary act of 1989, but the slow and transversal discursive struggle for hegemony that preceded it. Various German scholars have already emphasised this point. Cristiane Lemke, for example, believes that the crumbling of the Berlin Wall resulted from the continuously increasing gap between the official political culture (the one determined by the state) and the dominant political culture (the one prevailing in the heads of people).[16] Sigrid Meuschel advances similar propositions when examining changing levels of legitimacy that the communist regime enjoyed.[17]

Discursive transgressions were, of course, not the only factors responsible for the spectacular collapse of the Berlin Wall. No monocausal explanation can ever do justice to such a complex set of events. The Soviet alliance system, for instance, needed to become morbid enough for domestic forces of dissent to express themselves independently of externally imposed Cold War geopolitical restraints. Neither does an emphasis on the infiltration of 'subversive' ideas into East Germany suggest that processes of social change were merely influenced by changes in the external environment. Such a position would amount to the very structural and discursive determinism that annihilates the possibility of retaining a notion of human agency.

Many East Germans did, at various levels and in various forms, actively influence the transformation of societal values. Some commentators seek to reveal how everyday forms of resistance at the

---

[16] Christiane Lemke, *Die Ursachen des Umbruchs 1989: Politische Sozialisation in der ehemaligen DDR* (Opladen: Westdeutscher Verlag, 1991).

[17] Sigrid Meuschel, 'Wandel durch Auflehnung: Thesen zum Verfall bürokratischer Herrschaft in der DDR', in R. Deppe, H. Dubiel and U. Rödel (eds.), *Demokratischer Umbruch in Osteuropa* (Frankfurt: Suhrkamp, 1991), pp. 26–47

workplace gradually undermined the stability of the German system of domination.[18] Others, such as David Bathrick, focus more on how activities of the literary intelligentsia contributed to the peaceful occurrence of social change in East Germany.[19] He demonstrates how several generations of writers and public intellectuals, from the early reform oriented novelists and playwrights to the Prenzlauer Berg poets of the 1980s, broke taboos, challenged the official legitimisation discourse and were able to carve out dialogical spaces within a suffocating public realm. It is up to the remaining parts of this book to theorise such discursive terrains of dissent and the transversal dimensions that are entailed in them.

Summary

While the previous chapter explained why great revolutionary events do not always uproot discursive systems of domination, the present chapter suggested that transversal discursive dynamics are among the driving forces behind great events. Both of these arguments entail that commonly perceived instances of popular dissent, such as heroic uprisings and mass demonstrations, are much less influential in triggering social change than their spectacular appearance suggests. The events that deserve our analytical attention are not the moments when overthrowers hurl statues into the mud. Key historical events are more elusive, more inaudible in their appearance. They evolve around the slow transformation of societal values. Foucault:

> An event, consequently, is not a decision, a treaty, a reign, or a battle, but the reversal of a relationship of forces, the usurpation of power, the appropriation of a vocabulary turned against those who once used it, a feeble domination that poisons itself as it grows lax, the entry of a masked 'other'.[20]

In an attempt to comprehend processes through which this 'masked other' precipitates social change, this chapter has supplemented Foucault's approach to power with Gramsci's concept of hegemony.

---

[18] Jeffrey Kopstein, 'Chipping Away at the State: Workers' Resistance and the Demise of East Germany', *World Politics*, 48, April 1996, pp. 391–423.
[19] David Bathrick, *The Powers of Speech: The Politics of Culture in the GDR* (Lincoln: University of Nebraska Press, 1995), p. 2.
[20] Michel Foucault, 'Nietzsche, Genealogy, History', in P. Rainbow (ed.), *The Foucault Reader*, tr. D.F. Bouchard and S. Simon, (New York, Pantheon Books, 1984/1971), p. 88.

A discursive rereading of the East German case has served to illustrate the practical usefulness of this theoretical fusion. From such a perspective, the collapse of the Berlin Wall can be read as resulting from the slow and transversal transformation of values that preceded the more overt and spectacular acts of rebellion. Expressed in Gramscian terms, the resistance movement could only exert agency and establish a new and stable order once the classes or social groups that conducted the revolutionary struggle enjoyed widespread popular support. Without having first won this so-called 'war of position', and having achieved hegemonic leadership within civil society, dissident voices will most likely be silenced by the repressive state apparatus.

While appreciating the discursive dimension of social change, it is important not to separate civil society from spheres that lie beyond it. It is precisely in the fusion of the local and the global, in the spaces that lie between the domestic and the international that some of the most important discursive dynamics take place. Influential technological and communicative innovations have led to an increasing annihilation of space by time, to the blurring of conventional boundaries of sovereignty and identity. The fall of the Berlin Wall is a case in point. The infiltration of external media sources across the Iron Curtain into all aspects of East German life illustrates the far-reaching political dynamics that issue from discursive transgressions. It is in these transversal and discursive terrains that the interaction between domination and resistance is carried out today. But how can we possibly understand the manifestations of human agency that issue from these struggles? Can they actually be understood at all? Or are they simply too complex, too subtle, too elusive to be apprehended by the human mind?

184

Part III: Discursive terrains of dissent

> The power of what is erects the boundaries into which our consciousness crashes. We must seek to crash through them.[1]

Changes in political dynamics, particularly the advent of globalisation, have transformed the manner in which dissent operates today. Practices of resistance have taken on increasingly transversal dimensions. They ooze into often unrecognized, but nevertheless significant grey zones between domestic and international spheres. They fuse the local and the global.

The first two parts of this book have scrutinised these transformations from a variety of perspectives. The inquiry has focused, in particular, on whether or not a long modern tradition of theorising dissent remains adequate to understand the transversal context within which political dynamics are unfolding today. A reading of the events that led to the collapse of the Berlin Wall has demonstrated how instances of popular dissent, such as street demonstrations and protest migration, transgressed the spatial givenness of East German and international politics. While challenging the authoritarian regime and, ultimately, contributing to the dissolution of the Cold War order, these dissident practices were bound by limits too. A comparative analysis of gender relations before and after German unification served to illustrate this point. Despite active participation in the protest movement of 1989, women as a social group were in some ways worse off after unification. The institutionally and discursively entrenched patriarchal system of exclusion remained unaffected by practices of popular dissent. To understand these seemingly paradoxical dynamics,

[1] Theodor W. Adorno, *Negative Dialektik* (Frankfurt: Suhrkamp, 1992/1966), p. 29.

the inquiry then sought to rethink the interaction between domination and resistance in the context of transversal struggles. Emerging from this rethinking was the suggestion that processes of social change can be assessed more adequately by focusing not on great events, but on the slow and transversal transformation of values that precedes them. Necessary as well is a move away from grand theoretical and spatial forms of representing dissent towards a discursive understanding of how power relations operate in a multitude of interconnected domains that range from the local to the global.

Part III reveals how such a move towards a discursive and transversal understanding of social change makes room for various new ways of locating human agency in global politics. Agency is now no longer limited to the actions of statesmen or to great revolutionary events, but also takes place in countless daily and often mundane domains. The range of such dissident potential is unlimited and includes virtually every act that interferes with the transversal constitution and reconstitution of societal values. Rather than seeking a comprehensive treatment of the topic in question, the analysis will thus concentrate, representatively, on everyday forms of resistance that have to do with practices of speaking and writing.

The collapse of the Berlin Wall serves, once more, as a practical background against which theoretical discussions are carried out. This time the focus lies with a group of young poets who, during the 1980s, sought to interfere with the spatial, political and, above all, the discursive constitution of East German and Cold War politics (chapter 9). By dealing with the painful existence of boundaries (both political and linguistic), the work of these poets illustrates the potential and limits of exerting human agency through inferences with the construction of societal values. But before embarking on this inquiry, some theoretical groundwork is necessary. Chapters 7 and 8 thus provide an introduction to language and discourse that facilitates an active and non-essentialist understanding of dissent and social change. The key to this endeavour lies in saying no more about human agency than can possibly be known. Such a position recognises that human agency has no stable nature, but, rather, consists of the very perceptions that imbue human action with meaning. Transversal dissent, then, is the process of interfering with the discursive constitution and objectification of global politics.

7   Mapping everyday global resistance

> Resistance, or what one usually calls resistance, was in the beginning
> not a political gesture, but a *moral* gesture: an instinctive separation
> from the tiring ticking of the norm. It had to do with the words *truth*
> and *lie*, with *honesty* and *deceit*. . . It began in one's own head, in the
> solitude before one's own image.[1]

The terrain where discursive dissent takes place is the slow and cross-
territorial transformation of societal values. But how is one to understand the manner in which these terrains of dissidence function and
engender human agency? To engage with this question the analysis
now moves away from considering discourses as overarching monolithic forces that dominate all aspects of our lives. Without denying
their power, indeed, by drawing upon it, one must pay attention to
the fissures in them, theorise their fragmentation and their thinness.
By doing so, discursive terrains of dissent all of a sudden appear
where forces of domination previously seemed invincible.

   Some theoretical groundwork is necessary to conceptualise the complex linkages between discursive forces and transversal dissent. To
begin, one must analyse politics at the level of dailiness, especially at
the level of an individual's identity formation. At first sight, such an
inquiry seems of little relevance to the more grandiosely perceived
domain of global politics. Yet, in an age of globalisation, where space
becomes increasingly annihilated by time, the sphere of dailiness
always already contains the global within it. To theorise this domain
of dailiness, and the individual's place within it, is thus a crucial pre-

---

[1] Herta Müller, 'Das Ticker der Norm', in *Hunger and Seide* (Reinbeck: Rowolt, 1997),
   pp. 91–2.

187

requisite for understanding adequately how dissent and human agency are operative in contemporary global politics.

The discursive dynamics through which transversal dissent operates are located in the spaces that lie between the strong and the weak, between dominant and marginalised discourses. The power that lingers in this void is best understood by shifting foci from epistemological to ontological issues. This is to say that one must observe how an individual may be able to escape the discursive order and influence its shifting boundaries. Individuals have fragmented and hyphenated identities. By tapping into these multiple dimensions of Being, individuals can take the first step in resisting some aspects of discursive domination. The present chapter theorises this transformative potential of Being and then illustrates its functioning by drawing attention to ensuing everyday forms of resistance. Later chapters will then remove more layers of abstraction and demonstrate the practical relevance of discursive dissent and the possibilities for human agency that they open up in contemporary global politics.

The lingering power of discursive voids

When reading Nietzsche's *Genealogy of Morals*, Foucault offers a good way into the difficult task of recognising the significance of discursive practices and their bearing upon socio-political realities:

> What Nietzsche calls *Entstehungsherd* [the place of emergence]. . .is not specifically the energy of the strong or the reaction of the weak, but precisely this scene where they are displayed superimposed or face-to-face. It is nothing but the space that divides them, the void through which they exchange their threatening gestures and speeches.[2]

Why is this void between the energy of the strong and the reaction of the week so important? How can it explain the functioning of transversal dissent? Foucault identifies this interstice as the place where power relations are usurped. It hosts the entry of forces, their eruption, 'the leap from the wings to central stage.'[3] The discursive void contains, in short, the key to understanding historical discontinuities.

---

[2] Michel Foucault, 'Nietzsche, Genealogy, History', in P. Rainbow (ed.), *The Foucault Reader*, tr. D.F. Bouchard and S. Simon, (New York, Pantheon Books, 1984/1971), p. 84.
[3] Foucault, 'Nietzsche, Genealogy, History', p. 84.

But how are we to understand a void? How are we to appreciate the dynamics that evolve within it, the ways in which it plays out the forces that linger on all of its multiple points of entry and exit? The first step in this direction entails a departure from the deeply entrenched Western practice of viewing the world in dualistic terms. Much of modern thought has revolved around the juxtaposition of antagonistic bipolar opposites, such as rational/non-rational, good/ evil, just/unjust, chaos/order, domestic/international or, precisely, strong/weak. One side of the pairing is considered to be analytically and conceptually separate from the other. The relationship between them generally expresses the superiority, dominance or desirability of one entity (such as strong/order) over the other (such as weak/chaos). The crucial spaces between them, the grey and indefinable voids, remain unexplored. Departing from this long tradition would, by contrast, emphasise the complementariness of opposites and the overlapping relationships between them. Since one side of the pairing (such as order) can only exist by virtue of its opposite (such as chaos), both form an inseparable and interdependent unit.[4]

Non-dualistic conceptualising recognises that social dynamics cannot be understood by juxtaposing dominant and marginalised discourses, or local and global spheres. Discourses overlap, influence each other. They transgress boundaries. They are in a constant state of flux, and so are their multiple and cross-territorial relationships with political practice. A dominant discourse usually incorporates elements of discursive practices that are squeezed into the margins. The influence of these exiled discourses, in turn, may increase to the point of their becoming dominant. The dividing lines between discourses always changes and may be blurred to the point that one needs to accept, as Foucault does, that multiple discursive elements interact at various strategic levels.[5] What deserves our attention, then, is the discursive void, the space where these multiple and overlapping discourses clash, where silent and sometimes not so silent arguments are exchanged, where boundaries are drawn and redrawn.

The second step in appreciating how the discursive void influences transversal struggles requires a break with some aspects of Foucault's

---

[4] See, for instance, Jacques Derrida, *A Derrida Reader: Between the Blinds*, ed. P. Kamuf (New York: Columbia University Press, 1991), esp. pp. 259–76.
[5] Michel Foucault, La Volonté de Savoir, vol. I, *Histoire de la Sexualité* (Paris: Gallimard, 1976), p. 133.

thought. It may be the case that confrontations in the discursive void do not take place among equals, that, indeed, the only drama staged there is an endlessly repeated play of domination.[6] But resistance to these plays of domination is an equally constant theme. Foucault, of course, would not necessarily disagree, for he argues that 'wherever there is power, there is resistance'.[7] He is simply less optimistic about the chances of precisely locating and directing these forms of resistance. He even goes as far as arguing that because the dynamic in the space between the strong and the weak takes place in an interstice, a 'non-place' where adversaries do not meet directly, no one is responsible for its outcome.[8] Such an interpretation can easily lead to a fatalistic interpretation that annihilates altogether the concept of human agency – an interpretation that is neither compelling nor necessarily compatible with most of Foucault's remaining arguments.

If power and domination are so omnipresent, so invincible, how could anything ever change? If, as Foucault implies, there is no conversation, no common language, not even a visible discursive meeting between the inside and the outside, the centre and the margin, how could one explain all those challenges from below, the moments when people walk through walls, take to the street and shake, successfully or not, the foundations of the established domestic and international order?

Hegemonies may be increasingly global in scope, but they are not invincible. There are fissures, there are cracks, there are weak spots: windows of opportunity that lead to transformative pathways. The question is how to locate, theorise and explore them. James Scott has taken a decisive step in this direction by deconstructing the notion of hegemony. His logic is compelling, at least up to a certain point. Central to Scott's argument about the interaction between domination and resistance is the separation he draws between what he calls the 'public transcript' and the 'hidden transcript'. The public transcript displays various parallels with the concept of hegemony discussed in the previous chapter. It is that which is visible in public of the interaction between subordinates and those who hold power, in short, the self-

---

[6] Foucault, 'Nietzsche, Genealogy, History', pp. 84–5.
[7] Foucault, *La Volonté de Savoir*, p. 125. See also 'The Ethic of Care for the Self as a Practice of Freedom', in J. Bernauer and D. Rasmussen (eds.), *The Final Foucault* tr. J.D. Gauthier (Cambridge, Mass.: The MIT Press, 1988), esp. pp. 11–13.
[8] Foucault, 'Nietzsche, Genealogy, History', p. 85.

portrait of the dominant social group.[9] By controlling the public transcript, elites can establish an official ideological narrative that depicts how they want subordinates to see them. But this is not the whole story, Scott insists. Beside this hegemonic public conduct there is 'a backstage discourse consisting of what cannot be spoken in the face of power'.[10] The hidden transcript is where these 'offstage' opinions are revealed. Elites have their hidden transcripts, the gestures and words which, for example, reveal the contradictions of the public transcript or shed light on its instrumental and exploitative dimensions. But subordinates have hidden transcripts as well. Once they escape the eyes of power holders, they too engage in 'offstage' gesturing and talking that contradict the public transcript. These forms of speech are, of course, produced for a different audience and under very different circumstances than the public discourse. Scott illustrates where and how the hidden transcript renders possible a critique of power behind the back of domination:

> Here, offstage, where subordinates may gather outside the intimidating gaze of power, a sharply dissonant political culture is possible. Slaves in the relative safety of their quarters can speak the words of anger, revenge, self-assertion that they must normally choke back when in the presence of the masters and mistresses.[11]

The disguised practices of dissent that develop in these anonymous spaces will receive attention later in this chapter. At this point it is more important to note that Scott grants subordinates more cognitive autonomy than most theorists of hegemony do. For him, the powerless are well aware of their situation, but accept the status quo for strategic reasons. In one of his early studies on exploitation and peasant politics in South East Asia, Scott demonstrates, for example, that peasants, confined by basic problems of subsistence, often reject outright rebellion and deliberately choose risk-averse strategies to minimise the probability of disaster.[12] The powerless thus have good reasons for keeping up a public appearance that suggests acquiescence with the public transcript.

Scott's suggestion that subordinates, driven by self-interest, deliber-

---

[9] James C. Scott, *Domination and the Arts of Resistance: Hidden Transcripts* (New Haven: Yale University Press, 1990), pp. 2, 18.
[10] Ibid., p. xii.
[11] Ibid., p. 18. See also pp. xii and 1–69.
[12] James C. Scott, *The Moral Economy of the Peasant: Rebellion and Subsistence in Southeast Asia* (New Haven: Yale University Press, 1976).

ately reinforce hegemonic appearances, amounts to a major critique of the (neo)Marxist concepts of hegemony and false consciousness. Indeed, Scott engages directly with some of Gramsci's ideas. Scott is particularly critical of what he calls the thick theory of hegemony. He dismisses as untenable the argument that a dominant ideology is so powerful in concealing its logic of oppression that it persuades subordinate groups to espouse uncritically the values that explain and justify their own subordination.[13] Thick hegemony suggests that manufactured consent in the form of false consciousness sustains systems of domination and social dynamics in general. This position, Scott argues, gravely misjudges the ability of subordinates to learn from their daily material experiences, which allows them to penetrate and demystify the dominant ideology. He has more sympathies for a thin theory of hegemony and false consciousness. From this theoretical perspective, resignation is the key factor and consent is achieved without necessarily changing the values of subordinates. This is to say that hegemony does not alter people's minds, it only delineates the realistic from the unrealistic, the possible from the impossible by convincing subordinate groups that certain elements of the given social order are simply inevitable. Hence, some of the aspirations that the powerless have are relegated to the realm of idle dreams, of wishful thinking.[14]

Scott's analysis implies, much like Foucault's reading of Nietzsche, that it is important to focus not only on the actions of the strong or the reactions of the weak, but also on the space between them. Scott does not talk directly of a void, but his description of social dynamics renders supports for such a concept. For example, he considers the boundaries between the public and the hidden transcripts not a solid wall, but a 'zone of constant struggle between dominant and subordinate'. By observing the 'dialectic of disguise and surveillance' that unfolds in this space, he argues, one can understand better cultural patterns of domination and subordination.[15]

Scott's theorising of hidden transcripts constitutes an important step in locating contradictions and possibilities for dissent that would be missed by focusing solely on hegemony and discursive practices. But

---

[13] Scott, *Domination and the Arts of Resistance*, p. 72.
[14] Scott, *Domination and the Arts of Resistance*, p. 74, and 70–107; James C. Scott *Weapons of the Weak: Everyday Forms of Peasant Resistance* (New Haven: Yale University Press, 1985), pp. 304–50.
[15] Scott, *Domination and the Arts of Resistance*, pp. 4, 14.

an entire dismantling of the concept of hegemony is not necessary for this endeavour. Yes, subordinates are much more aware of their situation than their often accommodating public behaviour suggests, than, indeed, the Gramscian concept of hegemony suggests. Yes, discursive domination does not crush everything in sight. The powerless often deliberately reinforce hegemonic appearances for reasons of strategy or simple self-preservation. But this is not to say that their insight into a situation is authentic, that they enjoy some form of pre- or extra-discursive knowledge. Even while strategically maintaining a public posture of consent against their better judgement, subordinates do not derive this 'chosen' attitude from a position of authenticity. They, like anybody else, live in a community whose language, social practices and customs set limits to the thinking process. They too are part of a discursive order, one that provides the conceptual tools through which 'reality' makes sense. They too are confined by the edges of discursive practices, even if these practices are more subtle than an undifferentiated concept of hegemony suggests. Hidden transcripts revolve around their own hegemonies, discursive orders that may be markedly different from the public transcript, but nevertheless play a crucial role in influencing social dynamics that unfold in the void between the strong and the weak. Ignoring the restraining and enabling elements that are entailed in these crucial discursive factors is to miss out on what may well be the most potent forms of dissent, those that operate through a transformation of discursive practices.

Rather than dismantling the concept of discursive power, a reading of transversal dissent reinforces such a concept. One can theorise how cracks, contradictions and weaknesses in hegemonic orders are exploited such that their transformative potential may be employed to promote social change across boundaries of national sovereignty. While drawing upon Foucault's and Scott's opposing arguments, such a reading of transversal struggles is situated somewhere between the two. This is to say that one must manoeuvre back and forth between a Foucauldian emphasis on discourse, which runs the risk of annihilating human agency, and Scott's trust in the ability of subordinates to cut through the fog of hegemony, which may border on idealism and hinder an adequate understanding of discursive forms of domination and dissent.

How being is always already that which it is not

A shift of foci from epistemological to ontological concerns is necessary to explore the transformative and transversal potentials that are
contained in the discursive void. The main focus then no longer lies
with how knowledge is always mediated by discourse, but how, at
the level of Being, the subject may or may not be able to escape the
confines of this discursive order.

A discussion of Being is, of course, impossible without an engagement with Martin Heidegger. Yet, Heidegger is problematic. His writings are dense, by no means easy to digest. There are also the
(in)famous fascist overtones of his inaugural address as rector of the
University of Freiburg in 1933, the subsequent one year of open cooperation with the Nazi regime, and his unwillingness to discuss the
issue even long after the fall of the Third Reich. Yet, few would dispute the status of Heidegger's philosophical writings as one of the
most insightful and influential contributions of this century. Commentators as diverse as Fred Dallmayr, John Caputo or Leslie Thiele
vehemently criticise Heidegger's political position while drawing
heavily on his theoretical writings to advance such projects as a critical
ontology or a conception of justice and obligation. The main premise
of these and many other like-minded approaches is that one can separate the useful, non-ideological aspects of Heidegger's thought from
his fascist comments,[16] that one can discover a politics in Heidegger
that is at odds with the one he personally championed,[17] that one can
'read Heidegger against Heidegger'.[18] Without engaging the details of
this debate, one can employ Heidegger's ontology to derive various
useful insights into the role that transversal dissent plays in contemporary global politics. A certain level of abstract theorising is, however, necessary to recognise this usefulness.

Heidegger's concept of Dasein constitutes a good starting point.
Dasein is derived literally from a combination of the German words

---

[16] Fred Dallmayr, *Between Freiburg and Frankfurt: Toward a Critical Ontology* (Amherst:
University of Massachusetts Press, 1991) and *The Other Heidegger* (Ithaca: Cornell University Press, 1993).
[17] Leslie Paul Thiele, *Timely Meditations: Martin Heidegger and Postmodern Politics*
(Princeton: Princeton University Press, 1995), p. 9.
[18] John D. Caputo, *Against Ethics: Contribution to a Poetics of Obligation with Constant
Reference to Deconstruction* (Bloomington: Indiana University Press, 1993), p. 227.

'Das-sein', the that-it-is of a being, its existence, as opposed to its essence, the what-it-is (Was-sein) of a thing or person.[19] Dasein thus is the specific and concrete existence of a being as incorporated into a cultural setting and constituted through interactions with people and things in this world. It has always a temporal character, for it expresses the relationship between Being and time. Heidegger argues that Dasein derives its meaning in temporality, that it is only through time that Dasein can understand Being, that, indeed, 'the meaning of the Being of that being we call Dasein proves to be *temporality*'.[20]

Understanding Being through its temporality means that the past is not an epoque gone, but an integral part of the present of Being. In this sense, Dasein is always historical. One cannot separate who one is from how one grew up, from the education, the custom, the language and a whole set of other experiences and impressions that shaped our Being over time. Dasein is always circumscribed by the presence of past discursive elements. Moreover, Dasein not only regulates what it transmits from the past, but also conceals this very process of regulation. This, in turn, means that all actions of subjects and, indeed, the very notion of human agency, are always delineated by the boundaries of this temporal dimension of Being.

But the inevitable presence of its past is only one aspect of the temporal dimension of Being. Discourses do not overwhelm the subject entirely. Dasein also contains the future and all its various possibilities. In view of Heidegger's unconventional notion of time, this potential is not something that may or may not materialise. It is already contained in the very temporality of Being. Dasein, then, is not a stable and permanent aspect of Being. Rather, it is always in the process of becoming something else than what it is. This process of perpetual transformation is linked to such aspects as dialogue, consciousness and self-reflection. Expressed in Heidegger's somewhat idiosyncratic language:

> Dasein. . . is ontically distinguished by the fact that in its Being this being is concerned *about* its very Being. Thus it is constitutive of the Being of Dasein to have, in its very Being, a relation of Being to this Being. And this in turn means that Dasein understands itself in its

[19] See Martin Heidegger, 'Being and Time' in *Basic Writings* tr. D.F. Krell (New York: HarperCollins, 1993/1927), p. 48.
[20] Ibid., p. 60.

> Being in some way and with some explicitness. It is proper to this
> being that it be disclosed to itself with and through its Being. *Under-*
> *standing of Being is itself a determination of Being of Dasein.*[21]

The point, then, is not only that Dasein's awareness of Being influences the constitution of its own nature, but also that Being already
embodies the transformative potential of Dasein to be something else
than what it is. Dasein, Heidegger points out, always understands
itself 'in terms of its possibility to be itself or not to be itself'.[22] It is
up to the task of thinking to explore the range of options that are
contained in the double-edged character of Being. Self-reflection has
the potential, at least up to a certain point, to cut through the fog of
conventional temporality and thus undermine the forms of concealment by which Being resists the possibility of being something else
than what it is.

The task of this chapter entails searching for ways through which
this transformative potential of Dasein's relation to Being permit us to
conceptualise discursive terrains of transversal dissent and, by doing
so, articulate an alternative understanding of how human agency
functions in global politics. But how are we to bring the discussion to
a practical level without loosing the benefit of Heidegger's more
abstract insights into the question of Being? Recent post-positivist feminist literature leads us in the right direction. Hardly any feminist
reaches so blindly into abstraction that s/he loses sight of the more
immanent political task of addressing the concrete circumstances
within which women's lives are confined. Those who venture into
metatheoretical spaces, and many do so successfully, often feel the
need, unlike Heidegger, to justify their approach and draw attention
to its direct political and ethical relevance.[23] But before theorising the
differences between Heidegger and feminist authors, first a few
remarks on important similarities. They are not explicitly laid out.
While one finds abundant references to psychoanalytical perspectives
on the subject, especially via Freud, Jung, Lacan and Zizek, Heidegger's name is astonishingly absent from feminist debates. Only a few
isolated authors theorise Being through more than just fleeting and
symbolic footnotes to Heidegger. Yet, while his name is largely

---

[21] Ibid., pp. 53–4.
[22] Ibid., p. 54.
[23] For example, Kathy Ferguson, *The Man Question: Visions of Subjectivity in Feminist*
Theory (Berkeley: University of California Press, 1993), pp. ix–xi.

effaced, many of Heidegger's ideas are omnipresent in feminist literature. This is the case not only of his ontology, but also of his work on such topics as identity/difference, language, otherness, concealment, or *Destruktion* (handed down, via poststructuralism, as deconstruction). The presence of these insights, however, is (ironically) concealed and mediated via Heidegger's more 'sanitised' and 'de-Germanised' contemporary French interpreters, such as Derrida, Foucault, Levinas or Deleuze.

But where exactly do these Heideggerean residues linger in feminist theory? Where is his emptiest of all concepts, this Being that is not authentic and cannot even be grasped? The refusal to freeze and objectivise the subject, to transport the positivist discourse of science into the ontological realm, is also a key rallying point in postmodern feminism. Judith Butler, for instance, views the subject primarily as a Foucauldian regulatory practice, a normative rule that governs and upholds culturally constructed gender identities.[24] She thus rejects the notion of an authentic female identity, an essence that crystallises if one digs deep enough. Instead, she analyses the process by which subjects are constituted as essences, to then explore the possibilities that emerge from their multiplicities. Others argue along the same lines. Trinh Minh-ha believes that there is no permanent essence of wo/man, that, indeed, 'women can never be defined'.[25] Kathy Ferguson eschews the search for an 'essential reality to which our representations correspond'.[26] These assumptions about Being's elusiveness are probably best captured in Donna Haraway's metaphor of women as cyborgs. A cyborg is a hybrid of machine and organism, something that lies between social reality and fiction. In today's mythic and high-technological age, she argues, we all live as chimeras, we are all cyborgs, a 'condensed image of both imagination and material reality'.[27] Being, in this interpretation, is not only evasive and constructed, but, much as Heidegger argues, it actually is not. It happens. Being is a constant process of renewal. Moving along the same slippery lines, Butler considers gender not as a noun or a static cultural marker but,

---

[24] Judith Butler, *Gender Trouble: Feminism and the Subversion of Identity* (New York: Routledge, 1990), pp. 16–17.
[25] Trinh T. Minh-ha, *Woman, Native, Other* (Bloomington: Indiana University Press, 1989), pp. 95–6.
[26] Ferguson, *The Man Question*, p. 154.
[27] Donna J. Haraway, *Simians, Cyborgs, and Women: The Reinvention of Nature* (New York: Routledge, 1991), pp. 149–50.

rather, as an activity, an incessant action of some sort, something that one becomes but can never be.[28]

While working within these and other Heideggerean concepts, most feminist authors are reluctant to elevate the question of Being to a purely abstract level. Those who deal directly with Heidegger deplore that his concept of ontological difference does not include sexual difference, that he fails to pose the 'sexual question'. Braidotti, for example, reads Heidegger via Derrida's interpretation and criticises both of them for placing the emergence of the subject beyond sexual difference. Such a conceptual notion of Being above and beyond sexuality, she argues, makes the mistake of reducing sexual difference to a derived given that is not constitutive of the subject.[29]

Those feminists who grapple with the question of Being without dealing with Heideggerean dilemmas of abstraction focus (ironically, again) on Heideggerean themes of identity and difference.[30] Yet, the main focus of these authors lies not so much, or at least not only, with differences between men and women, not even with differences among women. Strategies of resistance are carved out by exploring differences within women. The terms fractured or hyphenated identities are most commonly used to convey the theoretical starting point for this innovative approach to difference. Being, here too, is a very complex issue. Braidotti speaks for many feminists when she argues that the synthesising power of the term 'I' is nothing but a 'grammatical necessity, a theoretical fiction that holds together the collection of differing layers, the integrated fragments of the very-receding horizon of my identity.'[31] Women (and men) have multiple, fractured and ambivalent subjectivities that move back and forth between such terrains of identity as class, race, gender, nationality, language and sexual preference. People's identities, then, cannot be reduced to an essence. They are situated fluidly along such lines, as, for instance, Afro-American-socialist-English-speaking-recently-divorced-father-and-factory-worker-man   or   Hispanic-lesbian-college-educated-

---

[28] Butler, *Gender Trouble*, p. 112.
[29] Rosi Braidotti, *Patterns of Dissonance: A Study of Women in Contemporary Philosophy* (New York: Routledge, 1991), p. 104.
[30] See Heidegger, *Identity and Difference*, tr. J. Stambaugh (New York: Harper & Row, 1969).
[31] Rosi Braidotti, 'The Politics of Ontological Difference', in T. Brennan (ed.), *Between Feminism and Psychoanalysis* (London: Routledge, 1989), p. 93.

198

abroad-in-Northern-Europe-residing-woman. The combinations, of course, are endless.

What is the potential for transversal dissent contained in these hyphenated identities? How can they lead to expressions of human agency? Some of the above feminist authors claim convincingly that a strategic use of hyphenated identities opens up chances for undermining the regulatory norms established by these very identities. They provide the individual with opportunities to escape the suffocating impact of hegemonies, seek out its cracks and weaknesses, and explore the enabling potential that lingers in the discursive void. And a major part of this process is carried out, as subsequent chapters will reveal, in a cross-territorial context.

A feminist exploration of multiple identities runs counter to many established approaches to dissent which, in Terry Eagleton's words, claim that 'a certain provisional stability of identity is essential not only for psychical well-being but for revolutionary political agency'.[32] While recognising the need for provisional foundations to articulate critique, a feminist and discursive rethinking of transversal dissent locates manifestations of human agency precisely in the fluidity of identity, in its constituted and multiple dimensions. Rather than sliding into 'an irresponsible hymning of the virtues of schizophrenia', as Eagleton fears,[33] an exploration of the discursive struggles that surround the pluralistic nature of identity is the very precondition for human agency and for an adequate assessment of the processes through which its transformative potentials are unleashed.

Ferguson employs the term 'mobile subjectivities' to capture the possibilities for transformation that arise from moving back and forth among a whole range of hyphenated identities and their corresponding mental resting places. Dissident potential emerges because this process not only entails travelling across and along axes of power, domination and resistance, but also destabilises the regulatory norms that have been constructed through the delineation of these identities.[34] By being aware of the arbitrariness and excluding tendencies embedded in identity constructions, such as class, race or gender, subjects become empowered and can take part in daily processes that

---

[32] Terry Eagleton, *Ideology: An Introduction* (London: Verso, 1991), pp. 197–8.
[33] Ibid., p. 198.
[34] Ferguson, *The Man Question*, pp. 158–63.

slowly but constantly redraw the political boundaries of identities. Haraway makes a similar point through a slightly different terminology that relies upon her cyborg metaphor. She talks of 'situated knowledges', of how moving back and forth between various subjectivities can open up multiple visions. The point is, Haraway emphasises, not to ground one's knowledge in stable standpoints, but to explore visions of change that unfold through multi-dimensional, shifting and always eluding hyphens of identity.[35]

The potential for change embedded in these visions of Being are as potent as the ones advocated by Heidegger. But this potential does not lie primarily in the temporal aspects of Being, future possibilities that are already contained in the existential self-awareness of Dasein. It is captured by drawing attention to the multiple dimensions of Being that exist simultaneously. Potential for human agency is then contained in the transgression of boundaries that has been enabled through an awareness of the flexibility contained in hyphenated identities. These two seemingly disparate visions of Being display important parallels. In both temporal or simultaneous dimensions, Being is always already that which it is not. Discursive domination is a crucial force to be reckoned with. But it is not the end of the story. There are ways of eluding discourse. There are glimmers of hope. There are fractured visions of human agency.

Networks of anti-discipline / everyday forms of resistance

To get closer to the objective of theorising the practical dimensions of discursive and transversal forms of dissent it is necessary to remove one more layer of abstraction. Required is another shift of foci, this time from ontological to tactical issues, from mobile subjectivities to the practices through which they turn into vehicles of dissent. The focus now rests with the domain of everydayness, the sphere of *Alltäglichkeit* that Heidegger theorised only in abstract terms. With this step the analysis returns, full circle so to speak, to the Nietzschean argument presented in the previous chapter, namely that our attention should be focused less on great historical events, and more on the seemingly insignificant slow and cross-territorial transformation of values that precede them.

---

[35] Haraway, *Simians, Cyborgs, and Women*, pp. 183–201.

There are many ways of searching for practices of transversal dissent and aspects of human agency hidden in the dailiness of life. Michel de Certeau's approach is one of the most productive conceptual entry points to explore everyday forms of resistance. His objective is to refute the widespread assumption that common people are passive onlookers, guided by the disciplinary force of established rules. He attempts to demonstrate that seemingly mundane daily practices are not simply background activities, not even mere forms of resistance, but are, indeed, an integral part of socio-cultural production.

De Certeau clearly detects human agency in everyday life. For him, normal people are not simply faceless consumers, they are '[u]nrecognised producers, poets of their own affairs, trailblazers in the jungles of functionalist rationality'.[36] De Certeau makes use of Foucault's research by turning it upside down. He strongly opposes Foucault's notion of a panoptical discourse, one that sees and controls everything. He considers it unwise spending one's entire energy analysing the multitude of minuscule techniques that discipline the subject and paralyse her/him in a web of micro-level power relations. Such an approach, de Certeau stresses, unduly privileges the productive apparatus. Instead, he proposes an anti-Foucauldian path to understanding domination and resistance:

> If it is true that the grid of 'discipline' is everywhere becoming clearer and more extensive, it is all the more urgent to discover how an entire society resists being reduced to it, what popular procedures (also 'minuscule' and quotidian) manipulate the mechanisms of discipline and conform to them only in order to evade them, and finally, what 'ways of operating' form the counterpart, on the consumer's (or 'dominee's'?) side, of the mute processes that organize the establishment of socioeconomic order.[37]

These 'ways of operating', are the practices by which people can re-appropriate the space controlled through the existing discursive order. It is not my intention here to provide an exhaustive account of everyday forms of resistance that take place in these 'networks of anti-discipline', as de Certeau calls them.[38] Such a task would be doomed from the start, for the range of daily acts of dissent is unlim-

[36] Michel de Certeau, Arts de Faire, vol. I, *L'Invention du Quotidien*, (Paris, Gallimard, 1990/1980), p. 57, tr. S.F. Rendall in *The Practice of Everyday Life* (Berkeley, University of California Press, 1984), p. 34.
[37] De Certeau, *Arts de Faire*, pp. xxxix–xl, tr. *The Practice of Everyday Life*, p. xiv.
[38] De Certeau, *Arts de Faire*, p. xl.

ited. I simply illustrate the persuasive aspects of de Certeau's argument via a few examples, leaving it to chapters 8 and 9 to analyse in detail more specific everyday forms of transversal dissent, those related to speaking and writing.

De Certeau focuses primarily on the uses of space in Western consumer societies, on how everyday practices like walking, shopping, dwelling or cooking become arts of manipulation that intervene with the prevalent discursive order. Other authors locate daily practices of subversion in different spheres of life. James Scott has dealt in detail with everyday forms of peasant resistance. For him too, the big events are not peasant rebellions or revolutions. They occur rarely anyway. What deserves our attention, he argues, is the constant everyday struggle between the peasantry and those who seek to extract labour, taxes, rents and the like from them.[39] Through extensive, detailed and highly compelling research Scott demonstrates the prevalence of low-profile forms of resistance. These are the critiques spoken behind the back of power, the utterances that make up the earlier-mentioned hidden transcript. Although such critique is never spoken openly, it nevertheless is in the open. Indeed, this form of critique is almost omnipresent in folk culture, disguised in such practices as rumours, gossip, jokes, tales or songs. They are the vehicles of the powerless by which they 'insinuate a critique of power while hiding behind anonymity or behind innocuous understandings of their conduct'.[40] We find a perfect example of such a practice in Margaret Atwood's fictional, but all too real authoritarian word:

> There is something powerful in the whispering of obscenities about those in power. There's something delightful about it, something naughty, secretive, forbidden, thrilling. It's like a spell, of sorts. It deflates them, reduces them to the common denominator where they can be dealt with. In the paint of the washroom cubicle someone unknown had scratched: *Aunt Lydia sucks*. It was like a flag waved from a hilltop in rebellion.[41]

The scene of an obscenity anonymously scribbled onto a bathroom wall is an act of subversion. Anonymity provided the security necessary to scream out what cannot even be whispered in the face of the oppressors. There is a clear target, but no visible author, no agitator

[39] Scott, *Weapons of the Weak*, pp. xv–xvi.
[40] Scott, *Domination and the Arts of Resistance*, p. xiii, 19, 136–82.
[41] Margaret Atwood, *The Handmaid's Tale* (London: Jonathan Cape, 1986), p. 234.

that could be prosecuted. The audience is potentially limitless. Scott insists that such a politics of hidden dissent, of disguise and anonymity, is neither empty posturing nor a substitute for real resistance. It is resistance of the most effective kind, for these subversive gestures eventually insinuate themselves, in disguised form, into the public discourse. They lead to a slow transformation of values, they nurture and give meaning to subsequent, more overt forms of resistance or rebellion. They may bring upon an explosive political situation during which the *cordon sanitare* between the hidden and public transcripts is torn apart.[42]

Everyday forms of resistance are, of course, not new. Indeed, one of the most famous illustrations of such dissent dates back to sixteenth-century France, to the Renaissance author François Rabelais. His very personality illustrates how he escaped aspects of discursive orders by navigating back and forth between various hyphenated identities: Franciscan monk, humanist, doctor of medicine and, in the function that interests us here, writer of grotesque and satirical stories. His five books on the adventures of Gargantua and his son Pantagruel are episodes of carnival, laughter, mockery and fantastical imagination. They include, for example, a chapter on how Pantagrual realised 'Gargantua's marvellous intelligence by his invention of an Arse-wipe' or how he 'set five chambers of hell on fire, sacked the great black hall, threw Proserpina into the flames, and broke four of Lucifer's teeth'.[43]

In his influential analysis of Rabelais' writings, Mikhail Bakhtin draws attention to the revolutionary potential hidden in these seemingly merely humorous stories. Indeed, Rabelais demonstrates that contrary to the position of la Boétie, his contemporary and fellow humanist, resistance does not need to be confined to heroic acts of mass dissent.

The popular culture of laughter was deeply subversive, for it opposed, even ridiculed, the seriousness and hypocrisy of the official feudal culture. It mocked the clergy and its rigid Christian rituals. In this sense, Bakhtin stresses, laughter was freedom because it 'celebrated temporary liberation from the prevailing truth and from the established order; it marked the suspension of all hierarchical rank,

[42] Scott, *Domination and the Arts of Resistance*, pp. 19–20, 183–227.
[43] François Rabelais, *The Histories of Gargantua and Pantagruel*, tr. J.M. Cohen (Penguin Books, 1966), pp. 66–9, 277.

privileges, norms, and prohibitions'.[44] This suspension and, in a more general sense, the language of the market place and of carnival, created possibilities for uninhibited speech. It carved out a space where, in late twentieth-century talk, those unpronounceable public-toilet-wall-scribblings could be screamed out into the streets.

Laughter opened up, at least for a short moment, a glimpse at utopian freedom, at a life beyond the heavy Christian mythology of death and eternal punishment in the form of Hell after death. Laughter, Bakhtin argues, liberates the mind from dogmatism and pedantry, from fear and intimidation. It shatters the belief that life has a single meaning.[45] In this sense, laughter, in both practice and writing, creates mobile subjectivities and situated knowledges. Carnival becomes a revolutionary act, one that slowly transforms values and norms, one that enters political spheres. Rabelais' satire, blessed with immediate popular success and equally swift condemnation from the leading clergy, rendered support for an emerging humanist movement and contributed to the eventual death of God, the gradual decay of an unchallenged theocentric world-view.

Despite engendering powerful and hidden mechanisms of change, everyday forms of resistance are not unproblematic. Like more open forms of dissent, they are certainly not immune from entrenching discursive forms of domination. Here too, the work of Rabelais is illustrative. For all his subversive carnivalesque writings, his views on women undoubtedly supported existing patriarchal practices. Consider the following famous passage in book I, when Rabelais describes Gargantua's arrival in Paris and his annoyed reaction to the curious crowd that surrounded him. The passage epitomises both the subversive aspects of Rabelais' grotesque satire and his refusal to grant women even the status of subjecthood:

> Then, with a smile, he [Gargantua] undid his magnificent codpiece and, bringing out his john-thomas, pissed on them so fiercely that he drowned two hundred and sixty thousand, four hundred and eighteen persons, not counting women and small children.[46]

Bakhtin overlooks the discursive consequences that arise from Rabelais' treatment of women as faceless objects. Instead, he primarily

---

[44] Mikhail Bakhtin, *Rabelais and His World*, tr. H. Iswolsky (Cambridge, Mass.: MIT Press, 1968), p. 10.
[45] Ibid., p. 123.
[46] Rabelais, *The Histories of Gargantua and Pantagruel*, p. 74.

analyses the various metaphorical aspects of scenes like the tossing of excrement, drenching in urine or, in general, Rabelais' repeated focus on 'images of the material bodily lower stratum'. Bakhtin draws links to circles of birth, life and death, fertility and renewal, but never touches upon the issue of gender relations and related systems of exclusion.[47] He never asks who laughs about whom in Rabelais' world. He never notices that only men laugh about masculine themes, like the drenching in urine. Women, by contrast, often refuse to ridicule themselves and 'view the laughter of others as an instrument of control over them'.[48]

Moving to more contemporary settings, we find scholars who attempt to locate everyday practices of resistance in domains where domination had hitherto been considered omnipresent. The historian Stephen Kotkin, for instance, analyses in great detail how the Soviet industrial city of Magnitogorsk emerged and expanded during the 1930s. Although life in the city almost perfectly epitomises the despotic character of Stalinism, Kotkin demonstrates how ordinary citizens constantly reshaped the environment in which they lived. 'New categories of thinking suddenly appeared, old ones were modified; nothing stood still'.[49] Thinking space was generated through seemingly insignificant acts, such as the process of naming and explaining new phenomena they encountered in the market place or their living quarters. Far more often than the coercive political climate would suggest, individuals were able to challenge, or at least circumvent, existing rules by engaging in 'resourceful, albeit localised, resistance to the terms of daily life that developed within the crusade of building socialism'.[50]

As has been the case with more heroic practices of popular dissent, everyday forms of resistance have undergone important transformations with the advent of globalisation. The prevalence of global media networks, in particular, has provided the struggle over values with almost immediate cross-territorial dimensions. Among the everyday forms of resistance that are operative in these transversal terrains are the increasing number of so-called new social movements. They are

[47] Bakhtin, *Rabelais and his World*, pp. 147–52, 368–436.
[48] Madelaine H. Caviness, 'Patron or Matron? A Capetian Bride and a Vade Mecum for Her Marriage Bed', *Speculum: A Journal in Medieval Studies*, 68, 2, April 1993, 361.
[49] Stephen Kotkin, *Magnetic Mountain: Stalinism as a Civilization* (Berkeley: University of California Press, 1995), p. 356.
[50] Ibid., pp. 21.

pressure groups and other loose organisations that do not challenge the prevailing political system as such, but contribute to a slow and constant transformation of values by focusing on the need to rethink specific issue areas. In an insightful and highly compelling study, R.B.J. Walker has demonstrated how such critical social movements engage local dynamics such that the ensuing creation of thinking space has the potential to engender transformation in a much wider spatial and political context.[51] The diffused activities of social movements are, in some ways, the quintessential form of postmodern politics, of local dissent against various forms of metanarrative impositions.[52] Critical social movements and other everyday forms of resistance operate, of course, in all parts of the world. Arturo Escobar and Sonia Alvarez, for instance, have shown how, in Latin America during the 1980s, various collective forms of protest were able to promote social change by engaging in the construction and reconstruction of collective identities.[53] Some also suggest that dissident potential is hidden in the seemingly homogenising and suffocating forces of popular culture, where some detect, much as Rabelais did half a millennium before, carnivalesque challenges to the narrow and single representation of reason in the public sphere.[54]

Summary

This chapter has mapped out some of the discursive terrains in which transversal dissent takes place. Discourses are not invincible monolithic forces that subsume everything in reach. Despite their power to frame social practices, a discursively entrenched hegemonic order can be fragmented and thin at times. To excavate the possibilities for dissent that linger in these cracks, a shift of foci from epistemological to ontological issues is necessary. Scrutinising the level of Being reveals how individuals can escape aspects of hegemony. Dasein, the existential awareness of Being, always already contains the potential to become something else than what it is. By shifting back and forth

---

[51] R.B.J. Walker, *One World, Many Worlds: Struggles for a Just World Peace* (London: Zed Books, 1988).

[52] Or so at least claims Stephen K. White, *Political Theory and Postmodernism* (Cambridge: Cambridge University Press, 1991), pp. 10–12.

[53] Arturo Escobar and Sonia E. Alvarez (eds.), *The Making of Social Movements in Latin America: Identity, Strategy and Democracy* (Boulder, Col: Westview Press, 1992).

[54] John Docker, *Postmodernism and Popular Culture* (Cambridge, Cambridge University Press, 1994).

between hyphenated identities, an individual can travel across various discursive fields of power and gain the critical insight necessary to escape at least some aspect of the prevailing order.

Transversal practices of dissent that issue from such mobile subjectivities operate at the level of dailiness. Through a range of seemingly mundane acts of resistance, people can gradually transform societal values and thus promote powerful processes of social change. Theses transformations are not limited to existing boundaries of sovereignty. The power of discursive practices is not circumscribed by some ultimate spatial delineation, and neither are the practices of dissent that interfere with them. At a time when the flow of capital and information is increasingly trans-territorial, the sphere of everyday life has become an integral aspect of global politics – one that deserves the attention of scholars who devote themselves to the analysis of international relations. The remaining chapters seek to sustain this claim and, in doing so, articulate a viable and non-essentialist concept of human agency.

Second interlude **Towards a discursive understanding of human agency**

> The kind of critique we need is one that can free it of its illusory
> pretension to define the totality of our lives as agents, without
> attempting the futile and ultimately self-destructing task of rejecting
> it altogether.[1]

The task of articulating such a critical position on human agency
towered over the entrance to this book and has never ceased to be its
main puzzle, a cyclically reccurring dilemma, the issue with which
each chapter had to struggle. How can we understand the processes
through which transversal dissident shapes contemporary global politics? Where is this fine line between essentialism and relativism,
between suffocating in the narrow grip of totalising knowledge claims
and blindly roaming in a nihilistic world of absences? How to walk
along this narrow path without taking a fatal step, either to the left or
to the right, into a bottomless epistemological pit? How to deal with
the death of God, to make a clear break with positivist forms of representing dissent without either abandoning the concept of human
agency or falling back into a new form of essentialism?

We have now arrived at the point where some preliminary answers
to these difficult questions are called for. A series of theoretical and
practical inquiries into transversal struggles have suggested that
human agency can still be exerted and conceptualised, even at a time
when global politics is characterised by a multitude of increasingly
complex cross-territorial interactions. Such a conceptualisation cannot
be based on a parsimonious proposition, a one-sentence statement that

---

[1] Charles Taylor, *Human Agency and Language* (Cambridge: Cambridge University
Press, 1995/1985), p. 7.

captures something like an authentic nature of human agency. There is no essence to human agency, no core that can be brought down to a lowest common denominator, that will crystallise one day in a long sought after magic formula. The point is, rather, to recognise the complexities that are involved in a formulation of human agency and to work through them, rather than against or around them.

One way of conceptualising human agency while recognising its elusiveness is to ground its articulation in a specification of what Michel de Certeau called 'operational schemes'.[2] As opposed to a systematic theory, an understanding of operational schemes recognises that human agency should be assessed in its fluidity and its constituted dimensions. Rather than trying to determine what human agency is, such an approach maps the contours within which human agency is carried out. These contours are best understood through three closely interconnected concepts: discourse, tactic and temporality. Each of these sites of investigation illustrates how transversal dissent is a process that transgresses, and in doing so also challenges, the spatial givenness of contemporary global politics. What follows briefly recapitulates the previous research steps in light of these three central concepts. Equipped with the ensuing conceptual map, the last two chapters then seek to illustrate how a specific, discursively based form of transversal dissent may be able to exert human agency.

Theorising cross-territorial transgression: discourse, tactic, temporality

Discourse is the most central concept in a non-essentialist assessment of human agency. A shift from grand theoretical representations of dissent towards a discursive understanding of power relations is necessary to reach a more adequate understanding of the role that human agency plays in contemporary global politics. A discursive approach is not only able to deal better with entrenched systems of exclusion, but also minimises the danger of imposing one's own subjective vision upon a series of far more complex social events. Instead of focusing on ahistorical theories of power, a discursive approach investigates how social dynamics have been imbued with meaning and how this process of rendering them rational circumscribes the

---

[2] Michel de Certeau, *Arts de Faire*, vol. I, *L'Invention du Quotidien*, (Paris: Gallimard, 1990/1980), p. 51.

boundaries within which the transversal interaction between domination and resistance takes place.

While providing compelling evidence of subtle forms of domination, a discursive approach may run the risk of leaving us with an image of the world in which the capacity for human agency is all but erased, annihilated by impenetrable discursive forces. This risk is particularly acute in a world that is characterised by increasingly heterogeneous and perhaps even elusive cross-territorial dynamics. But recognising these transversal complexities does not necessarily lead into a pessimistic *cul de sac*. Discourses, even if they take on global dimensions, are not as overarching as some analysts suggest. They contain fissures and cracks, weak points which open up chances to turn discursive dynamics against themselves. The previous chapter has outlined this position in detail. A brief rehearsal – even at the risk of appearing slightly repetitive – is necessary to provide the prerequisite for an adequate discursive conceptualisation of human agency in global politics. For this purpose we must, as the prologue has already stressed, seek to see beyond the levels of analysis problematique that has come to frame international relations theory. Rather than limiting the study of global politics to specific spheres of inquiry – those related to the role of states and the restraints imposed on them by the structures of the international system – an analysis of transversal struggles pays attention to various political terrains and the cross-territorial dynamics through which they are intertwined with each other. One of these terrains is the sphere of dailiness, which is all too often eclipsed by investigations that limit the domain of global politics to more visible sites of transversal struggle, such as wars, diplomatic negotiations, financial flows or trade-patterns. The domain of dailiness, though, is at least as crucial to the conduct of global politics, and an investigation into discursive dynamics illustrates why this the case.

Cracks and weaknesses in globalised discursive practices can be seen best by shifting foci from epistemological to ontological issues. This is to say that in addition to analysing how discourses mould and control our thinking process, we must scrutinise how individuals, at the level of Being, may or may not be able to escape aspects of the prevalent discursive order. Being is always a product of discourse. But Being also is becoming. It contains future potential, it is always already that which it is not. Being also has multiple dimensions. Hyphenated identities permit a person to shift viewpoints constantly, to move back and forth between various ways of constituting oneself. Resulting methods of mental deplacement, of situating knowledge, open up possibilities for thinking beyond the narrow confines of the transversally established discursive order. This thinking space provides the opportunity to redraw the boundaries of identity which control the parameters of actions available to an individual. Exploring this thinking space already is action, Heidegger claims, for 'thinking acts insofar as it thinks'. Such action, he continues, is 'the simplest and at the same time the highest, because it concerns the relation of Being to man'.[3] But how is one to understand processes through which critical thinking breaks through the fog of discourse and gives rise to specific and identifiable expressions of human agency?

The concept of tactic offers the opportunity to take a decisive step towards exploring the practical dimensions of Dasein, the existential awareness of Being, without losing the abstract insight provided by Heidegger. The sphere of dailiness is where such practical theorising is most effective. Entering this ubiquitous sphere compels us to one more shift, away from contemplating the becoming of Being towards investigating specific ways in which individuals employ their mobile subjectivities to escape discursive forms of domination. The focus now rests on everyday forms of resistance, seemingly mundane daily practices by which people constantly shape and reshape their environment. One can find such forms of resistance in acts like writing, laughing, gossiping, singing, dwelling, shopping or cooking. It is in these spheres that societal values are gradually transformed, preparing the ground for more open manifestations of dissent.

Before drawing attention to the inherently transversal character of everyday activities, it is necessary to point out that the effects they produce cannot be understood by drawing direct links between action and outcome. In this sense, the present analysis departs fundamentally from the manner in which agency in global politics has come to be theorised. Most approaches to international theory, including the influential constructivist contributions to the structure–agency debate, display a clear 'commitment to causal analysis'.[4]

Discursive dissent operates tactically, rather than strategically. And

---

[3] Martin Heidegger, 'Letter on Humanism', *Basic Writings* tr. D.F. Krell (New York: HarperCollins, 1993/1927), p. 217.
[4] Jeffery T. Checkel, 'The Constructivist Turn in International Relations Theory', *World Politics*, 50, January 1998, 347; Alexander Wendt, 'The Agent-Structure Problem in International Relations Theory', *International Organization*, 41, 1987, 351–6.

tactical action cannot be understood in causal terms. It is different from a strategic form of dissent, where agent and target can be separated and the attempt is usually made to articulate a causal relationship between them. Strategy envisages how an identifiable agent (such as a protest march) exerts influence on an identifiable target (such as a change in policy desired by the march). A discursive understanding of human agency in global politics cannot rely on such strategic and causal assumptions. In the context of complex transversal struggles, the duality of cause and effect, as it is commonly perceived, does not exist. What does exist, instead, is a continuum of interconnected cross-territorial dynamics from which we arbitrarily isolate a few pieces and then neatly fit them, as Nietzsche once expressed it, into the image we had already made for ourselves of the world.[5]

The link between action and outcome in discursive forms of dissent is impossible to articulate through a causal formula. As opposed to strategic action, de Certeau emphasises, tactical forms of resistance have no clearly specified target, no visible place to exert influence. There is no direct causal relationship between the subject of will and the exterior circumstances at which this will is directed. Tactical actions, de Certeau claims, cannot be autonomous from their target. They always insinuate themselves into the Other, without seizing it entirely, but yet without being able to keep their distance.[6]

Take the rather mundane example that could come from any industrialised society: a critical and environmentally aware consumer who, against prevalent practices of production and consumption, refuses to buy milk that is bottled in non-reusable containers. At first sight, such a localised protest act seems to be void of any political significance, yet alone a transversal one. Alone this shopper does not stand a chance of exerting human agency in the traditional sense. S/he does not cause particular events, does not physically transgress boundaries, does not walk through walls and iron curtains. But if a substantial part of the population engages in similar daily acts of protest, producers will eventually be compelled to adjust to changed market conditions. But where is the agent and the causal relationship in this form of protest? One cannot pick out a particular shopper who epitomises this tactical act of dissent. Consumers may also have multiple reasons for refusing

---

[5] Friedrich Nietzsche, *Die Fröhliche Wissenschaft* (Frankfurt: Insel Verlag, 1982/1882), §§ 110–12, pp. 127–31.
[6] De Certeau, *Arts de Faire*, p. xlvi.

to buy milk in non-reusable containers. They may, for example, have environmental related concerns, oppose commercial dairy farmers, or be vegetarian. Moreover, where is the target of this tactical form of dissent? Is it the supermarket? The retailer? The producer of non-reusable containers? The farmer who delivers milk? Government authorities who fail to impose sufficient environmental standards? Cross-territorial trade practices? Fellow shoppers who still buy milk bottled in non-reusable containers? Or even the global political economy as a whole, of which the said shopper is as much part as anybody else?

A tactic does not have the possibility of perceiving its adversary in a space that is distinct, visible and objectifiable. The space of tactic is always the space of the Other.[7] This is to say that a tactical form of dissent, like shopping, cannot keep its distance from the object of the action. It always operates in the terrain of the opponent. Tactical actions leave their assigned places, enter a world that is too big to be their own but also too tightly woven to escape from. Because tactic does not have a specific target and cannot separate between the I and the Other, it can never conquer something, it can never keep what it wins. Tactic must always seize the moment and explore cracks that open up within existing discursive orders. It must constantly manipulate its environment in order to create opportunities for social change.[8]

It is through the concept of temporality that we can appreciate the ways in which tactical actions unleash their transformative and transversal potential. The causality entailed in a discursive understanding of human agency, as far as one can speak of causality in this diffused context, is always mediated through time. But temporality is a slippery concept, an experience that is, according to Gaston Bachelard, never pure.[9] Tactical actions, de Certeau stresses, operate along 'indeterminate trajectories'. This means, in a first instance, that tactic works discursively, that it transforms values and becomes visible and effective only through maturation over time. In a second instance, the indeterminacy of the trajectory refers to the fact that tactical actions defy the spatial logic established by the organising procedures of a particular political or economic system. Expressed in de Certeau's somewhat

[7] Ibid., pp. 60–1.
[8] Ibid., pp. xlvi–xlvii, 61.
[9] Gaston Bachelard, *La Dialectique de la Durée* (Paris, PUF, 1989/1950), p. 113.

idiosyncratic language, tactical actions cannot be perceived as a conventional succession of events in space. They evoke a temporal movement, one that focuses on the diachronic succession of points, rather than the figure that these points establish on a supposedly synchronic and achronic space. The latter view, de Certeau stresses, would make the mistake of reducing a 'temporal articulation of places into a spatial sequence of points'.[10]

Tactical action contains transversal potential. The above mentioned refusal to buy milk bottled in non-reusable containers illustrates how tactical manifestations of human agency are not bound by the spatial logic of national sovereignty. The consumer who changes his/her shopping habits engages in an action that escapes the spatial controlling mechanisms of established political and economic boundaries. The effect of such a tactical action is not limited to a localised target, say, the supermarket. Over an extended period of time, and in conjunction with similar actions, such tactical dissent may influence globalised practices of production, trade, investment, advertisement and the like. The transversal manifestations that issue from such actions operate along an indeterminate trajectory insofar as they promote a slow transformation of values whose effects transgress places and become visible and effective only by maturation over time.

Having introduced, through notions of discourse, tactic and temporality, the conceptual tools for a discursive understanding of human agency, the analysis now proceeds to examine how a specific everyday form of resistance may exert human agency in a cross-territorial manner. Language, and the dissident potential contained within it, will be the main focal point. Once more, the inquiry moves back and forth between domination and resistance, abstraction and dailiness, theory and practice, epistemology and ontology. While navigating through these circular mechanisms of revealing and concealing it is crucial to resist the temptation of endowing human agency with specific attributes. Rather, the task must revolve around theorising dissent in a way that recognises how the nature of human agency cannot be separated from how we perceive human action and its ability to shape global politics.

[10] De Certeau, *Arts de Faire*, pp. 58–9

8   Resistance at the edge of language games

> We who would see beyond seeing
> see only language, that burning field.[1]

Language is one of the most fundamental aspects of human life. It is omnipresent. It penetrates every aspect of transversal politics, from the local to the global. We speak, Heidegger stresses, when we are awake and when we are asleep, even when we do not utter a single word. We speak when we listen, read or silently pursue an occupation. We are always speaking because we cannot think without language, because 'language is the house of Being', the home within which we dwell.[2]

But languages are never neutral. They embody particular values and ideas. They are an integral part of transversal power relations and of global politics in general. Languages impose sets of assumptions on us, frame our thoughts so subtly that we are mostly unaware of the systems of exclusion that are being entrenched through this process.

And yet, a language is not just a form of domination that engulfs the speaker in a web of discursive constraints, it is also a terrain of dissent, one that is not bound by the political logic of national boundaries. Language is itself a form of action – the place where possibilities for social change emerge, where values are slowly transformed, where

---

[1] Charles Wright, 'Looking Outside the Cabin Window, I Remember a Line by Li Po,' in *Chickamauga* (New York: The Noonday Press, 1995), p. 21.

[2] See Martin Heidegger, *Unterwegs zur Sprache* (Stuttgart: Verlag Günter Neske, 1959), p. 11; *Beiträge zur Philosophie (vom Ereignis)* (Frankfurt: Vittorio Klostermann, 1989), p. 510; 'Letter on Humanism', *Basic Writings*, tr. D.F. Krell (New York: HarperCollins, 1993/1977), p. 217.

individuals carve out thinking space and engage in everyday forms of resistance. In short, language epitomises the potential and limits of discursive forms of transversal dissent.

This chapter provides the theoretical basis necessary to appreciate the far-reaching political and transversal potential that is entailed in everyday forms of dissent that engage the linguistic constitution of global politics. The subsequent, final chapter will then examine, through an additional reading of the events that led to the fall of the Berlin Wall, the practical potential of such dissident practices.

To scrutinise the role of language in global politics is not simply to examine the clash of values between different national languages. Interactions between them, as for instance in translating activities at diplomatic summits, is of course a central aspect of international relations. But the political struggle over language also occurs in an array of other, far more subtle domains. Consider how a key event in global politics, such as the fall of the Berlin Wall, can be represented through different types of speech, each of which embodies a subjective but discursively objectified way of looking at the world. The turbulent events of 1989 can, for instance, be understood through the vocabulary of high politics, which revolves around great power relations and diplomatic negotiations; or through the vocabulary of strategic studies, which stresses military capacities, state repression and relations of coercive force; or through the vocabulary of international political economy, which places emphasis on market performances and their impact on political stability; or through the vocabulary of peace studies, which focuses on popular dissent and its ability to uproot systems of domination; or through the vocabulary of feminist theory, which illuminates the gendered dimensions of crumbling walls; or through the vocabulary of the common men and women in the street, which epitomises the daily frustrations of living in a suffocating society; or through any other vocabulary that expresses the subjective dimensions of interpreting events. In each case, though, the specific vocabulary that is used embodies and objectifies a particularly, discursively embedded world-view – one that is inherently political, even though it presents its view-points, often convincingly, as unbiased representations of the real. But all of these view-points, no matter how detached and impartial they seem, do more than merely interpret the events that led to the collapse of the Berlin Wall. In rendering

216

it meaningful, they are not only describing and representing, they are actually intervening in the events.[3]

A sustained engagement with the philosophy of language is necessary to recognise the potential for transversal social change that is entailed in dissident practices that interfere with the linguistically entrenched objectification of global politics. This chapter is, of course, unable to survey this complex issue in an exhaustive way. The focus will rest with two authors, Nietzsche and Wittgenstein, who represent key elements of an approach that perceives language not as a way of representing the world, but as an activity, a way of life. An engagement with this approach serves to prepare the ground for a practical and more overtly political reading of language and its relation to transversal struggles. Language, then, is no longer seen as a mere medium of communication. It is also the very site where politics is carried out. Critiquing practices of global politics is thus a process that cannot be separated from critiquing the languages through which these practices have become normalised and objectified. To outline how such a rethinking of politics may engender human agency, this chapter focuses on dissident potentials that are entailed in the practice of writing, understood not in its narrow sense as a mere act of inscribing signs, but as everything which makes this act possible – in short, language itself.

The metaphorical structure of language as social practice

It would be far beyond the scope of this chapter to provide even a highly condensed summary of the major writings on the philosophy of language and its relevance to the analysis of transversal struggles. Ruminations about language date at least as far back as ancient Greek philosophy. More recently, differences have been particularly pronounced between an Anglo-Saxon tradition, which focuses on the logical clarification of linguistic statements, and a continental approach that pays more attention to the socially embedded dimen-

---

[3] See Gilles Deleuze and Félix Guattari, *A Thousand Plateaus: Capitalism and Schizophrenia*, tr. B. Massumi (London: The Athlone Press, 1996/1980), p. 86; and Paul Patton, 'The World Seen From Within: Deleuze and the Philosophy of Events', *Theory and Event*, 1, 1, January 1997, http://muse.jhu.edu/journals/t+ae, §§ 1–9.

sions of language, to its function of providing meaning and embedding forms of life. I will engage only with the latter tradition. But even within this more restricted domain, I cannot possibly do justice to the complexities of the debates that are being waged. My objective is limited to outlining a few central arguments that are crucial in the attempt to read transversal dissent in a way that facilitates a positive but non-essentialist conceptualisation of human agency.

Nietzsche played an important role in the debate about language, for he opened up, Foucault stresses, the possibility of connecting philosophical tasks with radical reflections on language.[4] Language, Nietzsche argues, can never provide us with pure, unmediated knowledge of the world. Thinking can at best grasp imperfect perceptions of things because a word is nothing but an image of a nerve stimulus expressed in sounds. It functions, to simplify his argument, as follows: a person's intuitive perception creates an image, then a word, then patterns of words, and finally entire linguistic and cultural systems. Each step in this chain of metaphors entails interpretations and distortions of various kinds. When we look at things around us, Nietzsche illustrates, we think we know something objective about them, something of 'the thing in itself'. But all we have are metaphors, which can never capture an essence because they express the relationship between people and things.[5] For Nietzsche, language systems are sets of prejudices that are expressed via metaphors, selectively filtered images of objects and phenomena that surround us. We cannot but live in conceptual 'prisons' that permit us to take only very narrow and sporadic glimpses at the outside world, glimpses that must entail, by definition, fundamental errors of judgement.[6]

But there is more to the problem of language than its imperfections as a medium of expression. Languages embody the relationship between people and their environment. They are part of a larger discursive struggle over meaning and interpretation, an integral element of politics. We are often not aware of this function of language. The process of forgetting that we have been conditioned by linguistically

---

[4] Michel Foucault, *Les Mots et les Choses* (Paris: Gallimard, 1966), p. 316.
[5] Friedrich Nietzsche, 'Über Wahrheit und Lüge im aussermoralischen Sinn', in J. Habermas (ed.), *Erkenntnistheoretische Schriften*, (Frankfurt: Suhrkamp, 1968/1873), esp. pp. 100–1.
[6] Friedrich Nietzsche, *Morgenröte: Gedanken über die moralischen Vorurteile* (Frankfurt: Insel Taschenbuch, 1983/1881), § 117, p. 100. See also *Die fröhliche Wissenschaft* (Frankfurt: Insel Verlag, 1982/1882), §§ 57–8, 110–12, 354–5, pp. 83–4, 127–31, 235–40.

entrenched values largely camouflages the systems of exclusion that are operative in all speech forms. We become accustomed to our distorting metaphors until we 'lie herd-like in a style obligatory for all'.[7] As a result, factuality, observation, judgement and linguistic representation blur to the point that the boundaries between them become all but effaced:

> This has given me the greatest trouble and still does: to realize that what things *are called* is incomparably more important than what they are. The reputation, name, and appearance, the usual measure and weight of a thing, what it counts for – originally almost always wrong and arbitrary, thrown over things like a dress and altogether foreign to their nature and even to their skin – all this grows from generation unto generation, merely because people believe in it, until it gradually grows to be part of the thing and turns into its very body. What at first was appearance becomes in the end, almost invariably, the essence and is effective as such.[8]

As soon as one problematises the existence of objectified values one must recognise that there cannot be authentic knowledge of the world, knowledge that is not in one way or another linked to the values of the perceiver and the language through which s/he gives meaning to social practices. Truth, Nietzsche thus says in a famous passage, is no more than 'a mobile army of metaphors, metonyms and anthropomorphisms – in short, a sum of human relations, which have been enhanced, transposed, and embellished poetically and rhetorically, and which after long use seem firm, canonical, and obligatory to a people: truths are illusions about which one has forgotten that this is what they are'.[9]

The importance of Nietzsche's position on language becomes clearer when placed in comparison with Wittgenstein's approach. While Nietzsche made language a philosophical and political issue, Wittgenstein turned philosophy and politics into the study of language. A brief elucidation of the differences between his earlier and later work, both highly influential in shaping contemporary philosophical discussions, underlines the importance of approaching language as social

---

[7] Nietzsche, 'Über Warheit und Lüge', p. 103.
[8] Nietzsche, *Die fröhliche Wissenschaft*, § 58, p. 84, tr. W. Kaufmann in *The Gay Science* (New York: Vintage Books, 1974), pp. 121–2.
[9] Nietzsche, 'Über Warheit und Lüge', p. 102, tr. W. Kaufmann as 'On Truth and Lie in an Extra-Moral Sense', in *The Portable Nietzsche* (New York: Penguin Books, 1982/ 1954), pp. 46–7.

practice, rather than a mere representation of them. Like Nietzsche, Wittgenstein believed that we can never reach something like an authentic bottom of things. We cannot advance fundamental proposi- tions because the boundaries set by language prevent us from asking further, more profound questions.[10] Wittgenstein's early work was concerned with delineating what can be said about the world and what cannot be said. For that purpose he intended to correct the short- comings of ordinary language and search for clearer forms of expres- sion. From this perspective the main task of philosophy is 'the logical clarification of thoughts'.[11] The assumption behind this search for clar- ity is that language represents the world to us, that a proposition is a 'picture of reality', 'a model of reality as we think it is'.[12] In a radical turnaround three decades later, Wittgenstein considered his earlier work on language seriously flawed and embarked on an entirely dif- ferent path.

The position of the later Wittgenstein, which is of particular relev- ance for a discursive understanding of transversal dissident practices, abandons the search for a perfectly logical language and returns words from their metaphysical use back to the context of everyday life.[13] Wittgenstein considers futile the attempt to clarify or reveal a hidden logic underlying the relationship between words and reality, for the very process of naming can only be carried out in the context of rules that are operative within an established language. These rules of naming are not embedded in a form of logic, but in social interac- tions. They are part of an ensemble of human practices from which an author cannot escape. Wittgenstein starts his journey towards this perspective by outlining the problems entailed in Augustine's approach to language, which draws a direct link between words and the objects they refer to. The words 'red apple', for example, signify a fruit labelled as apple and displaying the colour characteristic com- monly defined as red. This practice of naming may work in the case of nouns, such as 'apple', 'table' or chair', where one can point towards an object that corresponds to the word. But the issue becomes

---

[10] Ludwig Wittgenstein, *Wittgenstein's Lectures: Cambridge 1930–1932*, ed. D. Lee (Oxford: Blackwell, 1980/1931), p. 34.
[11] Ludwig Wittgenstein, *Tractatus Logico-Philosophicus*, tr. C.K. Ogden (London: Rout- ledge, 1990/1922), § 4.112, p. 77.
[12] Ibid., § 4.01, p. 63.
[13] Ludwig Wittgenstein, *Philosophische Untersuchungen*, in *Werkausgabe Band I*, (Frankfurt: Suhrkamp, 1993/1952), § 116, p. 300.

problematic with more tangible nouns, or with verbs, pronouns, pre-positions and other grammatical subtleties. For instance, one cannot point towards 'morality', 'thinking', 'whether', 'but' or 'of'. These words have no referent. They express such intangible factors as activities, functions, feelings, opinions, relationality. In short, they do not correspond to some object in the real world. They are part of a social convention, of shared linguistic rules that embody a particular approach to life.[14]

For the later Wittgenstein, then, language is no longer a picture of the world. The speaking of a language 'is part of an activity, or a form of life'.[15] This does not mean, however, that there is no life outside language. David Pears emphasises that the position of the later Wittgenstein

> is not that our view of the world owes nothing to its nature. That would be absurd. Wittgenstein's point is only that, if we try to explain our view of the world by saying something about its nature, what we say will necessarily belong to our view of it. We have no independent standpoint from which to assess the relation between our usual standpoint and the world.[16]

From this perspective, one does not try to grasp the meaning and representational aspects of words, but instead pays attention to their function, to the 'workings of our language'.[17] Wittgenstein uses the term 'language game' to draw attention to the ways in which languages are part of culturally specific forms of life. There are countless language games that come and go. He mentions such examples as giving orders and obeying them, translating from one language to another, or asking, thanking, cursing, greeting, praying.[18]

An approach that perceives language as human activity, rather than a way of categorising phenomena, opens a whole range of opportunities to study the relationship between language and human agency. Hanna Pitkin, for instance, shows how our understanding of action may be enriched by asking no longer what action is or how it functions, but how we talk about it, how language games guide the implementation of this particular aspect of practice. Language thus becomes

---

[14] Ibid., §§ 1–15, pp. 237–44.
[15] Ibid., § 23, p. 250.
[16] David Pears, *The False Prison: A Study of the Development of Wittgenstein's Philosophy*, vol. I (Oxford: Clarendon Press, 1987), p. 12.
[17] Wittgenstein, *Philosophische Untersuchungen*, § 109, p. 298.
[18] Ibid., § 23, p. 150.

action itself because 'we use language not merely to talk about action, but to act – to carry on actions, to teach actions, to plan or produce actions, to assess actions done and redress any ways in which they have gone wrong'.[19]

With Wittgenstein, language is revealed as one of the most central aspects of our lives and, by extension, of politics. It is self-evident that in today's age of globalisation this political dimension entails very explicit transversal components. At a time when media-networks and other technological features facilitate an immediate and global flow of information, the political struggle over language is a worldwide struggle. Language has thus become one of the central features that fuses the local with the global, and elevates the transversal linkages between them to the site where many decisive political battles are waged. The key is to recognise the centrality of these largely inaudible sites of contestation, and to find ways of understanding how they shape our lives.

Critique of language as an everyday form of global resistance

How exactly can a Wittgensteinean understanding of language illuminate the transversal dissident potential that is entailed in interfering with everyday forms of speech? How can language turn into a discursive form of dissent?

Language and discourse overlap in many ways, but are by no means the same. Michael Shapiro points out how a postmodern interpretation of global politics emphasises 'discourse rather than language because the concept of discourse implies a concern with the meaning- and value-producing practices in language rather than simply the relationship between utterances and their referents'.[20] The concept of discourse may thus illuminate the arbitrariness of the seemingly inevitable evolution and conduct of global politics. It is a way of examining, in Mikhail Bakhtin's words, 'language in its concrete living totality'.[21]

---

[19] Hanna Fenichel Pitkin, *Wittgenstein and Justice: On the Significance of Ludwig Wittgenstein for Social and Political Thought* (Berkeley: University of California Press, 1972), p. 164.

[20] Michael J. Shapiro, 'Textualizing Global Politics', in J. Der Derian and M.J. Shapiro (eds.), *International/Intertextual Relations: Postmodern Readings of World Politics* (Lexington, Mass: Lexington Books, 1989), p. 14.

[21] Mikhail Bakhtin, *Problems of Dostoevsky's Poetics*, tr. C. Emerson (Minneapolis: University of Minnesota Press, 1984), p. 181.

Discourse and language are forms of concealment that offer opportunities to reveal. They are transversal forms of domination that offer
opportunities to resist and transform. These practices of concealing
and revealing must be examined in their cyclical existence. Without
paying attention to the domineering aspects of language one cannot
understand its potential for resistance. This is not unproblematic. For
many authors the subjugating power of language is overwhelming.
According to Heidegger 'man acts as though he were the shaper and
master of language, while in fact language remains the master of
man'.[22] Benjamin Lee Whorf, in his path-breaking study of Hopi con-
ceptualisations of time and space, object and subject, argues that the
individual is utterly unaware of the power of language to construct
his/her consciousness and 'constrained completely within its
unbreakable bonds'.[23] Roland Barthes goes even further in his notorious remarks during the inaugural lecture at the Collège de France. For
him, freedom can exist only outside language. But languages have
no outside. A language always imposes. It is, in this sense, 'neither
reactionary nor progressive, it is simply fascist, for fascism does not
prevent speech, it forces speech'.[24] Barthes' claim, largely dismissed as
polemics, has the merit of reminding us that there is always an aspect
of subjugation in the use of languages, no matter how objective, neutral and open they may appear.

George Orwell's fictional world provides a perfect illustration for
this subjugating power of languages. Consider how Oceania introduced Newspeak to accommodate its official ideology, Ingsoc. New
words were invented and undesirable ones either eliminated or
stripped of unorthodox meanings. The objective of this exercise was
that 'when Newspeak had been adopted once and for all and Old-
speak forgotten, a heretical thought – that is, a thought diverging from
the principles of Ingsoc – should be literally unthinkable'.[25] By then
history would be rewritten to the point that even if fragments of documents from the past were still to surface, they simply would be unintelligible and untranslatable.

[22] Martin Heidegger, '. . .Poetically Man Dwells. . .', in *Poetry, Language, Thought*, tr. A. Hofstadter (New York: Harper & Row, 1971/1951), p. 215.
[23] Benjamin Lee Whorf, *Language, Thought, and Reality* (Cambridge, Mass.: The MIT Press, 1974/1956) p. 256.
[24] Roland Barthes, *Leçon Inaugurale de la Chaire de Sémiologie Littéraire du Collège de France* (Paris: Editions du Seuil, 1978), pp. 14–15.
[25] George Orwell, 'The Principles of Newspeak', Appendix to *Nineteen Eighty-Four* (Oxford: Clarendon Press, 1984/1949), p. 417.

We find similar dynamics at work in the more 'real' (but equally Orwellian) world of defence intellectuals. Carol Cohn demonstrates how the particular language that they employ not only removes them from the 'reality' of nuclear war, but also constructs a new world of abstraction that makes it impossible to think or express certain concerns related to feelings, morality, or simply 'peace'. The consequences, Cohn stresses, are fateful because the language of defence intellectuals has been elevated to virtually the only legitimate medium of debating security issues.[26] The fact that this language is male dominated is widely recognised at least since Dale Spender has claimed that the English language is man made and largely under male control. This, she argues, has constructed language and thought patterns that define the male as norm and the female as deviant. Spender reinforces her point by showing how the introduction and legitimisation of 'man' and 'he' as terms to denote both male and female 'was the result of a deliberate policy and was consciously intended to promote the primacy of the male as a category'.[27]

Noam Chomsky provides another example of the links between language and transversal politics. He argues that mainstream discourses linguistically presented the American 'involvement' in Vietnam such that the actual thought of an 'aggression' or 'invasion' was unthinkable, and this despite readily available evidence in support of such an interpretation.[28] The same linguistic dynamic of exclusion is at work in international relation theory, where the dominant realist language renders discussions of epistemology virtually impossible. Consider how Robert Gilpin criticises the post-structuralist language of Richard Ashley by declaring entirely unintelligible his claim that 'the objective truth of the discourse lies within and is produced by the discourse itself'.[29] The concepts used in this sentence not only make perfect sense to any critical social theorist, but also are essential for the articulation of an epistemological critique. Yet, read through the Newspeak of scientific realism, the very idea of epistemological critique is a her-

[26] Carol Cohn, 'Sex and Death in the Rational World of Defense Intellectuals', in L.R. Forcey (ed.), *Peace: Meanings, Politics, Strategies* (New York: Praeger, 1989), pp. 39–71.
[27] Dale Spender, *Man Made Language* (London: Routledge & Kegan Paul, 1985/1980), p. 150.
[28] Noam Chomsky, *Knowledge of Language: Its Nature, Origin, and Use* (New York: Praeger, 1986), pp. 276–87.
[29] Robert G. Gilpin, 'The Richness of the Tradition of Political Realism', in Robert O. Keohane (ed.), *Neorealism and its Critics* (New York: Columbia University Press, 1986) p. 303.

etic thought and the sentence thus becomes simply untranslatable. The language of realism has rendered any challenge to its own political foundations unthinkable.

How can one turn language from a system of exclusion to a practice of inclusion, from a method of domination to an instrument of resistance? And how can one appreciate the transversal dimensions that are entailed in these sites of everyday struggle? The starting point lies with what is aptly called *Sprachkritik* in German. Literally translated as 'critique of language', *Sprachkritik* is, at least according to the linguist Fritz Mauthner, 'the most important task (*Geschäft*) of thinking humanity'. The poet Paul Valéry probably captured its objective best when claiming that 'the secret of well founded thinking is based on suspicion towards language'.[30] If challenges to practices of domination and attempts to open up thinking space are to avoid being absorbed by the dominant discourse, then they must engage in a struggle with conventionally recognised linguistic practices, or at least with the manner in which these practices have been constituted. The form of speaking and writing becomes as important as their content. Dissent cannot be separated from critique of language, for it remains ineffective as long as it does not interfere with the ways in which linguistic systems of exclusion constitute and objectivise social practices.

But can a language so easily be appropriated as a tool of dissent against its own subjugating power? Is it enough, as Nietzsche suggests, to 'create new names, estimations and probabilities to create eventually new "things."'[31] Of course not.

One can never be free within language. One can never break free from language. The point is, rather, to acknowledge that an individual has no possibility to function as an authentic perceiver or agent, that the spaces for action opened up by critique are still circumscribed by the larger boundaries of linguistic structures. Moreover, critique of language must be careful not be trapped in an idealism that suggests the world exists only because it is perceived by our mind, that objects outside this mental sphere have no qualities of their own. Such a working assumption would go astray in a futile search for the perfect language and, by doing so, fall back into the logical positivism from which the later Wittgenstein so carefully tried to escape. Because there

---

[30] Mauthner and Valéry cited in Hans-Martin Gauger, 'Sprachkritik', in *Deutsche Akademie für Sprache und Dichtung*, January 1991, pp. 23–4.
[31] Nietzsche, *Die fröhliche Wissenschaft*, § 58, p. 84.

is no direct and logical correspondence between words and meaning, between a name and a thing, a spear-heading into unexplored linguistic terrains can only be socially meaningful if it stretches the rules of existing language games while never losing sight of the ways in which these language games constitute and are constituted by concrete forms of life.

The point, then, is to articulate resistance at the edge of language games, that is, to avoid lifting words out of their social and dialogical context while, at the same time, exploring to the utmost the unstable and transformative nature of languages. This is best done, I argue, by interfering with the ways in which languages constitute sites of political practice, sites where realities are formed, reformed, legitimised and objectivised through a series of transversal discursive dynamics.

To illustrate the dissident potential contained in language the focus now turns more specifically to practices of writing. A few preliminary remarks are necessary for this purpose. A prevalent position in the philosophy of language suggests, exemplified by Wittgenstein and de Saussure, that speaking and listening constitute the key to understanding language. What, then, is the exact role of the written word? Derrida is of help here, especially his engagement with de Saussure's influential theory of linguistics. For Saussure, the study of the abstract concept of language (*le langage*) can roughly be divided into two subject areas, *la parole*, which are individually spoken or written utterances, and *la langue*, the particular socialised language system that establishes the codes and conventions by which these individual messages can be realised.[32] Derrida points out that the term *la parole*, literally translated as speech, gives clear precedence to voice, hearing, sound and breath. This Saussurean position constitutes writing as a simple supplement to the spoken word, as an activity that consists merely of derivative functions.[33] Derrida vehemently rejects as ethnocentric the Western practice of logocentrism, the study of language based on phonetics, on the spoken word, the logos. He even goes as far as claiming that writing, defined in a broad sense, came before speech. Once we free ourselves from the artificially constructed link between writing and a phonetic alphabet, we recognise writing in

[32] Ferdinand de Saussure, *Cours de linguistique général* (Paris: Payot, 1987/1915), pp. 138–9.
[33] Jacques Derrida, *Of Grammatology*, tr. G.C. Spivak (Baltimore: The Johns Hopkins University Press, 1976/1967), pp. 7–8, 30–44.

inscriptions of any kind, such as in the pictographic, the ideographic or the hieroglyphic.[34] One can, of course, argue with such a position, but this is besides the point here.

Two of Derrida's positions on language are particularly important for an appreciation of the dissident potential contained in the written word. First, he claims, rather boldly, that the written word exceeds in some ways the spoken one.[35] Speech may be more elusive than writing for it can be erased or refuted. It is not engraved once and for all. But face-to-face speech is often severely constrained by the necessity to reinforce hegemonic appearances, to restrain one's criticism in the face of power. The process of writing, by contrast, is removed from the immediacy and performative pressure of face-to-face speech. Thus, writing creates enough distance from the eye of power to facilitate critique and nurture the confidence to express it. Second, and more importantly, Derrida convincingly argues that writing designates 'not only the physical gestures of literal pictographic and ideographic inscription, but also the totality of what makes it possible'.[36] Writing thus stands for everything that enables it, in short, language itself. Scrutinising the forms of dissent that are hidden in practices of writing has thus relevance beyond this immediate realm, for it represents the potential for discursive and transversal resistance contained in language per se.

Writing dissent I: disenchanting the concept

The domain of global politics contains an unlimited number of terrains that offer possibilities for linguistic forms of dissent to interfere with the course of transversal struggles. Before scrutinising a particular, linguistically based site of transversal dissent (the subject of the subsequent chapter), it is necessary to theorise in more detail how the written word offers opportunities to engender human agency. For this purpose an engagement with the work of Theodor Adorno is useful, particularly with his reading of Nietzsche. Adorno is ideally suited for this task because he epitomises both the strengths and dangers of writing dissent.

Adorno's approach to language emerges out of opposition to what

---

[34] For a concise discussion see John Docker, *Postmodernism and Popular Culture* (Cambridge: Cambridge University Press, 1994), pp. 135–43.

[35] Derrida, *Of Grammatology*, pp. 8–9.

[36] Ibid., p. 9.

he calls identity thinking. 'To think,' he claims, 'is to identify.'[37] It is a process through which we try to understand the bewildering world that surrounds us. Thinking expresses a will to truth, a desire to control and impose order upon random and idiosyncratic events. When we think we identify choices, privilege one interpretation over others, and, often without knowing it, exclude what does not fit into the way we want to see things. There is no escape from the subjective dimension of thought, no possibility of extracting pure facts from observation.

Thinking cannot be done without language. And language, of course, has always already established a preconceived conceptual order prior to what thinking is trying to understand.[38] In fact, Adorno even claims that before dealing with specific speech contents, languages mould a thought such that it gets drawn into subordination even where it appears to resist this tendency.[39] Identity thinking, he points out, is the form of thinking that ignores these unavoidable socio-linguistic restraints. It embarks on a fatal search for essences, seeks to extract the general out of the particular and thus forces unique things into an artificial unitary system of thought.

But thinking, Adorno claims, is not only obeying the power of language and discourse. Thinking also contains critical potential, for it is in itself already a process of negating, of resisting what is forced upon it.[40] Stretching the boundaries of language games, engaging in *Sprachkritik*, is the key to realising this potential. It permits us to break loose from the claws of the established order and to venture beyond the givenness of life. Adorno's conceptual starting point for this journey is negative dialectics, the refusal to subsume the particular under the general. This entails creating thinking space without succumbing to the temptation of searching for a Hegelean synthesis, a new totalising and exclusionary system of thought that would drift us back into the dangerous waters of identity thinking. Negative dialectics is the constant awareness of non-identity. It refuses to rely upon a preconceived standpoint. It rescues and develops what does not fit into prevailing totalising practices or what may emerge as a potential alternative to

---

[37] Theodor W. Adorno, *Negative Dialektik* (Frankfurt: Suhrkamp, 1992/1966), p. 17.
[38] Ibid., p. 15.
[39] Theodor W. Adorno, *Jargon der Eigentlichkeit*, Gesammelte Schriften, vol. VI (Frankfurt: Suhrkamp, 1973/1964), p. 416.
[40] Adorno, *Negative Dialektik*, p. 28.

them.[41] Adorno tries to open up such thinking spaces through a critique of language that calls for a radical departure from both the traditional usage of concepts and the style in which they are presented.

To talk and write we need concepts to express our ideas. Yet, concepts can never entirely capture the objects they are trying to describe. A concept is always a violation, an imposition of static subjectivity upon complex, interconnected and continuously changing phenomena. A concept is part of a language game. It fulfils a variety of constantly shifting functions. The meanings that concepts produce cannot be captured by the assertion of a static link between the concept and what it represents, between the sign and what it signifies. Nietzsche has hit the nail on its head when arguing that 'all concepts that semiotically subsume entire processes defy definition. Only that which has no history can be defined'.[42] Adorno illustrates this inevitable phenomenon by showing how the judgement that one is free depends on the concept of freedom. But this concept is both less and more than the object or subject it refers to.[43] It is less because it cannot adequately assess the complexities of the individual's expectations and the contexts within which s/he seeks freedom. It is more because it imposes a particular interpretation of freedom upon and beyond the conditions for freedom sought after by the individual. Thus, Adorno argues that 'the concept of freedom always lags behind itself. As soon as it is applied empirically it ceases to be what it claims it is.'[44] Here too we hear the echo of Nietzsche, who already claimed that liberal institutions cease to be liberal as soon as they are established, that, as a result 'there is nothing more wicked and harmful to freedom than liberal institutions'.[45]

Acknowledging and dealing with the political dimension of concepts is essential in articulating an adequate understanding of transversal dynamics. But how can one resist the subjugating power of concepts. How can one turn them into tools of dissent? At least two strategies offer transformative potential. First, one can appropriate the meaning of existing concepts. Consider how German and English

---

[41] Ibid., p. 15 and 'Einleitung zum Positivismusstreit', in *Soziologische Schriften I*, Gesammelte Schriften, Vol. VIII (Frankfurt: Suhrkamp, 1972/1969), pp. 292–5.
[42] Nietzsche, *Zur Genealogie der Moral* (Frankfurt: Insel Taschenbuch, 1991/1977), pp. 71–2. See also 'Über Warheit und Lüge', pp. 101–2.
[43] Adorno, *Negative Dialektik*, p. 153.
[44] Ibid., p. 154.
[45] Nietzsche, *Götzen-Dämmerung* (Berlin: Walter de Gruyter, 1969/1889), p. 133.

speaking gay/lesbian activists were able to transform the terms *'schwul'* and 'queer', once derogative and discriminatory expressions, into positively imbued assertions of identity that created possibilities for more inclusive ways of thinking and acting.[46] In almost diametrically opposed terrains we find Australia's pre-eminent poet, Les Murray, trying to reshape and de-vilify the term 'redneck'.[47] During the East German revolution we witnessed how citizens turned the expression 'we are the people' from a dogmatic governmental claim to legitimacy into a slogan that condensed all the resentments against this claim and, indeed, into a highly effective battle cry that contributed substantially to the downfall of the authoritarian regime. In the domain of international theory we can observe struggles over the meaning of such concepts as 'state', 'anarchy', 'hegemony', 'diplomacy', 'security' and 'ethics'. Take the concept of 'power'. Some traditional realists view(ed) it, in Hans Morgenthau's words, as 'man's control over the minds and actions of other men'.[48] In this definition, power is the capacity to act, something someone (a man) has and others do not. But diverging opinions pressed for a more broad conceptualisation, one that is also linked to functions of consent and legitimacy. Others again view power as a complex structure of actions that permeate every aspect of society. Power then is, as chapter 4 has demonstrated, not simply a subjugating force, but at least as much an enabling opportunity.

A second dissident strategy consists of creating new concepts in order to avoid the subjugating power of existing ones. The challenge of conceptualising forms of dissent that transgress the spatial givenness of international politics is a case in point. How is one to designate this novel political dynamic and the transformed context within which they unfold? The term 'international', initially coined by Jeremy Bentham, appears inadequate, for it semantically endows the nation-state with a privileged position – a privilege that no longer corresponds, at least in many instances, to the realities of global politics. In an effort to obtain an understanding of the word that reaches beyond state-centric visions, various authors have searched for more

---

[46] See, for example, Lisa Duggan, 'Making it Perfectly Queer', *Socialist Review*, 22, 1, 1992, 11–31; and Steven Epstein, 'A Queer Encounter: Sociology and the Study of Sexuality', *Sociological Theory*, 12, 2, July 1994, 188–202.

[47] Les Murray, *Subhuman Redneck Poems* (Potts Point, NSW: Duffy & Snellgrove, 1996).

[48] Hans J. Morgenthau, *Politics among Nations: The Struggle for Power and Peace* (New York: Alfred Knopf, 1949), p. 26.

adequate concepts. R.B.J. Walker, for instance, speaks not of international relations, but of 'world politics', which he defines 'as an array of political processes that extend beyond the territoriality and competence of a single political community and affect large proportions of humanity'.[49] Christine Sylvester employs the term 'relations international', thereby placing the emphasis on the various relational aspects of world politics, rather than the perceived centrality of nation-states.[50] James Rosenau scrutinises the domain of 'post-international politics' – a sphere in which interactions are carried out not by states and non-state actors, but by 'sovereignty bound' and 'sovereignty free' actors.[51] While endorsing these various conceptual innovations, this book has primarily relied on the term 'transversal' to capture the increasingly diffused and cross-territorial nature of contemporary dissident practices.

New concepts can help to widen the purview of traditional perceptions of international relations, but it is important to emphasise that the issue of representation can never be solved, or even understood, at a purely terminological level. From the perspective of the later Wittgenstein, there is no logical and authentic relationship between, for instance, the meaning of term 'international' and a state-centric view of the world. 'International' is only what we make of the term. The main problem is a discursively entrenched language game in which the term 'international' embodies social practices that assign nation-states priority and thus legitimise and objectivise ensuing political practices, no matter how violent they may be.

Knowing the dangers of exclusion and objectification inherent in any form of conceptualising does not release us from the need to employ concepts in order to express our thoughts. What, then, is the point? Adorno claims that we must not turn the necessity to operate with concepts into the virtue of assigning them priority.[52]

The daring task is to open up with concepts what does not fit into concepts, to resist their distorting power and return the conceptual to the non-conceptual. This disenchantment with the concept is the anti-

[49] R.B.J. Walker, 'History and Structure in the Theory of International Relations', *Millennium*, 18, 2, 1989, pp. 181–2; *Inside/outside: International Relations as Political Theory* (Cambridge: Cambridge University Press, 1993), pp. 99–103.
[50] Christine Sylvester, *Feminist Theory and International Relations in a Postmodern Era* (Cambridge: Cambridge University Press, 1994).
[51] James N. Rosenau, *Turbulence in World Politics: A Theory of Change and Continuity* (Princeton: Princeton University Press, 1990).
[52] Adorno, *Negative Dialektik*, p. 23.

dote of critical philosophy. It prevents the concept from becoming an absolute in itself.[53] The first step towards disenchanting the concept is simply refusing to define it monologically. Concepts should achieve meaning only gradually, in relation to each other. Adorno even goes as far as intentionally using the same concept in different ways in order to liberate it from the narrow definition that language itself had already imposed upon it.[54] That contradictions could arise out of this practice does not bother Adorno. Indeed, he considers them essential. One cannot eliminate the contradictory, the fragmentary and the discontinuous. Contradictions are only contradictions if one assumes the existence of a prior universal standard of reference. What is different appears as divergent, dissonant, and negative only as long as our consciousness strives for a totalising standpoint, which we must avoid if we are to escape the dangers of identity thinking.[55]

Just as reality is fragmented, we need to think in fragments. Unity is not found by evening out discontinuities. Contradictions are to be preferred over artificially constructed meanings and the silencing of underlying conflicts. Thus Adorno advocates writing in fragments, such that the resulting text appears as if it always could be interrupted, cut off abruptly, any time, any place.[56] Here too we hear the advice of Nietzsche, who recommends that one should approach deep problems like taking a cold bath, 'quickly into them and quickly out again'.[57] The belief that one does not reach deep enough this way, he claims, is simply the superstition of those who fear cold water. But Nietzsche's bath has already catapulted us into the vortex of the next linguistic terrain of resistance, the question of style.

Writing dissent II: thoughts on the substance of form

Conventional wisdom holds that good writing is concise, clear and to the point. Many activists, for instance, stress how important ease in communication is for purposes of organising popular resistance. Gramsci emphasised time and again the crucial importance of

[53] Adorno, *Negative Dialektik*, pp. 23–5, 156–8; 'Der Essay als Form', in *Noten zur Literatur*, Gesammelte Schriften, vol. XI (Frankfurt: Suhrkamp, 1974/1958), pp. 9–33.
[54] Adorno, 'Der Essay als Form', pp. 19–20.
[55] Adorno, *Negative Dialektik*, pp. 17–18.
[56] Adorno, 'Der Essay als Form', pp. 24–5.
[57] Nietzsche, *Die fröhliche Wissenschaft*, § 381, p. 278.

bridging the communicative gap between intellectuals and the working class. Philosophy, he argued, is not a strange or difficult thing, not something that is confined to the activities of specialists.[58] The Brazilian educator Paulo Freire argued along the same line. For him questions of language and human agency are directly linked. They are essential in the attempt to unveil the dehumanised world of oppression, to transform the dispossessed into responsible subject that can enter and forge historical processes.[59] If an intellectual speaks in a language that is not attuned to the concrete situation of the people s/he is trying to reach, then the talk is nothing but alienated and alienating rhetoric.[60] The ones who are devoted to liberation but unable to communicate with the people only impose a monologue, the very instrument of domination and domestication from which the people have to liberate themselves in order the make the transition from object to subject.[61] Thus, the intellectual's task is not to preach to the people, but to listen to them, to enter into a dialogue and open up space for the people to think and act themselves. To facilitate this process, the intellectual must trust in the oppressed and their ability to reason. S/he must understand the day-to-day conditions that frame the language of the people. Only words that have meaning in this context contain a potential for change. All other words are not true words, they are deprived of the dimension of action, their transformative power.[62]

But is the link between language and human agency as unproblematic as Freire suggests? Is clear language all that is needed to express dissent? Or is not clear language only clear because we have acquired fluency in it over the years, because we have rehearsed it time and again as part of a system of shared meanings that channels our thinking into particular directions? Do we not appreciate clarity only because we have already been drawn into a language game that is integral to the discursive practices of domination that silently frame and subjugate our mind? Adorno certainly thinks so, and his argument is compelling, at least up to a certain point.

---

[58] Antonio Gramsci, *Prison Notebooks*, tr. Q. Hoare and G.N. Smith (New York: International Publishers, 1985/1971), pp. 323, 347–7.

[59] Paulo Freire, *Pedagogy of the Oppressed*, tr. M.B. Ramos (New York: Continuum, 1983/1970), pp. 20–40.

[60] Ibid., p. 85.

[61] Ibid., pp. 47–52.

[62] Ibid., pp. 28, 38–9, 42, 53, 75–7, 85–6.

We easily forget, for instance, that the language of realism, which has for long dominated the study of global politics, only appears clear because we have acquired familiarity with it. Abstract realist concepts like 'unit', 'actor', 'system', 'regime', 'Realpolitik', 'dependent/independent variable' and 'relative/absolute gains', are not clear and intelligible by some objective standard, but only because they have been rehearsed time and again as part of a system of shared meanings that channels our thinking into particular directions. By contrast, the new terminology applied by recent critiques of international relations theory is often perceived as needless jargon, assaults on language,[63] a rambling and conceptual menace that is employed 'not to reinforce argument, but to compensate for the lack of it'.[64] However, the disturbing new concepts in question – such as 'genealogy', 'foundationalism', 'reification', 'logocentrism', or 'incommensurability' – only appear dissonant because they diverge from or subvert the linguistic conventions that legitimise dominant perceptions of global politics. But this is only the beginning. Nietzsche and Adorno suggest that the question of style reaches much further.

For Adorno, standard modes of communication are inadequate to express a critical thought. He even goes as far as arguing – rather provocatively – that clear language is domination. It imposes closure. Even if critical, an argument presented in a straightforward writing style can, at best, articulate an alternative position and replace one orthodoxy with another one. It is unable to open up thinking space. If a reader is to break free from the subtle repression that the dominant discourse disguises through its linguistic practices, s/he has to struggle with a text, grapple for the meaning of words, and be torn away, painfully, from a deeply entrenched form of communicative subjugation. If a reader is to come to terms with her/his own prejudices, a text must challenge, puzzle, shake, uproot, disturb, even frustrate and torment her/him.

'Slack and sleeping senses must be addressed with thunder and heavenly fireworks.'[65] So preaches Zarathustra and so believes Adorno, who defies all Cartesian methodological rules and rejects as dangerous the proposition that one ought to move from the simple to

---

[63] Gilpin, 'The Richness of the Tradition of Political Realism', p. 303.
[64] Fred Halliday, *Rethinking International Relations* (Vancouver: UBC Press, 1994), p. 39.
[65] Nietzsche, 'Thus Spoke Zarathustra', tr. W. Kaufmann in *The Portable Nietzsche*, p. 205.

the complex and that one must demonstrate clearly and explicitly each step that leads to the articulation of a particular idea.[66] He justifies this unusual position with the argument that the true value of a thought is measured according to its distance from the continuities of orthodox knowledge. This is to say that the closer a thought gets to the generally accepted standards of writing and representing, the more it loses its dialectical and antithetical function. Adorno thus attempts to open up thinking space by writing in an unusual style, unusual in word choice, concept usage, syntax, sentence flow and many other aspects.[67] Style is at the core of Adorno's thought. It leads him to a position where, expressed in Eagleton's ironically disapproving voice, every sentence is 'forced to work overtime; each phrase must become a little master-piece or miracle of dialectics, fixing a thought in the second before it disappears into its own contradictions'.[68]

Adorno's provocative and controversial claims on language visualise important terrains of dissent, but they also engender various dangers. The difficulty of his style severely limits possibilities for the expression of dissent and human agency. As long as a critical text is only accessible to a small circle of intellectuals who invest the time to decipher it, solve its puzzles and explore its contradictions, critical knowledge will continue to reside in the margins, hegemonies will remain unchallenged, and practices of dominating will persist. The semantics of negative dialectics do not constitute a suitable linguistic tool of dissent at a time when the spread of global media networks increasingly fuse information with the language of entertainment. Besides being obscure, Adorno also comes dangerously close to a linguistic idealism or a heroic avant-garde elitism. By freeing himself radically from the totalising forces of identity thinking, he paradoxic-ally runs the danger of falling back into the positivist pitfalls from whence he is so desperately trying to escape, for his position on style implies, much like the one espoused by the early Wittgenstein, that ordinary language is insufficient, in need of correction.

The point is not to search for a more perfect representation of global

[66] Adorno, 'Der Essay als Form', pp. 22–5.
[67] Adorno, *Minima Moralia: Reflexionen aus dem beschädigten Leben* (Frankfurt: Suhrkamp, 1980/1951), pp. 88–9; *Jargon der Eigentlichkeit*, pp. 440–2. For discussions of the crucial importance that Adorno grants to the question of style see Gillian Rose, *The Melan-choly Science: An Introduction to the Thought of Theodor W. Adorno* (London: MacMillan, 1978), pp. 11–26.
[68] Terry Eagleton, *The Ideology of the Aesthetic* (Oxford: Basil Blackwell, 1990), p. 342.

political realities, but to acknowledge that language games are an integral part of transversal politics. Peter Bürger illustrates the centrality of this problem when comparing Adorno's and Lukács' approach to aesthetics. Adorno advocates avant-gardiste art in a radical form that rejects all false reconciliation with what exists. Lukács, by contrast, opposes such a form of dissent, for it remains too abstract, void of historical perspective, and thus unable to promote social change.[69] An adequate understanding of linguistically based transversal dissent accepts some elements of the Adornean position but has overall many more parallels with Lukács' rejection of an avant-garde search for radical and authentic expression. Words, even if they dissolve into their own contradictions, can never be more than what we make out of them. One can never guess how a word functions, Wittgenstein claims. One must first examine how it is used and then learn from it.[70]

Any attempt to assert human agency through a critique of language that reaches beyond the ways in which words are embedded in their social and dialogical contexts, is in danger of ending up in an idealist cul de sac. Adorno runs this danger when he searches for utopia in avant-garde aesthetics. This is the defeatist side of Adorno, which deplores that truth can never be plausible or directly communicable to everyone because each communicative step distorts and falsifies.[71] But one can reject Adorno's futile search for perfect expression and still accept the importance of the issue that feeds his dilemma, namely the recognition that writing styles, and language in general, are intrinsically linked to politics.

Writing styles are issues of substance, sites of contestation. Critique of global politics cannot be separated from a critique of the language through which the constitution and conduct of global politics has become objectified. The form of writing is as important as its content. Indeed, form is content.

Any dissident practice that seeks to resist the encroachment of thought by dominant discursive practices must grapple with this issue. This does not mean that a writing style necessarily needs to be difficult. The key is to write within the communicative restraints of

---

[69] Peter Bürger, *Theory of the Avant-Garde*, tr. M. Shaw (Minneapolis: University of Minnesota Press, 1984), p. 88.
[70] Wittgenstein, *Philosophische Untersuchungen*, § 340, p. 387.
[71] Adorno, *Negative Dialektik*, pp. 50–2.

existing language games while at the same time pushing their boundaries. To recognise this necessity is to do away with the myth that
dissent can be articulated best by relying merely on a clear writing
style. Michael Shapiro is among the authors who have most convincingly argued – and demonstrated – that resorting to this 'old epistemology of "clarity"' fails to recognise and deal with practices of
domination that are embedded in language.[72] He draws attention to
the importance of style, to how literary forms of writing, that is those
who are self-conscious about their own figural practices, constitute
important politicising practices:

> Literary discourse. . . is hyper-politicising. By producing alternative
> forms of thought *in* language, it makes a political point. By virtue of
> its departures from linguistic normality, it points to the way that
> institutions hold individuals within a linguistic web. But it goes
> beyond this demonstration. It deforms image to show how accepted
> models of the real are productions of grammatical and rhetorical con-
> structions, and it forms antagonistic imagery that provides sites for
> resistance to domination.[73]

There are, of course, many literary styles that have the potential to
serve as discursive forms of dissent. Before focusing in detail on one
of them – poetry – I illustrate, via a few examples, the range of possibilities for exploring the crucial links between form and substance,
writing and dissent, literature and politics.

APHORISMS: Nietzsche and Adorno are, as already mentioned,
among various authors who write in fragments to avoid practices
of domination that emerge from totalising representations of the
world. This substantive dimension of style is why many authors
consider Nietzsche's resort to aphorisms as one of the most important
contributions of his work. Just as Eagleton describes Adorno's
language as 'rammed up against silence where the reader has no
sooner registered the one-sidedness of some proposition than the
opposite is immediately proposed',[74] one never finds Nietzsche engaging in concealment by upholding the correctness of a viewpoint

---

[72] Michael J. Shapiro, 'Literary Production as Political Practice', in his *Language and
Politics* (Oxford: Basil Blackwell, 1984), p. 230. See also his *Language and Political
Understanding: The Politics of Discursive Practices* (New Haven: Yale University Press,
1981).
[73] Ibid., p. 239.
[74] Eagleton, *The Ideology of the Aesthetic*, p. 342.

without drawing attention to its contradictions, to the voices that linger in its shadows. This is why many prominent commentators, from Thomas Mann to Giorgio Colli, argue that to take Nietzsche literally is to be lost, for 'he said everything, and the opposite of everything'.[75]

The key to Nietzsche does not lie in his viewpoints, but in the style through which he opened up thinking space, celebrated diversity and came to terms with the death of God. His thought is inseparable from his particular writing style. There are, of course, many other authors who relied upon aphorisms to push the boundaries of writing. Wittgenstein, for example, recognised the dangers of welding his ideas into an artificial whole, of forcing them against their will into an unbroken chain of coherent sequences. The best he could do, Wittgenstein claimed, would always remain philosophical remarks, fragments that defy the logic of a totality.[76]

THE ESSAY: An old practice of dissident writing is the essay, which defies totalising forms of representation by refusing to rely on methodological procedures that pretend to lead towards an authoritative form of knowledge. Montaigne was one of the earliest authors who employed this style to express his sceptical Humanism. Other well-known representatives are the early Frankfurt School writers, in particular Lukács, Benjamin and Adorno.

An essay must fulfil a number of strict requirements, or so at least argues Adorno, who considers this genre as 'the critical form par excellence'.[77] An essay is explicitly anti-authoritarian insofar as it recognises no first principles, no standpoint outside itself. It negates everything that is systematic, that drifts towards a totalising claim. To acknowledge that there are no transcending forms of knowledge is to accept the historical dimension of truth contents, it is to abandon the illusion of thought breaking through layers of masking facades towards some sort of objectivity.[78] The result, then, is a form of writing that makes its hostility towards totalising thought an integral part of

[75] Thomas Mann and Giorgio Colli, cited in Volker Gerhardt, 'Philosophie als Schicksal', postscript to Nietzsche's *Jenseits von Gut und Böse* (Stuttgart: Philipp Reclam, 1988/1886), p. 236. See also David B. Allison (ed.), *The New Nietzsche: Contemporary Styles of Interpretation* (Cambridge, Mass.: The MIT Press, 1990/1985).
[76] Wittgenstein, *Philosophische Untersuchungen*, p. 231.
[77] Adorno, 'Der Essay als Form', p. 27.
[78] Ibid., pp. 10, 19.

its existence. The essay begins where it wants to begin, discusses what it wants to discuss, ends where it feels itself completed, rather than where there is nothing left to say.[79] Such positions on style are, of course, often dismissed as relativism. Adorno counters by arguing that the essay intends to free thought from its arbitrariness precisely by accepting arbitrariness into the essay's own procedures, instead of masking it as spontaneity.[80]

THE NOVEL: There is room for diversity in the novel, a genre that is, like aphorisms and the essay, freed from the compulsion to present the world from only one viewpoint. Lukács points out that in the novel a totality can only exist in abstract terms. The relatively independent and unconnected parts of a novel endow it with an unfinished form, one that is always in the process of becoming.[81] Mikhail Bakhtin argues along the same lines and considers the novel as an anarchic, insubordinate genre, a site of popular resistance against the hegemony of official and centralised authority. Here too style is considered not an innocent or neutral aesthetic dimension, but a political expression, an 'epistemic choice'.[82] Bakhtin deals specifically with Dostoevsky and the so-called polyphonic novel, a genre of writing that refuses to rely on a unifying authorial position and instead permits a 'plurality of independent and umerged voices and consciousnessses, a genuine polyphony of fully valid voices'.[83]

The transversal application of these subversive stylistic devises is, of course, unlimited. We know, for instance, of contemporary African novelists, like Gabriel Okara, Chinua Achebe, Yvonne Vera or Ayi Kwei Armah, who 'decolonise' the English language in an attempt to break free from the repressing and transversal forces of imperialism. This entails, as in the case of Armah, deliberately handling directions and time not through European concepts, but

---

[79] Ibid., pp. 10, 26.
[80] Ibid., p. 27.
[81] Georg Lukács, *The Theory of the Novel*, tr. A. Bostock (Cambridge, Mass.: The MIT Press, 1971/1920), pp. 70–83. See also J.M. Bernstein, *The Philosophy of the Novel: Lukács, Marxism and the Dialectics of Form* (Minneapolis: University of Minnesota Press, 1984).
[82] Josephine Donovan, 'Style and Power', in D.M. Bauer and S.J. McKinstry (eds.), *Feminism, Bakhtin, and the Dialogic* (Albany: State University of New York Press, 1991), pp. 85–6.
[83] Bakhtin, *Problems of Dostoevsky's Poetics*, p. 6.

via localised terms like 'the falling' and 'the rising' (instead of west and east) or 'seasons' and 'moons' (instead of years and months).[84] This simple example of stylistic dissent illustrates that the boundaries of language can be pushed without relying upon a difficult and obscure Adornean writing style. Franz Kafka's novels are written in simple and direct German. Yet, Kafka's metaphorical imagination allowed him to pierce through linguistic domination with such ease that he managed to advance one of the most powerful critiques of the modern condition.

DIALOGUES: The resort to dialogues is another, more direct way of accepting fragmentation and resisting impositions from monological thought forms. Theatre is the most explicit expression of this genre. It is not surprising that Jean-Paul Sartre, Simone de Beauvoir, Berthold Brecht, Hélène Cixous and many other prominent social critics engaged in this form of stylistic dissent. Tom Stoppard claims to write plays because dialogue is the most respectable way of contradicting himself.[85] But the notion of dialogue goes further than the theatre. Many authors search for stylistic ways of articulating thoughts such that they do not silence other voices, but co-exist and interact with them. I have already mentioned Bakhtin's dialogism, a theory of knowledge and language that avoids the excluding tendencies of monological thought forms. Bakhtin accepts the existence of multiple meanings, draws connections between differences, and searches for possibilities to establish conceptual and linguistic dialogues among competing ideas, values, speech forms, texts, validity claims and the like.[86] Jürgen Habermas attempts to theorise the preconditions for ideal speech situations. Communication, in this case, should be as unrestrained as possible, such that 'claims to truth and rightness can be discursively redeemed'.[87] We also know of feminists, like Christine Sylvester, who employ a method of empathetic co-operation, which aims at opening up questions of gender by a 'process of positional slippage that occurs when one listens seriously to the concerns, fears,

---

[84] See Emmanuel Ngara, *Stylistic Criticism and the African Novel* (London: Heinemann, 1982), p. 140.
[85] Tom Stoppard cited in *The New Yorker*, 17 April 1995, p. 111.
[86] Bakhtin, *Problems of Dostoevsky's Poetics*.
[87] Jürgen Habermas, 'A Philosophico-Political Profile', in *New Left Review*, 151, May/ June 1985, p. 94.

and agendas of those one is unaccustomed to heeding when building social theory'.[88]

Summary

Disenchanted concepts, aphorisms, the essay, the novel, satire and dialogue are only examples of stylistic devices that can be employed to seek dialogue and transformation, to escape the encroaching grip of a totality and subvert transversal practices of domination. There is no correct style, no language that solves the problem of representation and related practices of exclusion.

Through an engagement with the philosophy of language, this chapter has sought to provide the prerequisite for understanding the crucial role that linguistic practices play in transversal struggles. At a time when the cross-territorial flow of information is among the most central features of global politics, the linguistic dimensions of transversal struggles has become a domain where important interactions between domination and resistance are carried out. To recognise the political centrality of this domain not only brings into view a range of hitherto obscured dissident potential, but also facilitates an alternative, discourse-oriented understanding of transversal struggles. Such an understanding underlines how the role of human agency in global politics is intrinsically linked to the manner in which this role is perceived and objectified.

Language-based forms of transversal dissent operate through complex and often contradictory processes. An author who tries to exert human agency by engaging in linguistic dissent must defy the language of dominant political perspectives in order not to get drawn into their powerful vortex. But s/he must also articulate alternative thoughts such that they are accessible enough to constitute viable tools to open up dialogical interactions. This can, of course, only be achieved if alternative knowledge can break out of intellectual obscurity, if it can reach and change the minds of most people. However, a text that breaks with established practices of communication to escape their discursive power has, by definition, great difficulties in doing this. Hence, writing is, as Roland Barthes claims, always a compromise between memory and freedom, between, on the one hand, being con-

---

[88] Christine Sylvester, 'Empathetic Cooperation: A Feminist Method for IR', *Millennium*, 23, 2, 1994, 317.

strained by the long history of words, by the power of language to penetrate every single aspect of our writing, and, on the other hand, affirming one's freedom by an act of writing that is not just communication or expression, but a leap beyond the narrow confines of existing language games.[89]

A contemporary reading of Nietzsche is particularly suited to recognise these intricate links between language and politics. Zarathustra is constantly torn back and forth between engaging with people and withdrawing from them. The masses fail to comprehend his attempts to defy herd instincts and problematise the unproblematic. 'They do not understand me; I am not the mouth for these ears', he hails. 'Must one smash their ears before they learn to listen with their eyes?'[90] At times he appears without hope: 'what matters a time that "has not time" for Zarathustra?. . .why do I speak where nobody has *my* ears? It is still an hour too early for me here'.[91] Succumbing to the power of language, Zarathustra returns to the mountains, withdraws into the solitude of his cave. But thoughts of engaging with humanity never leave him. He repeatedly climbs down from his cave to the depths of life, regains hope that monological discourses will give way to dialogue, that the herds will understand him one day: 'But *their* hour will come! And mine will come too! Hourly they are becoming smaller, poorer, more sterile – poor herbs! poor soil! and *soon* they shall stand there like dry grass and prairie – and, verily, weary of themselves and languishing even more than for water – for *fire*.'[92]

No dissenting writer can hope to incinerate immediately the dry grass of orthodox linguistic prairies. Discourses live on and appear reasonable long after their premises have turned into anachronistic relics. More inclusive ways of thinking and acting cannot surface overnight. There are no quick solutions, no new paradigms or miraculous political settlements that one could hope for.

Discursive forms of resistance, even if they manage to transgress national boundaries, do not engender human agency in an immediate and direct way. Writing dissent is a long process, saturated with obstacles and contradictions. It operates, as outlined in the Interlude preceding this chapter, through tactical and temporal transformations of

---

[89] Roland Barthes, *Le degré zéro de l'écriture* (Paris: Éditions du Seuil, 1972/1953), pp. 7–24.
[90] Nietzsche, *Thus Spoke Zarathustra*, pp. 128–30.
[91] Ibid., pp. 280, 284.
[92] Ibid., p. 284.

discursive practices. But this lengthy and largely inaudible process is not to be equated with political impotence. The struggles over the linguistic dimensions of transversal politics are as crucial and as real as the practices of international Realpolitik. They affect the daily lives of people as much as so-called 'real-world issues'. Language, in both speech and writing, is a disguised but highly effective political practice. With this recognition emerges a new kind of activist, situated, as Barthes notes, 'half-way between militant and writer', taking from the former the commitment to act and from the latter the knowledge that the process of writing constitutes such an act.[93] The task now consists of removing one more layer of abstraction, so that the practical and transversal dimensions of language-based forms of dissent can become visible. For this purpose the next chapter now examines how a specific stylistic form of resistance, usually thought to be the most esoteric of all – poetry – may be able to engender human agency by transgressing the spatial and discursive boundaries of global politics.

---

[93] Barthes, *Le degré zero de l'écriture*, p. 23.

9 Political boundaries, poetic transgressions

> To be a poet in a destitute time means: to attend, singing, to the trace
> of the fugitive gods. This is why the poet in the time of the world's
> night utters the holy.[1]

Truth vanished once one came to terms with the death of God,
once one accepted the impossibility of understanding the world in
its totality, once one laid to rest the search for Archimedean foundations, be they theological, scientific or moral. 'No god any longer
gathers men and things unto himself', Heidegger observes with a
slight tone of regret.[2] People have lost the ability to grasp, taste,
apprehend, even imagine the location of the holy source of knowledge. Truth fell into a bottomless pit. But the fugitive gods still
linger around the holy source and provide us with hints about its
location – hints full of ambiguities and contradictions. Poetry, Heidegger claims, is the instrument that comes closest to apprehending
these hints. It is the voice that senses the trace of the fugitive gods,
stays on their tracks and shows to its kindred mortals 'the way
toward the turning'.[3]

Heidegger's claims for poetry are, of course, overstated. Lyrics
cannot leap beyond language games. But poetry is unique, and
offers valuable insight, insofar as it engages the relationship

---

[1] Martin Heidegger, 'What Are Poets For?', in *Poetry, Language, Thought*, tr. A. Hofstadter (New York: Harper & Row, 1971/1936), p. 94.
[2] Ibid., p. 91.
[3] Ibid., p. 94. See also L.M. Vail, 'Revealing and Concealing', in *Heidegger and Ontological Difference* (University Park: Pennsylvania State University Press, 1972), pp. 25–46.

between language and socio-political reality in a highly self-conscious manner. This is why it is worthwhile to preoccupy oneself with a form of speaking and writing whose impact remains confined, in most cases, to a small literary audience. What one can learn from observing poetic subversions of linguistically entrenched forms of domination can facilitate understanding, at least to some extent, of how dissent functions in more mundane daily contexts, which, by definition, mostly elude the eyes and ears of intellectual observers.

This chapter illustrates the potential and limits of poetic dissent by engaging in one more rereading of the events that led to the collapse of the Berlin Wall. The focus now lies with a young generation of poets that emerged in the late 1970s and flourished, mostly underground, until the communist regime began to disintegrate in late 1989. Epitomising the activities of this generation is the area around Prenzlauer Berg, a run-down workers' quarter in East Berlin which, during the 1980s, turned into a Bohemian artist and literary scene. Out of it emerged a counter-culture, a kind of ersatz public sphere that opened up possibilities for poetry readings, art exhibitions, film showings and the publication of various unofficial magazines. Handwritten at times, they were produced in only small editions; copies were passed on directly from person to person.

Vibrant and symbolic as the Bohemian underground scene at Prenzlauer Berg was, it soon came to stand as a metaphor to capture the sprit of an entire generation of East German writers. It must be noted, however, that underground scenes developed in other cities too, in Dresden and Leipzig, for instance. The poets of the 1980s were a heterogeneous group of individuals, whose visions and forms of expression cannot be lumped together into a common movement, or even be captured with the term 'generation'. They ranged from urban punks to rural housewives, from poets who were able to publish their texts in an officially sanctioned form (in the East or West) to those many more who were driven out of the public sphere.

The spirit of the young poets revolved, by and large, around an intensive engagement with the spatial and linguistic constitution of the society they lived in. The contention of boundaries became, as Karen Leeder emphasises, the central theme of Prenzlauer Berg poetry. This ubiquitous theme not only expresses an awareness of boundaries, namely 'encroaching political and geographical horizons,

245

walls, barriers, frontiers, perimeters, barbed wire, stone – but also a yearning for the open spaces beyond'.[4]

It is this *Entgrenzung*, this breaking out of boundaries, this yearning for a world beyond the spatial givenness of Cold War politics, that rendered Prenzlauer Berg poetry inherently transversal. The poets of the 1980s shaped and were shaped by various cross-territorial struggles. Many of their texts were influenced by images projected through Western mass media, by recent trends in French literary theory, or by a range of other discursive aspects that transgressed the Iron Curtain and penetrated East German society despite the government's attempt to shield its population from such subversive influences. The work of the poets, in turn, generated similar cross-territorial dynamics. It led to various reactions from the outside world that put pressure back on the East German government.

The poems written at Prenzlauer Berg are forms of transversal dissent, for they not only traverse boundaries but, to borrow from David Campbell, they also 'are about those boundaries, their erasure or inscription, and the identity formations to which they give rise'.[5] This discursive subversion of political boundaries seems, at first sight, void of direct political significance. Dissent, for most of the Prenzlauer Berg poets, was apolitical. As opposed to previous generations of dissident writers, they did not directly engage the authoritarian regime. The purpose was, rather, to elude its political and linguistic spell altogether. Instead of getting entangled in the agitation that permeates heated political manoeuvrings, dissent was supposed to engage the forces that had already framed the issue, circumvented the range of discussions and thus pre-empted fundamental political debates. Dissent thus dealt with language, with the discursive construction and objectification of Cold War political realities.

Some authors advance rather bold claims on behalf of the Prenzlauer Berg poets. David Bathrick, for instance, believes that they succeeded in creating a counter-public sphere that challenged the one-dimensionality of the official political discourse. They were part of a literary intelligentsia whose activities, he stresses, 'contributed to the process of peaceful social change, even "revolution" in [East Ger-

---

[4] Karen Leeder, *Breaking Boundaries: A New Generation of Poets in the GDR* (Oxford: Clarendon Press, 1996), p. 55.

[5] David Campbell, 'Political Prosaics, Transversal Politics, and the Anarchical World', in Michael J. and Hayward R. Alker (eds.), *Challenging Boundaries: Global Flows, Territorial Identities* (Minneapolis: University of Minnesota Press, 1996), p. 23.

many]'.[6] Although Bathrick's arguments are compelling, it is too early to suggest, in a definitive manner and backed up with concrete evidence, that the poets of the 1980s have directly contributed to the fall of the Berlin Wall. Too diffused are the links between cause and effect to endow an underground and thus relatively marginal literary movement with such revolutionary credentials. But this is not to say that poetic forms of dissent were ineffective. The literary scene of the 1980s undoubtedly exerted a transversal form of human agency. The challenge now consists of recognising the complexities through which these poetic activities have possibly shaped socio-political dynamics. Needless to say, such a momentous task cannot possibly be laid to rest in a chapter-length inquiry.

The purpose of this chapter is thus limited to a micro-level study that illustrates, through a few selective examples, how a group of poets struggled with the discursive boundaries of the society they lived in; how this struggle took on transversal dimensions; and how these dimensions challenged the spatial constitution of Cold War politics. The analysis begins by introducing the context within which the East German poetry scene of the 1980s emerged. By closely reading and examining passages of several poems, I then demonstrate how a deliberate stretching, even violating, of linguistic conventions can open up spaces to think and act. The limits of this process will be outlined in relation to damaging revelations that document how the Prenzlauer Berg subculture had, after all, been penetrated by the *Staatssicherheit*, the state's notorious security service.

The politics of living in a socio-linguistic order

Most observers of Cold War politics stress that East Germany was characterised by an unusual absence of prominent dissident intellectuals. The communist regime in Berlin never had to deal with critics as outspoken as, say, Alexander Solzhenitsyn, Vaclav Havel or Adam Michnik.[7] The absence of radical dissidents is said to have multiple reasons. Among the older generation of East German writers the regime enjoyed a certain level of legitimacy because several of its leaders, including Erich Honecker, had stood at the forefront of the

[6] David Bathrick, *The Powers of Speech: The Politics of Culture in the GDR* (Lincoln: University of Nebraska Press, 1995), pp. 2, 240.
[7] See, in particular, Christian Joppke, *East German Dissidents and the Revolution of 1989* (London: Macmillan, 1995).

fight against fascism. Many intellectuals also shared the desire to find a societal order more just and egalitarian than capitalism. The dissidents that did exist were therefore often not radicals – they wanted to reform the communist system, rather than destroy it altogether. Some poets, playwrights and novelists took a more confrontational line during the 1960s and 1970s. But most of them ended up, for one reason or another, in West Germany – a country that could provide them not only with political, but also with linguistic asylum. A case in point is the forceful expatriation, in 1976, of the prominent satirist and songwriter Wolf Biermann.[8]

The writings of the subsequent generation of East German authors emerged in response to a new set of issues. Those who were active in the poetry scene of the 1980s differed sharply from previous East German intellectuals, in part because they had actually been born into an already existing socialist edifice; that is, as opposed to their fathers and mothers, the writers of Prenzlauer Berg did not witness the spread of fascism, the end of the war and the division of their country into two separate states. They were born in the 1950s and 1960s, long after the post-war redrawing of geopolitical maps. Theirs was a struggle for meaning, a desire to think and live outside the prescribed boundaries of political and social acceptability. Uwe Kolbe, one of the most active poets at Prenzlauer Berg, explains in his much cited 'Born into it':

> Tall wide green land,
> Fence-scattered plain.
> Red
> Sun-tree at the horizon.
> The wind is mine
> And mine the birds.
>
> Small green land narrow,
> Barbed-wire-landscape.
> Black
> Tree besides me.
> Harsh wind.
> Strange birds.[9]

---

[8] See Bathrick, *The Powers of Speech*, esp. pp. 70–7.

[9] Uwe Kolbe, 'Hineingeboren', in *Hineingeboren: Gedichte 1975–1979* (Berlin and Weimar: Aufbau, 1980), p. 47. 'Hohes weites grünes Land, / zaundurchsetzte Ebene. / Roter / Sonnenbaum am Horizont. / Der Wind ist mein / und mein die

There is disillusionment in these lines, an unresolved tension between youthful dreams and the realities in which they have failed to materialise. There is a clear recognition of boundaries, and the painful impositions they have imposed on people's lives. One can hear the frustrated voice of an individual who simply wanted to live his life. Nothing more. Nothing less.

Born into the political boundaries of an already existing socialist order meant a variety of things: born into a country that built walls to keep its citizens from voting with their feet; born into a bi-polar vision of global politics; born into a dichotomy of barbed-wire-landscapes on the inside and a vast, mostly unseen world on the outside; born into a political idea at a time when its contradictions became increasingly visible; born into a society that had, despite its crumbling foundations, allegedly solved all major social problems and arrived, so to speak, at the end of history. There was nothing left to deal with, except the immobility of daily routines. Kurt Drawert, trying to figure out how to live a historical moment that was not his:

> What was it worth, my
> presence in an already thought through world,
>
> ordered, in definitions, tables,
> headlines delivered?
> Ready-made-conditions and ready-made-judgements.
> History was over. The present
>
> was over, the future, the revolution,
> the answers were over.[10]

Drawert, like many of his fellow poets, searched for an 'I' in a void, for a purpose in a world where the individual had no more historical task to fulfil. The frustration of feeling homeless at home was only amplified by a perceived lack of alternatives. It was this loss of meaning and the attempt at working through it, futile as it may have

---

Vögel. // Kleines grünes Land enges, / Stacheldrahtlandschaft. / Schwarzer / Baum neben mir. / Harter Wind / Fremde Vögel.'

[10] Kurt Drawert, 'Zweite Inventur', in *Zweite Inventur* (Berlin und Weimar: Aufbau, 1987), p. 12. 'Was war sie wert, meine / Anwesenheit in einer Welt die dekliniert war, // geordnet, in Definitionen, Tabellen, / Schlagzeilen gebracht? / Fertigbedingungen und Fertiggerichte. / Die Geschichte war fertig. Die Gegenwart // war fertig, die Zukunft, die Revolution, / die Antworten waren fertig.'

seemed at times, that provided the younger writers with a poetic raison d'être.

One could say that the dilemmas they dealt with arose from being born into a language whose boundaries had already circumscribed the range of their possible experiences. The language they had was simply not adequate to express their agonies, frustrations and confusions, in short, the world they lived in. Neither did it permit the development of a critical attitude towards either domestic or international politics.

The existing language had thrown sheet after sheet of silence over a generation of writers long before even one of its members could have raised her voice in protest. 'People are formed by language – if one has devoured the language, then one has eaten the order as well', says the poet Stefan Dörig.[11] Uwe Kolbe goes even further. The frustration of being sucked into the political vortex of an existing language led him to believe that there had never been an authentic opposition in East Germany. This, he claimed, was true of prominent dissident writers like Christa Wolf, Heiner Müller, Rudolf Bahro and Wolf Biermann. Although some of them were imprisoned and suffered extensively as a result of their opposition to the authoritarian regime, they cannot be considered genuine opposition because they articulated their critique from within the dominant world-view, and especially from within the dominant Marxist language.[12] Kolbe may have somewhat overstated the case, but he was certainly not the only one who struggled with the inadequacy of the language the younger generation had inherited. Two poetic examples. Kurt Drawert:

> I did not want to speak like my father (or grandfather, for instance)... to use this language would have been a form of subjugation... I felt that whenever father (or grandfather, for instance) spoke, it was not really father (or, for instance, grandfather) who spoke, but something distant, strange, external, something that merely used his (or her) voice... I had no choice but to speak and thus to be forced into misunderstandings or lies, to feel observed,

---

[11] Dörig, translated by Bathrick in *The Powers of Speech*, p. 239. For a detailed discussion see Leeder, *Breaking Boundaries*, pp. 19–76.

[12] Kolbe, 'Die Heimat der Dissidenten: Nachbemerkungen zum Phantom der DDR-Opposition', in K. Deiritz and H. Krauss (eds.), *Der deutsch-deutsche Literaturstreit oder 'Freunde es spricht sich schlecht mit gebundener Zunge* (Frankfurt: Luchterhand, 1991), pp. 33–9.

influenced and dominated by something distant, strange and external.[13]

Jayne-Ann (formerly Bernt) Igel uses a more lyrical form to emphasise the silences that are imposed by the inadequacies of existing speech forms. S/he was among those who not only struggled for voice, but also voiced the very process of this struggle. 'The Pupil':

> was i caught forever, as i learned their language, my
> voice a bird-squeak, keeping me under their spell; they held
> me near the house like a vine, whose shoots they clip
> ped, so that they do not darken the rooms
>
> and close to the wall of the house i played, under the light
> of drying sheets, the fingers pierced through the plaster, i
> did not want to miss the personified sound of my name, which
> smelled like urine; those who carried my name in their mouth,
> held me by the neck with their teeth[14]

Igel refuses to close a question ('was I caught forever, as I learned their language') with an appropriate question mark. One is inevitably thrown into a continuous questioning mood that lasts until the end of the poem. The sense of suspense is further accentuated by the fact that Igel merges sentences with commas, semi-colons or a simple 'and' where they normally would be terminated with a full stop. Indeed, the suspense of the initial question even continues beyond the end of the poem, for Igel refuses to close it with any sort of punctuation. The desperate scream 'was i caught forever, as i learned their language' echoes long after the last word is read.

---

[13] Kurt Drawert, *Spiegelland: Ein deutscher Monolog* (Frankfurt: Suhrkamp, 1992), pp. 25–7. 'aber wie mein Vater (or Großvater, beispielsweise) wollte ich nicht sprechen... diese Sprache zu benutzen wäre zugleich eine Form der Unterwerfung gewesen... Ich spürte, sobald Vater (oder Großvater, beispielsweise) sprach, daß nicht tatsächlich Vater (oder beispielsweise Großvater) sprach, sondern dass etwas Fernes, Fremdes, Äusseres gesprochen hatte, etwas, das sich lediglich seiner (oder ihrer) Stimme bediente... Also blieb nur, zu sprechen und damit dem Mißverständnis oder der Lüge zu verfallen und im Sprechen sich beobachtet, beeinflußt und beherrscht zu wissen von etwas Fernem, Fremden und Äusseren...'

[14] Jayne-Ann Igel, 'Der Zögling', in T. Elm, *Kristallisationen: Deutsche Gedichte der achtziger Jahre* (Stuttgart: Reclam, 1992), p. 158. 'war ich endültig gefangen, als ich ihre sprache lernte, meine / stimme ein vogellaut, der mich ihnen bewahrte; sie hielten / mich am hause gleich dem rebstock, dessen triebe sie be / schnitten, dass er die zimmer nicht verdunkele // und dicht bei der mauer des hauses spielte ich, unterm lichte / trocknender laken, die finger durchlöcherten den putz, nicht / missen mochte ich den leibhaftigen klang meines names, der / nach urin roch; die meinen namen in ihrem munde führten, / hielten mich mit den zähnen fest am genick.'

Needed: a radical critique of language that could pierce through the plaster of existing speech, break its spell, slip away from the linguistic teeth drilled into one's neck. Needed: language that is not a vine, confined to the wall of the house and constantly trimmed, but a freestanding and freely growing tree, pushing its branches up into the open sky.

Transgressing the boundaries of normalised thought

The younger generation of East German poets stretched the boundaries of language with a high degree of self-awareness. They assumed that language had to be critiqued before one could even begin to critique the social and political structures of domestic or international politics. This is why the notion of *Sprachkritik*, presented in the previous chapter, became the key feature around which the literary scene at Prenzlauer Berg revolved.[15]

Poetry is critique of language *par excellence*. A poem is a conscious transgression of existing linguistic conventions, a protest against an established language game and the systems of exclusion that are embedded in it. In this sense poetry sets itself apart from prose because it negates, not by chance or as a side effect, but because it cannot do otherwise, because this is what poetry is all about.[16] A poet renders strange that which is familiar and thus forces the reader to confront what s/he habitually has refused to confront. For Julia Kristeva, poetic language disturbs, transgresses rules, fractures meaning. In doing so it 'breaks up the inertia of language habits' and 'liberates the subject from a number of linguistic, psychic, and social networks'.[17] Nicole Brossard argues likewise that poetic practices, such as shaking the syntax, breaking grammatical rules, disrespecting punctuation and using blank space, have a profound effect on readers. They offer new perspectives on reality

---

[15] Michael Thulin, 'Sprache und Sprachkritik: Die Literatur des Prenzlauer Bergs in Berlin / DDR', in H.L. Arnold (ed.), *Die andere Sprache: Neue DDR Literatur der 80er Jahre* (Munich: Text und Kritik, 1990), pp. 234–42.

[16] Ulrich Schödlbauer, 'Die Modernitätsfalle der Lyrik', in *Merkur*, No 551, vol. 49, No 2, Feb 1995, p. 174.

[17] Julia Kristeva, *Recherches pour une sémanalyze* (Paris: Seuil, 1969), pp. 178–9, tr. L.S. Roudiez in the introduction to Kristeva's *Revolution in Poetic Language* (New York: Columbia University Press, 1984), p. 2.

and make room for alternative ways of perceiving life and its meanings.[18]

By trying to break through the existing web of language and power, the young East German poets of the 1980s purposely wrote in ways that violated both poetological traditions and guidelines of ideological correctness. They tried to 'formulate what language does not yet contain'.[19] They searched for ways of expression that go 'beyond the vocabulary of power and assimilation'.[20] In some sense these experiments with language were simply meant to shock, to serve as an avant-gardist confrontation with the establishment. But many of the poems undoubtedly did more than just provoke. They sought to articulate a different form of dissent.

The poetic and political purpose of the Prenzlauer Berg writers was no longer to critique the existing system in order to replace it with something else, a superior ideology or a more adequate way of advancing the old one. The writer was no longer supposed to confront the system, as most previous dissidents had seen their vocation, but to refuse it, to step outside of it altogether. Years of dialogue had led nowhere. Resistance was now perceived to be a matter of eluding the system altogether, of breaking the old dichotomy of dissident/collaborator. Elke Erb, the co-editor of an influential early anthology of works by the young authors of the 1980s, characterises the transgression of linguistic conventions that mark their work as the result of 'an exit from the authoritarian system, a liberation from the tutelage of predetermined meanings'.[21] The textual landscape of the poet thus looked somewhat like a caravan of refugees, trying to leave behind a world whose main premises ceased to offer hope long ago. The poems written in the 1980s were traces of flight that featured strikingly little direct criticism of politics and ideology. There were hardly any references to historical struggles and class conflict. Critique became a process of forgetting, as in eluding the spell of the old world by not even naming it. But

---

[18] Nicole Brossard, 'Poetic Politics', in C. Bernstein (ed.), *The Politics of Poetic Form: Poetry and Public Policy* (New York: ROOF, 1990), p. 79.

[19] *ariadnefabrik*, IV/1987, cited in Olaf Nicolai, 'die fäden der ariadne,' in Arnold, *Die Andere Sprache*, p. 91.

[20] Editorial of *Mikado*, cited in K. Michael and T. Wohlfahrt (eds.), *Vogel oder Käfig sein: Kunst und Literatur aus unabhängigen Zeitschriften der DRR 1979–1989* (Berlin: Galrev, 1991), p. 348.

[21] Elke Erb, 'Vorwort' to E. Erb and S. Anderson, *Berührung ist nur eine Randerscheinung: Neue Literatur as der DDR* (Cologn: Kiepenheuer & Witsch, 1985), p. 15.

this apoliticality rendered the ensuing poetic forms of dissent all the more political.

Most striking, from both a political and a poetological point of view, is the persistent use of spatial metaphors. They signify the transversal aspirations of the Prenzlauer Berg scene, the willingness to transgress and challenge the constitution of Cold War international politics. Constantly recurring tropes like 'horizon', 'wall', 'border', 'narrow land', and 'barbed-wire landscapes' suggest a strong desire to break out of an entire way of living and thinking. Bert Papenfuß-Gorek, one of the more radical poets of the 1980s, destroyed linguistic conventions in an attempt to envisage what may lie beyond the horizon:

> scream against the wall
> scribble it at the wall
> stroll through the wall
>
> varieti not simpliciti
> & you sighter of varieti
> are not simpliciti but
> stand and stem of varieti[22]

Papenfuß-Gorek's poetry is characterised by a disregard for existing orthographic conventions. At times he ventures into a nearly incomprehensible (and untranslatable) private language. He breaks up words into their components or experiments with grammar, syntax and style. There are moments, however, where his misspelled adventures and his play with words and double-meanings manage astonishingly well to open up dialogical spaces by transgressing linguistically fixed modes of thinking.

Papenfuß-Gorek's desire to 'stroll through the wall', to leave the old world behind without the least trait of melancholy, did, indeed, anticipate the explosions and implosions that were to take place in November 1989, the moment when, after months of sustained mass demonstrations, hundreds of thousands of East Germans literally strolled through the Berlin Wall to take their first glimpse of the West. The image of the disintegrating Wall remains deeply

---

[22] Bert Papenfuß-Gorek, 'SOndern,' in S. Anderson and E. Erb (eds.), *Berührung ist nur eine Randerscheinung*, p. 162. 'schrei gegen die wand / schreib es an die wand / schreite durch die wand // fielfalt anstatt einfalt / & du einsteller der fielfalt / bist nicht einfalt sondern / baustein & bein der fielfalt'.

engraved in our collective memories of late twentieth-century global politics. It must be remembered, though, that at the time the Prenzlauer Berg poets wrote, in the early and mid 1980s, there was little hope for such a spectacular turnaround. Hardly anybody in the East or West, neither international relations scholars nor Cold War politicians, had expected the foundations of the Soviet alliance system to crumble like a house of cards. Papenfuß-Gorek's transversal persistence is thus all the more astonishing. Nineteen-eighty-four, from the 'underground' in East Berlin:

> pOwer will fall
> down, i.e. over
> thrown until stum-
> bling, ignored it will
> turn into motherearth[23]

Various modernist and postmodernist themes resonate in the approach to language that became central to the work of Papenfuß-Gorek and other Prenzlauer Berg poets. Indeed, Sascha Anderson, one of the key figures of the underground literary scene, emphasises the strong influence that writers such as Foucault, Baudrillard and Barthes exerted on him and fellow writers.[24] The prevalence of these themes testify to the regime's inability to shield its population from 'subversive' outside influences. The transversal nature of contemporary cultural and political struggles rendered the Iron Curtain porous, to the extent that the formation of domestic opinion has become intrinsically linked to the cross-territorial flow of ideas.

As a result of these transversal dynamics, the discursive dimension of power, particularly its link with the production and diffusion of knowledge, is an ever-present theme in Prenzlauer Berg poetry. And so is the challenge of any truth claims. The poets of the 1980s relied on what could be called a later Wittgensteinean view of language and politics. Words were no longer perceived as representations of an externally existing reality. Rather, language

---

[23] Papenfuß-Gorek, *vorwärts im zorn &sw. gedichte*, cited in Jürgen Zenke, 'Vom Regen und von den Traufen. Bert Papenfuß-Gorek: die lichtscheuen scheiche versunkener reiche', in W. Hinck (ed.), *Gedichte und Interpretationen*, vol. VII (Stuttgart, Philipp Reclam, 1997), p. 146. 'die mAcht wir runter- / kommen, d.h. gestürzt / werden bis sie stol- / pert, liegengelassen / wird sie zu muttererde'.

[24] Sascha Anderson, interviewed in Robert von Hallberg, *Literary Intellectuals and the Dissolution of the State: Professionalism and Conformity in the GDR* (Chicago: University of Chicago Press, 1996), p. 263.

was seen as an activity in itself – an activity that already contained, by definition, various political dimension. Rainer Schedlinski, one of Prenzlauer Berg's most articulate theorists, speaks of the 'resistance of forms', of a protest culture that attacks the sign itself, rather than merely the meaning that it arbitrarily imposed on us (or, more precisely, on other signs).[25]

For many observers, though, this transversally inspired avant-gardist move was everything but dissent. Its so-called postmodern aesthetic was said to lack both moral integrity and the power to oppose a very real political force, the authoritarian East German government. Clearly, the Prenzlauer Berg writers were not dissidents in the normal sense, nor did they want to be seen as such. But dissent has, as argued throughout this book, too often been understood only in romantic and masculine terms, as heroic rebellions against authority, exemplified by demonstrating masses, striking workers, brick-throwing students and fasting dissidents. Dissent is often a far more intricate and far more mundane phenomenon.

If poets, as those at Prenzlauer Berg, explore their own poetic world, then this is not necessarily to search for a perfect language or to ignore the multiple realities of social and political life. If a poem speaks only in its own matter it draws attention to the fact that words are arbitrary signs. By refusing to go beyond the poem, the poet subverts the often unquestioned link between the sign and the referent, the non-linguistic reality that the sign designates. The previous chapter has already debated the relative merits and problems of such a non-referential view of language, and later sections of the present chapter will do so again. At this point, however, it is more important to keep in mind that when pursuing their form of subversive writing, the poets of the 1980s considered language itself as a site where important political and social struggles take place. Schedlinski:

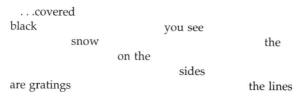

[25] Rainer Schedlinski, 'Die Unzuständigkeit der Macht', *neue deutsche literatur*, 40, 474, June 1992, 97.

```
            of humanity
                          language
   prison                            an open
             where
                     there is
                         no
                        outside²⁶
```

This poem does not only speak of spatial and linguistic prisons, but actually visualises them through its appearance on the page. The text is like a grating. Confinement, however, is only one aspect that is evoked by this particular spatial arrangement of words. One discovers, at the same time, an array of escape routes. Because the poem can be read in a variety of ways – horizontally, vertically, diagonally – it offers an alternative to the monological thought form that dominated much of the political rhetoric in East Germany. Prison and polyphony at once, Schedlinski's poetic grating accepts the limits of language but urges us to search for the multitude of voices that can be heard and explored within these limits. In this sense, the poem resembles what Gilles Deleuze and Félix Guattari called a rhizome: a multiplicity that has no coherent and bounded whole, no beginning or end, only a middle from where it expands and overspills. Any point of the rhizome is connected to any other. It has no fixed points to anchor thought, only lines, magnitudes, dimensions, plateaus, and they are always in motion.[27]

The transversal subversion of naming dailiness

In a political context where the voice of the subject had all but vanished, poetry became a way of defending individuality against the collectivisation of experience. This section reads three poems in an attempt to illustrate the manner in which poetry was used as a tool to describe the daily realities that were unspeakable, perhaps even unthinkable, through the medium of the official socio-political discourse.

[26] Rainer Schedlinski, 'die unvordenkliche lichtung der worte', *die rationen des ja und des nein: Gedichte* (Berlin und Weimar: Aufbau, 1988), cited in Leeder, *Breaking Boundaries*, p. 67. 'verdeckt / schwarzen siehst du / schnee den / auf den / seiten / sind gitter die zeilen / des menschen / sprache / gefängnis ein offenes / dort / gibt es / kein / draussen.'

[27] Gilles Deleuze and Félix Guattari, *A Thousand Plateaus: Capitalism & Schizophrenia*, tr. B. Massumi (London: The Athlone Press, 1996/1980), pp. 3–25, 377.

Durs Grünbein, although never really part of any collective poetic movement, is among those who most successfully vented frustrations that had been blocked out of prevalent ways of speaking. His poetry is grey, grim and ironic. His sources are explicitly cross-cultural. They are testimonies for the increasingly transversal nature of contemporary life. His politics, however, is not about grand historical struggles. It is about the daily realities imposed by political boundaries. It is about the search for words that can describe the East German urban and industrial wastelands. In this sense his poems appear like verbal mirror images of Anselm Kiefer's massive and unrelentingly desolate canvases.

Mid 1980s. The wall still intact. No cracks in sight. The East German landscape obfuscated by more than just industrial fumes. A poem from Grünbein's first collection, *Grey-zone at dawn*:

> So many days during which nothing
>   happened, nothing but the
> narrow manoeuvres of the winter, a few
>
> piles of snow, long melted at
>   night and the strange
> moment in the barrack region was
>
> an exotic flyer: as this
>   small squad of Russian soldiers in
> green feltwear silently
>
> guarded a bundle of newspapers and I read
>   KOMMYHИCT on top of it and
> I remembered the line 'Think
>
> of the watch at the wrist of
>   Jackson Pollock.'[28]

A strange poem, indeed. One that seems very real but at the same time plays with surrealist images – a tendency that is not surprising

---

[28] Durs Grünbein, 'Nimm es An!', in *Grauzone morgens* (Frankfurt: Suhrkamp, 1988), p. 48. 'Soviele Tage in denen nichts sich / ereignete, nichts als die / knappen Manöver des Winters, ein paar // Schneehügel morgens, am Abend längst / weggetaut und der seltsame / Augenblick im Kasernenviertel war // ein exotisches Flugbatt; als dieser / kleine Soldatentrupp Russin in / grünem Filzzeug schweigend ein // Zeitungsbündel bewachte und ich las / KOMMYHИCT obendrauf und / es fiel mir die Zeile ein ''Denk // an die Uhr am Handgelenk / Jackson Pollocks.'

given that the environment in which he wrote was itself marked by rather pronounced surrealist traits. But Grünbein neither escapes into surreal fantasies nor stays with a pure description of reality. He interweaves both of them in an attempt to break through to a different way of perceiving and living the world.

The poem goes through several stages. Its initial stanzas describe the monotone dailiness of life in East Germany, a life 'during which nothing happened'. But what are we to make of the 'exotic flyer' that turns the poem around at the beginning of the third stanza? Does it -refer to the 'small squad of Russian soldiers'? Not likely. Their silent but suffocating presence is part of East Germany's daily monotony, its well-established integration into the Cold War international order. The КОММУНИСТ (communist) written on top of the bundle of newspapers is hardly exotic, hardly exciting. Indeed, the misspelling of the Russian word COMMYHИCT as КОММУНИСТ suggests either disinterest or disrespect. Grünbein's transgression is a form of political critique that refuses even to engage the political topic it destabilises. He silently evokes the decay of an ideology, a misspelled idea that snowed in at dawn but melted long before dusk. He critiques the existing spatial arrangement of Cold War global politics – an arrangement that persists only because it is guarded by a squad of soldiers in feltwear.

The fourth stanza of Grünbein's poem ends abruptly with the admonition to 'think.' Think? Cut through the fog of the East German wasteland? Break out of the language that has been forced upon his generation? To be precise: 'think/of the watch at the wrist of/Jackson Pollock'! Rather bizarre, but judged by the spatial arrangement of the poem, a suggestion that the author clearly endowed with great importance. Does the watch signify the senseless passing of time, the vanishing of a youth ill-spent in a suffocating society? Or does Pollock simply become one of these mysterious but somehow glamorous and exotic Western symbols that so many East Germans longed for? The desire for the excitement of the strange, the transversal, for what was believed to be, often very naively, the materially abundant world on the other side of the unyielding Wall?

And what does Grünbein know about Pollock? What does the average reader of the poem know about him? Western media sources were available all over East Germany, but how adequately did they represent life beyond the Iron Curtain? Was the average East German aware of the early Cold War days, when American foreign policy, through the help of New York's Museum of Modern Art, promoted the paintings of Pollock and other abstract expressionists as a way of demonstrating the cultural superiority of the 'free world', the boundless existential opportunities of the new liberalism?[29] Does the poem maybe evoke Pollock's chaotic drip paintings as signs of disintegration, announcing the collapse of the Soviet empire? Is abstract expressionism presented as opposition to socialist realism? And can we assume the reader should know that Pollock himself flirted with socialism when he was part of a group of left-wing, avant-gardist artists in New York city during the 1930s?

We cannot assume. We do not know. Grünbein does not give answers. He stays ambiguous on purpose. His poem expresses dissatisfaction with the status quo. It silently screams out a desire to leap over the Wall and embrace the excitement of the West, its unknown and mystical dimensions. But the author's position cannot be nailed down. The few references to politics and ideology are too slippery and inconclusive.

Grünbein's poetic critique was grey shaded. It was named without being named, spoken and yet not spoken. David Bathrick, in his attempt to show how power in East Germany was articulated and contested through discourse and language, argues that poetry was subversive precisely because of the refusal to be narrowed down to a single meaning, precisely because of the absence of an 'I' that can be held responsible.[30] 'In a hierarchical society or in a dictatorship', another observer points out, 'nonsystematic thought [was] a form of threat'.[31] The poet's constant ambivalence directly undermined the state's promotion of a black-and-white, one-dimensional and teleological approach to history. There was no progress in Grünbein's lyrics, only depressing circularity and its ideological subversiveness.

Barbara Köhler's poem 'Rondeau Allemagne' launched a similar attack, but did so differently, both in terms of form and content. Instead of relying on experimental styles, as most Prenzlauer Berg poets did, Köhler shows that traditional verse forms can advance powerful linguistic critiques as well. She was not concerned with Pol-

---

[29] See Eva Cockcroft, 'Abstract Expressionism, Weapon of the Cold War', in F. Frascina (ed.), *Pollock and After: The Critical Debate* (London: Paul Chapman, 1985), pp. 125–33.
[30] Bathrick, *The Powers of Speech*, p. 73.
[31] Patricia Anne Simpson, 'Entropie, Ästhetik und Ethik im Prenzlauer Berg', in P. Böthig and K. Michael (eds.), *MachtSpiele: Literatur und Staatssicherheit im Fokus Prenzlauer Berg* (Leipzig: Reclam Verlag, 1993), p. 51.

lock's representation of American superiority. Her transversal gaze
was directed inwards. She observed how the unfulfilled desire to leap
beyond the Wall had transformed her and her immediate environment:

> I hold out in this land and grow, estranged,
> With that love pushing me beyond the verge
> Between the skies. To each his own urge;
> I hold out in this land and grow estranged.
>
> With that love pushing me beyond the verge;
> Entrenched agreements do I want to thwart
> And laugh, tearing to pieces my own heart.
> With that love pushing me beyond the verge;
>
> Between the skies to each his own urge:
> A bloody cloth is raised, the airship sinks.
> No land in sight; maybe a rope that swings
> Between the skies. To each his own urge.[32]

One cannot but walk away from this poem with a certain sense of
despair. It is a rondeau in which the last stanza does not resolve the
puzzle that was presented in the previous ones. The tension between
sky and land, desire and restraint, dream and reality, inside and outside, remains unresolved. Does the poem's estrangement from the
existing political and social system advocate a retreat into the self, a
sort of neo-liberal individualism? Is it the testimony of someone who
opted against trying to slip through the Iron Curtain into the West?
Someone who decided to stay and make the best out of what
remained? And what did remain? Only 'a rope that swings between
the skies', and only maybe. We discover a similar feeling of lost time
as in Grünbein's poem. The same despair. The desire to thwart
entrenched agreements. But Köhler does not express her frustration
through the senseless ticking away of the mysterious, imaginative
watch of Jackson Pollock.

---

[32] Barbara Köhler, 'Rondeau Allemagne', in T. Elm, *Kristallisationen*, pp. 158–9. 'Ich
harre aus im Land und geh, ihm fremd, / Mit einer Liebe, die mich über Grenzen
treibt, / Zwischen den Himmeln. Sehe jeder, wo er bleibt; / Ich harre aus im Land
und geh im fremd. // Mit einer Liebe, die mich über Grenzen treibt, / Will ich die
Übereinkünfte verletzen / Und lachen, reiß ich mir das Herz in Fetzen / Mit einer
Liebe, die mich über Grenzen treibt. // Zwischen den Himmeln sehe jeder, wo er
bleibt: / Ein blutig Lappen wird gehißt, das Luftschiff fällt./ Kein Land in Sicht;
vielleicht ein Seil, das hält / Zwischen den Himmeln. Sehe jeder wo er bleibt.'

'Rondeau Allemagne' conveys a sense of time through form and unusual juxtapositions. The rondeau's strict rules and its rhyme are not there to please the reader or to celebrate poetic conventions. They mark boundaries, restraints and rising tension. They represent the various components of a straight-jacket. Rhythm, Octavio Paz says, always conveys something, it is more than simply time divided into parts. It provokes expectation, it puts us in a state of waiting. Through rhythm time is no longer an abstract entity. It is endowed with meaning, a sense of direction, even if one does not know what this meaning is, where this direction leads.[33]

Köhler's poem speaks through its rhythm. It evokes, at one level, the monotonous passing of time, a voyage from nowhere to nowhere, and then back to nowhere. Repetition and repetition and repetition. Hopes and dashed hopes. Again. And again. But there is more to 'Rondeau Allemagne' than monotony. The rhyming conjunctions of verge and urge, which echo through the poem, provide an additional sense of urge(ncy). Tension is rising. There is impatience, rage, despair – the futility of being born into a social, spatial and linguistic order that refuses to acknowledge its own anachronistic nature. Imprisonment in a world of circularity that preaches linear progress. Sascha Anderson:

> go across the border
> on the other side
> stands a man and says:
> go across the border
> on the other side
> stands a man and says:
> go across the border
> on the other side
> stands a man and says:[34]

Poetic dissent and the limits of aesthetic autonomy

Anderson's transversal roaming into absurdity brings us to some of the more controversial aspects of Prenzlauer Berg. He was one of its

---

[33] Octavio Paz, *The Bow and the Lyre*, tr. R.L.C. Simms (Austin: University of Texas Press, 1973/1956), pp. 46–7.

[34] Sascha Anderson, *Jeder Satelit hat einen Killersateliten* (Berlin West: Rotbuch, 1982), p. 25. 'geh über die grenze / auf der anderen seite / steht ein mann und sagt: / geh

most illustrious representatives, the unofficial spokesperson of the avant-garde poets, an active and extroverted personality who organised readings, publication arrangements and the like. But Anderson was more than that. He also stood at the centre of a scandal that broke out a couple of years after the fall of the Berlin Wall.

The archives of the disintegrated old regime have revealed that various poets were paid informants of the *Staatssicherheit or Stasi*, the notorious state security service. Anderson and Schedlinski were the most prominent among them. Anderson's role was particularly damaging. As opposed to his more elusive poetry, his Stasi reports, filed over a period of twenty years, were precisely articulated and contained incriminating evidence against his fellow writers who often took great personal risks in articulating their avant-garde poetry. Intensive and emotional debates emerged in Germany. The Stasi affair not only questioned how successful the younger generation of writers were in breaking out of boundaries, but also shattered the cliché of the Bohemian underground poet. Of course, virtually all oppositional activities were infiltrated by the Stasi. But Prenzlauer Berg poets were supposed to be different. The whole premise of their activities was based on refusal and flight, on stepping altogether outside the system and its realm of influence. This strategy had contributed to the high level of integrity that the Prenzlauer Berg poets enjoyed during the 1980s, particularly in the West. They stood for 'a seemingly intact critical identity'.[35] They appeared 'to have successfully stepped free of the burden of complicity with which older writers had to come to terms after 1989'.[36] The fall from grace was thus all the harder when the Stasi revelations gradually emerged in November 1991.

Many writers from the previous generation were particularly harsh in their judgements of the Prenzlauer Berg scene. There was talk of hypocrisy and betrayal. Wolf Biermann, who dismissed the Prenzlauer Berg poets as 'late-dadaistic garden gnomes with pencil and brush',[37] was the most outspoken, but certainly not the only hostile voice. He and others spoke of lacking responsibility, of a genera-

---

über die grenze / auf der anderen seite / steht ein mann und sagt: / geh über die grenze / auf der anderen seite / steht ein mann und sagt.'

[35] Peter Böthig and Klaus Michael, 'Der 'Zweite Text," in their *MachtSpiele*, p. 12.

[36] Robert von Hallberg, 'Introduction' to *Literary Intellectuals and the Dissolution of the State*, p. 24.

[37] Biermann, cited by Alison Lewis, 'Power, Opposition and Subcultures: The Prenzlauer Berg "Scene" in East Berlin and the Stasi', *UTS Review*, 3, 2, November 1997, 139.

tion that had abandoned the commitment of revolutionary poetry for a naive and impotent avant-gardism. The fact that Anderson and Schedlinski put some of their fellow writers at risk signified for many the moral bankruptcy of the postmodernism that drove the writings of the 1980s. The autonomy of the aesthetic sucked back from its theoretical loftiness to the sump-hole of dirty politics?

Anderson's and Schedlinski's response to the accusations further intensified the debate. Anderson first downplayed his involvement with the Stasi. Even after the extent of his collaboration could no longer be denied he was rather blasé about the role he had played as a paid informant of the authoritarian regime. 'To me it's all the same', he declared without remorse. 'To me it meant nothing. . . I had no moral problems.'[38] Schedlinski then consolidated this culture of indifference by legitimising it through an analysis of postmodern theory. In a notorious 1992 essay he points towards the radically different understandings of resistance that separated the writers of the 1970s from those of 1980s. The former embraced a direct and explicit critique of society which, Schedlinski claims, led not only to a futile dialogue with the authorities, but also to an entanglement with existing power regimes. The latter, by contrast, lived in a postmodern age – a time when the object of resistance was no longer the meaning of something, but the sign itself, that is, the power-knowledge nexus that has already circumscribed the range of possible meanings.[39]

Schedlinski's reading of postmodern theory is highly problematic, for it revolves more around self-serving justifications than an attempt to grapple with the important ethical issues that the Stasi affair brought to the forefront. The fact that people in the opposition talked to the Stasi, Schedlinski says, 'does not necessarily mean that the Stasi controlled this opposition'.[40] Relying on a quasi-Foucauldian notion of complex and stratified power relationships, he portrays the Stasi as an institution that was as much enabling as it was repressive. The notorious State Security Service, so the argument goes, 'took decisions not only with regard to prohibition, censorship and persecution, but also with regard to permission, non-censorship and tolerance'.[41] To ignore the Stasi then or to demonise it now, in retrospect, is thus a

---

[38] Sascha Anderson, interviewed by von Hallberg in *Literary Intellectuals and the Dissolution of the State*, pp. 28, 295, 298.
[39] Schedlinski, 'Die Unzuständigkeit der Macht', pp. 96–8.
[40] Ibid., p. 82.
[41] Ibid., pp. 80, 84.

sign of naiveté, Schedlinski says. That may be right, and so is his argument that transformation can only come from within. But this hardly justifies the claim that he 'could, with the best of intentions, not imagine how it would have been more honourable to submit to an authority than to arrange oneself with it'.[42] Such and other self-absolving trivialisations of the Stasi did, of course, leave Schedlinski and Anderson wide open to various critiques. In fact, Schedlinski falls at times into clichés that are more characteristic of an uninformed anti-postmodern polemic than anything that has ever been said or written by the great variety of authors who are indiscriminately labelled as postmodern. Particularly problematic is Schedlinski's and Anderson's implicit equation of postmodernism with relativism, which suggests that those who reject an essentialist view of the world can neither pronounce ethical judgements nor occupy standpoints from whence it is possible to advance critique. This book has demonstrated in a variety of ways that far from disabling critique and normative judgements, an acceptance of multiplicities is in fact the very prerequisite for the formulation of a politics and ethics that does not objectify problematic practices of exclusion.

The accusations against Anderson and Schedlinski, and their self-serving theoretical defence, go to the core of the problem of language and human agency. Can poetry that refuses to engage direct political issues have any validity as a practice of dissent? Is the amoral poet-collaborator a necessary consequence of an approach that assumes language has to be critiqued before a fundamental political critique becomes even possible? More generally, can a position that rejects any objective truth claims still retain an ethics of responsibility in a destitute time?

These are difficult questions and, as such, beg for difficult answers. They certainly cannot be put to rest by a stereotypical lashing out against something called postmodernism. Such a polemic is unable to understand not only the complexities of the theoretical issues at stake, but also the contradictions that characterised the lives of a generation that was born into an existing socialist state. It trivialises the centrality of political boundaries and the attempts that were undertaken to transgress them. Most of the Prenzlauer Berg poets had, in fact, never claimed to be conventional dissidents. And to dismiss an entire generation of writers by the behaviour of two of its members is a highly

---

[42] Ibid, p. 89.

problematic exercise, especially if done from a comfortable position of hindsight. A personal act of an author, no matter how ethically questionable, does not provide sufficient ground to dismiss every-thing s/he has ever said or written, yet alone everything an entire tradition of thought has ever produced.[43]

The writers of the 1980s were not the uniform generation of poets that some of their critics want them to be. There were always tensions and disagreements, even within Prenzlauer Berg. Jan Faktor, for instance, left the scene in disgust over its lack of political commitment, its 'panic fear to produce texts in which anything could be fixed clearly and definitely'.[44] And even those who stayed had strong reser-vations about the actions of Anderson and Schedlinski. Hardly any fellow poet thought that 'it was all the same', or accepted as normal the paralysing atmosphere of mistrust that resulted from the constant Stasi-threat.[45] Perhaps it is simply too early to evaluate the contribu-tion of the Prenzlauer Berg poets. Too close and emotionally laden are the grim wastelands of East German communism and the turbulent events of 1989 to allow for even remotely detached judgements about these writers and the difficult situation they faced. What is needed, however, is a commitment towards a continuous and differentiated inquiry into the multiple and transversal dimensions that makes up the complex relationship between language and politics.

There are various reasons why the Prenzlauer Berg poets, and the younger East German writers in general, have to be taken seriously, why their work must be viewed through lenses that are more refined than those that are being applied by an anti-postmodern polemic. The relative merits of an autonomous aesthetic sphere is an old and much debated issue – one that certainly cannot be put to rest with the Prenzlauer Berg case. Its origins perhaps lie with the work of the nine-teenth-century French poet Stéphan Mallarmé, who tried to move away, much like Wittgenstein did later, from a perception of language

---

[43] Parallels exist here with how Paul de Man's sympathies for the fascist regime have been employed to discredit not only all of his remaining work, but also the entire literature on deconstruction. For an analysis that engages this difficult theoretical and ethical issue in more complex terms see Campbell, 'Political Prosaics, Transversal Politics, and the Anarchical World', pp. 14–16.
[44] Jan Faktor, 'Sechzehn Punkte zur Prenzlauer-Berg-Szene', in Böthig and Michael, *MachtSpiele*, p. 98.
[45] See, for instance, Drawert, 'Sie schweigen. Oder sie lügen', in Bötig and Michael, *MachtSpiele*, pp. 74–82; and Kolbe, *Die Situation* (Göttingen: Wallstein Verlag, 1994), p. 23; 'Offener Brief an Sascha Anderson', in *MachtSpiele*, pp. 318–20.

as a mere representation of the world. 'One does not make a poem with ideas, but with words',[46] argued Mallarmé in a famous letter to the painter Edgar Degas. A poet thus was no longer supposed to search for motives exterior to words. This idea gained momentum through the modernist movement, which sought to detach aesthetics from society and carve out an autonomous sphere within which art is pursued solely based on its own grounds: l'art pour l'art. In such a situation, says the art critic Clement Greenberg, 'content is to be dissolved so completely into form that the work of art or literature cannot be reduced in whole or in part to anything but itself'.[47] Art that severs all links to the world and represents nothing outside of itself has, of course, always been under harsh criticism by those who seek a more committed form of political engagement. By contrast, authors who defend the autonomous work of art locate its political relevance precisely in the attempt to create a critical distance from moral norms and social practices. Theodor Adorno, for instance, fears that committed and overtly political art is already a form of accommodation, for it often merely struggles in the name of a noble cause that has already become a political trend. Autonomous art thus contains critical potential precisely because of its refusal to identify itself with the sociopolitical, because of its hidden 'it should be otherwise'.[48]

The Prenzlauer Berg scene demonstrates that a linguistic form of dissent risks becoming either problematic or impotent if pursued in a too radical avant-gardist manner, that is, if its message bears no relationship to the social practices from which it seeks to distance itself. The key, as already suggested in the previous chapter, lies in retaining some form of aesthetic autonomy without losing contact with the language of existing social and political realities. The ensuing tightrope walk is an intricate affair, and the poets of the 1980s were not always successful in pursuing it. Perhaps most impressive is their achievement at the level of language itself. Despite their unusual styles (or maybe because of them?), there was a sense of reality in much of their work, a feeling of place and time that cannot be dismissed as a naive avant-gardist spearheading into unexplored linguistic terrains. Kolbe's 'Small green land narrow, / Barbed-wire-landscape'

---

[46] Mallarmé cited in Jean-Louis Joubert, *La Poésie* (Paris: Armand Colin, 1988), p. 86.
[47] Clemence Greenberg, 'Avant-Garde and Kitsch', in C. Harrison and P. Wood (ed.), *Art in Theory: 1900–1990* (Oxford: Blackwell, 1992/1939), pp. 531–2.
[48] Theodor W. Adorno, 'Commitment', in Harrison and Wood, *Art in Theory*, pp. 762–4.

was more than just a metaphor. It gave voice to the reality of everyday life and its confinement by the boundaries of Cold War international relations. And by naming this reality, the poem turned into a form of local resistance against the spatial delineation of global politics. It is in this sense that the poetry of the 1980s was meant as an 'existential answer', rather than a mere experiment with language.[49] By engaging in poetic subversion the younger generation tried to bring consciousness from the level of ideological doctrines and high politics down to the sobering level of dailiness. It is in this attempt to describe the undersides of East German life that the young writers of the 1980s were transversal dissidents of the most subversive kind.

The Prenzlauer Berg poets seemed less successful, at least at first sight, in creating a critical distance from power. The Stasi revelations demonstrated that the aim of eluding the authoritarian system, of avoiding its spell through the creation of an independent underground art and literary scene, had failed. The presence of informants amidst the allegedly autonomous and subversive poets ensured that the state was aware of all major movements that took place. But this does not necessarily mean that the scene was ineffective or entirely controlled by the state. In fact, East German security files reveal the extent to which state authorities were concerned by the activities of subversive writers. Consider a letter by the Minister of Culture, Kurt Hager, to the head of the Ministry for State Security, Erich Mielke. Dated 13 October 1986, the letter presents the poet Lutz Rathenow as a 'provocateur' who agitates against socialism and whose writings should be punished as a 'defamation of the state'. There are two possibilities to deal with Rathenow, Hager writes. One is to expatriate him (as was done with Biermann and others in the 1970s), the other is to pay no attention to his activities. Since the former would provide Rathenow with dangerous international public attention, the preferred option was simply to 'ignore him henceforth'.[50]

Rather than invalidating poetic dissent, the attitude of high-ranking politicians and security officials reveals how fearful the state was of the political and transversal potential of Prenzlauer Berg poetry. The forceful expatriation of Biermann and other dissident writers in the 1970s had brought the regime much unwanted publicity abroad. The Stasi thus resorted to a more thoughtful, more complex attempt to

---

[49] Thulin, 'Sprache und Sprachkritik', p. 235.
[50] Letter by Kurt Hager, cited in Lewis, 'Power, Opposition and Subcultures', p. 130.

minimise the challenges that could emerge out of the burgeoning underground poetry scene of the 1980s. Surveillance, co-optation and pre-emption were the key pillars of this strategy. It succeeded only insofar as the state was able to monitor, via paid informants such as Anderson and Schedlinski, some activities of the avant-garde writers and artists. The state's strategy certainly failed, as many commentators stress convincingly, in controlling the underground scene entirely.[51]

No political system, no matter how authoritarian, is ever able to dominate all aspects of a society. And no form of dissent, no matter how radical, is ever entirely autonomous from the political practices it seeks to engage or distance itself from. There is no easy way out of an existing web of power and knowledge. Poetic resistance, even if it contains transversal dimensions, cannot achieve success overnight. Indeed, a mere decade, which is the rough life span of the Prenzlauer Berg scene, can hardly be expected to do more than highlight the difficulties and contradictions entailed in breaking though a linguistically entrenched political order. It would have been naive, even absurd, to think that a group of disillusioned underground poets could escape the claws of power and lift themselves and their society into a state of perpetual emancipatory triumph.

Linguistic dissent works slowly, by changing the way we speak and think about ourselves and the world we live in. The young poets of the 1980s were part of this constant process of reframing meaning. They may not have been the heroic freedom fighters they were sometimes taken to be, but their works and lives can shed light on the complexities that make up the increasingly cross-territorial interaction between domination and resistance. Some of their poetic engagements with daily life in East Germany will remain important, if only because they captured a certain zeitgeist, the spirit of a decaying regime. And, for better or for worse, the Prenzlauer Berg writers have triggered a series of controversies that led to considerable public debate. The best we can hope for, in a sense, is that the ensuing issues, difficult as they are, remain debated in a serious and sustained manner. It is through the creation of such a debate that the Prenzlauer Berg writers have transcended their immediate sphere of activity. By embarking on a self-conscious exploration of form, the poets of the 1980s have opened

[51] For instance, Bathrick, *The Powers of Speech*, p. 240; Lewis, 'Power, Opposition and Subcultures', p. 139; Wolfgang Ullmann, 'Kontext: Über die Rolle der Kunst im Zeitalter antagonistischer Diktaturen', in Bötig and Michael, *MachtSpiele*, p. 25.

up opportunities to rethink the crucial relationship between language and politics in spaces that lie far beyond the gradually fading memory of East German wastelands.

Summary

This chapter was the last step in a journey that theorised human agency through an examination of various transversal practices of dissent. The chosen route has led away from great revolutionary acts towards an appreciation of less spectacular but equally effective daily practices of resistance. Their potential to engender transformation comes into view as soon as one conceptualises global politics not only in terms of interactions among sovereign states, but also, and primarily, as a complex and discursively conditioned site of transversal struggles.

Poetry is one of the dissident practices that become visible through this reframing of global politics. Poetic engagements with the linguistic constitution of political practices testify to the transversal and transformative potential that is contained in everyday forms of resistance. But poetry is, of course, only one of many linguistic and discursive sites of dissent. At a time when the local and the global become ever-more intertwined, a great variety of activities, often of a daily and mundane nature, have the potential to acquire significant transversal dimensions. An analysis of poetic dissent provides insight into the processes through which these sites of struggle operate. In doing so, poetry draws attention to a multitude of increasingly important transversal spheres that have all too often been ignored by international relations scholars, whose purview has tended to be confined to the domain of high politics.

The poetic imagination not only illustrates why global politics cannot be separated from the manner in which it has been constituted and objectified, but also reveals how linguistic interferences with these objectifications can exert human agency and engender processes of social change. Rather than attacking direct manifestations of power, poetic dissent seeks to undermine the linguistic and discursive foundations that have already normalised political practices. The potential of such interferences can only be unleashed through a long process. This is true of critique of language in general, whatever form it takes. There are no quick and miraculous forms of resistance to discursive domination. Dissent works by digging, slowly, underneath the foundations of authority. It unfolds its power through a gradual and largely inaudible transversal transformation of values.

But how can something as inaudible as transversal poetic dissent possibly be evaluated? How can a form of resistance that engages linguistic and discursive practices be judged, or merely be understood, by the very nexus of power and knowledge it seeks to distance itself from? These difficult questions beg for complex answers. I do not claim to have solved them here, nor do I believe that they can actually be solved, at least not in an absolute and definitive way. The impact of discursive dissent on transversal social and political dynamics is mediated through tactical and temporal processes. A poem, for instance, does not directly cause particular events, it does not visualise an opponent in space and time. A linguistic expression of dissent works by insinuating itself into its target – the population at large – without taking it over, but also without being separated from it. Even the agent becomes gradually blurred. The effect of a poem cannot be reduced to its author or even to the poem itself. Those who have read it may have passed altered knowledge on to other people, and thus influenced the transversal constitution of societal values.

Discursive forms of transversal dissent will always remain elusive. But this does not render their effects any less potent or real. Neither does this recognition invalidate efforts to assess the role of language in interfering with the constitution of global politics. It does, however, call for a more sensitive and modest approach to the question of evidence and human agency.

The East German poetry scene at Prenzlauer Berg, particularly its attempt to challenge the political, spatial and linguistic constitution of Cold War international politics, has served to illustrate the complexities that are entailed in transversal struggles. In some ways the young writers of the 1980s have shown that poetic dissent can be politically relevant even though, or, rather, precisely because it refuses to be drawn into narrow political debates. Their works were transgressions, attempts to stretch language such that a more critical view of daily life in East Germany could be expressed. While having succeeded in subverting various linguistic aspects of the existing order, the poetry scene at Prenzlauer Berg also epitomises some of the difficulties that are entailed in discursive forms of transversal dissent. The fact that the underground poetry scene was penetrated by the State Security Service has challenged both the credibility of the poets and their attempt to carve out an autonomous aesthetic space. But rather than

271

undermining the validity of their activities altogether, the Stasi revelations highlight the need to come to terms with the complex and transversal elements that are entailed in breaking out of existing webs of power and discourse. It is in this sense that the Prenzlauer Berg poetry scene – precisely because of its mixed success, precisely because of its controversies and failures – has contributed a great deal to our understanding of the transversal struggles that make up contemporary global politics.

Conclusion *The transitional contingencies of transversal politics*

> We stand in the middle of a transition where we cannot remain standing[1]

A series of fundamental transformations in global politics calls for an equally fundamental rethinking of how we have come to understand this central aspect of contemporary life. Processes of globalisation have led to various cross-territorial interactions that render the political and mental boundaries of the existing international system increasingly anachronistic. Nation-states no longer play the only role in a world where financial, productive and informational dynamics have come to disobey, transgress and challenge the deeply entrenched political principle of state sovereignty. This book is to be read in the context of recently undertaken efforts to understand these and other changing dimensions of global politics. Its prime task has been to scrutinise the role that dissent plays at a time when the transgression of boundaries has become a common feature of life.

A conceptual break with existing understandings of global politics is necessary to recognise trans-territorial dissident practices and to comprehend the processes through which they exert human agency. A long tradition of conceptualising global politics in state-centric ways has entrenched spatial and mental boundaries between domestic and international spheres such that various forms of agency have become virtually unrecognised, or at least untheorised. The centrality of dissent can thus be appreciated only once we view global politics, at least for a moment, not as interactions between sovereign states, but as 'a

---

[1] Rainer Maria Rilke, *From Letters to a Young Poet*, tr. M.D. Herter Norton (New York: W.W. Norton, 1934/1993), p. 64.

transversal site of contestation'.[2] This is to say that one's investigative gaze must be channelled less on national boundaries and the discursive practices that legitimise and objectivise them, but more on various forms of connections, resistances, identity formations and other political flows that transgress the spatial givenness of global politics.

With such a conceptual reorientation in mind, the present book has embarked on a disruptive reading of the agency problematique in international theory. This is to say that it has tried to understand transversal dissent and its influences on global politics by employing epistemological and methodological strategies that one would not necessarily expect in an investigation of an international relations theme. Cross-territorial manifestations of human agency have thus been scrutinised, for instance, not by engaging the well-developed structure–agency debate in international theory, but by employing a form of inquiry that illuminates the issues in question from a novel set of theoretical and practical perspectives. The following concluding remarks now reflect on the benefits that such a disruptive reading engenders for an understanding of contemporary global politics.

Visualising transversal dissent

Various practices of resistance, ranging from street protests to the publication of poetic underground magazines, have come to play an increasingly important role in global politics. To visualise these terrains of dissent and to appreciate their significance two steps are necessary.

First: Transversal dissent cannot be understood adequately through spatial modes of representation that divide global politics into several distinct levels of analysis. The very dynamics that drive transversal dissent unfold in the cross-flows and interstices of global life, in the grey zones that lie unexplored along the lines of geopolitically perceived necessity. At a time when global media networks can transform a local protest act into an instantaneous worldwide event, a spatially delineated understanding of social phenomena is no longer adequate to represent the dynamics of global politics. Cross-territorial flows must constitute the focal point of the analysis. Their significance can

---

[2] David Campbell, 'Political Prosaics, Transversal Politics, and the Anarchical World', in Michael J. Shapiro and Hayward R. Alker (eds.), *Challenging Boundaries: Global Flows, Territorial Identities* (Minneapolis: University of Minnesota Press, 1996), p. 23.

be appreciated only once we recognise how a variety of political spheres, from the local to the global, have become intertwined through processes of globalisation.

Second: Modern thinking patterns have engendered an urge to discover an authentic essence of dissent. The result is a compulsion to comprehend, once and for all, how dissent functions and how it exerts human agency in a variety of historical and cultural contexts. This desire must be viewed in the context of a long tradition of seeking replacements for what Nietzsche called the death of God, the disappearance, at the end of the medieval period, of a universally accepted way of looking at the world. As is the case with spatial forms of representation, approaches that revolve around a search for essences will never understand or even recognise transversal forms of dissent. Transversal dissent has no essence, it has not nature, for it consists of the very processes that challenge the manner in which the prevalent practices of global politics have come to be constituted as natural.

Rethinking human agency in global politics: theoretical puzzles, methodological trajectories

If transversal dissent has no nature, how do we recognise it? If transversal dissent cannot be assessed through spatial forms of representation, how can its ability to exert human agency be understood at all?

A certain level of abstraction, I argued, is necessary to deal with these difficult questions. Abstraction is needed not to remove oneself from political reality, but to get closer to it. Through deeply entrenched practices of speaking and writing we have grown accustomed to familiar representations of global politics, often to the point that these representations have become global politics itself. Theorising this objectification can increase awareness of the choices we have made or the ones that have been made for us. The language of such inquiries may, at first sight, seem removed from the everyday realities that are supposedly being addressed. But it is through this very process of estrangement that abstraction can reveal different facets of factual occurrences, and thus open up possibilities to rethink and redirect political practice. The journey that issued from this premise has led along the following path:

First, by opposing pessimistic attitudes that permeate some of the literature on structures and discourses, I have argued that human agency can still be exerted, even in a complex and transversally

275

operating world. The most powerful practices of dissent consist of processes that interfere with the manner in which global politics has been constituted. They work in discursive ways, that is, by engendering a slow transformation of values. Yet, it is one thing to identify transversal forms of dissent. It is an entirely different, and far more difficult thing to conceptualise them such that they can be positively endowed with the capacity to exert human agency. Such endeavours must be careful not to say more than what we could possibly know, not to pronounce anthropocentric judgements about what lies beyond human comprehension.

Second, confronting these limits to cognition, I have advanced a positive concept of human agency that is neither grounded in an essence nor dependent upon a presupposed notion of the subject. Such a conceptualisation opposes a body of literature which stipulates that stable foundations are necessary to assess human agency in global politics. I have demonstrated, by contrast, that accepting the contingent character of foundations is the very prerequisite for an adequate understanding of transversal dissent. A contingent foundation can be provided by a specification of operational schemes. As opposed to a theory that attempts to comprehend what human agency is, a specification of operational schemes is content with facilitating understanding of how human agency functions in a specific spatio-temporal context. It is a set of guidelines about how to approach the complexities that arise from posing the question of human agency in a non-essentialist way.

Third, the above puzzles are understood most adequately through an interdisciplinary approach, which is necessary to deal with circles of revealing and concealing that surround transversal struggles. Such an approach entails constant moving back and forth not only between unconnected bodies of literature and different levels of analysis, but also between theory and practice, abstraction and everydayness, epistemology and ontology, space and time, discursive domination and possibilities for dissent that arise from fissures in them. Each of these sites is crucial. Each offers a unique vantage point, but none of them holds the key to ultimate insight. Indeed, every process of revealing is at the same time a process of concealing. This is to say that by opening up a particular perspective, no matter how insightful it is, one conceals everything that is invisible from this vantage point. The enframing that occurs by such processes of revealing, Heidegger argues, runs the risk of making us forget that enframing is a claim, a disciplinary act which 'banishes man into that kind of revealing that is an ordering'. And where this ordering holds sway, Heidegger continues, 'it drives out every other possibility for revealing'.[3] This is why each chapter in this book has moved back and forth between different, sometimes incommensurable, insights into the question of human agency in global politics. A multi-layered and interdisciplinary approach recognises that the key to circumventing the ordering mechanisms of revealing is to think in circles, not to rest too long at one point, but to pay at least as much attention to linkages between than to contents of mental resting places.

Fourth, the ensuing exploration of dissent in global politics has led along the following circular trajectory of revealing and concealing: discourses are powerful forms of domination. They frame the parameters of thinking processes. They shape political and social interactions. They disregard national boundaries and take on increasingly transversal and global dimensions. Yet, discourses are not invincible. They may be thin. They may contain cracks. By moving the gaze from epistemology to ontology, I explored ways in which individuals can use these cracks to escape aspects of discursive domination. To recognise the potential for human agency that lingers in these cracks, I shifted foci again, this time from the level of Being to an inquiry into tactical behaviours. Individuals can draw upon the thinking spaces opened up by mobile subjectivities and engage in countless daily acts of dissent, which gradually transform societal values. Many of these tactical forms of dissent defy the spatial logic of national sovereignty. They enter transversal grey zones and, over an extended period of time, may alter the discursive practices that frame the constitution of global politics. I then scrutinised, by returning to epistemological levels, how these discursive interferences may engender processes of social change.

Moving along these constantly shifting transversal terrains of dissent is to resurrect a notion of human agency from a discursive viewpoint. Yet, it is not a notion based on a causal understanding – a perspective that presupposes an autonomous agent and a clearly separable and identifiable object upon which agency is projected. It is not a notion that embodies claims to totality, that believes every process of social change requires an agent to trigger it. Many aspects of social

---

[3] Martin Heidegger, 'The Question Concerning Technology', tr. D.F. Krell, in *Basic Writings* (New York: HarperCollins, 1993/1977), p. 332.

dynamics are beyond the influence of human agency, and certainly far beyond our ability to understand them adequately. Aspirations that deny these limits to cognition must be put to rest, filed ad acta as social science fiction.

The elusive nature of human agency renders conventional concluding remarks impossible. This is why I am not recapitulating in detail the findings of each research step. To gaze beyond these partial insights, to raise them to a higher level by squeezing each of the fragments into an overarching whole, would annihilate the unique vantage-point from whence they sought to shed light on global politics. The result: a preconceived and subjective mental image imposed upon a set of idiosyncratic social dynamics, one more act of concealing, the closing of the very thinking space I have tried to open throughout this book.

These concluding remarks are thus not to be seen as a synthesis of my findings, a final word on human agency. They are, rather, designed to underline the inherently open character of the agency problematique in global politics. They deal with the consequences that emerge from recognising that a conceptualisation of human agency can never be complete, that the very power of human agency is based on a constant process of becoming something else than what it is.

Thinking past the givenness of global politics: insights from the poetic imagination

Once one conceptualises global politics as a series of overlapping transversal struggles, various new forms of dissent come into view. Human agency is then no longer limited to the deliberations of statesmen or the strategic victories of military commanders, but takes place in a variety of other, often mundane and unrecognised domains. Dissent, likewise, is no longer solely associated with mass uprisings and other heroic acts of defiance. It is also operative in powerful but largely inaudible processes that take place against the backdrop of great events. Indeed, more than anywhere else, transversal dissent is located in countless non-heroic practices that make up the realm of the everyday and its multiple connections with contemporary global life.

The possible range of transversal sites of dissent is virtually unlimited. This book has thus focused on one representative domain: language. In a media infused contemporary world, where the local can become instantly global, the written and spoken word no longer

278

follow the dictum of national sovereignty. Messages that are carried by, in and through languages easily slip through iron curtains and other unsuccessful attempts to uphold divisions between the domestic and the international that no longer correspond to the political and spatial realities of globalised life.

Insight into the processes that transgress the spatial logic of global politics has come from a rather unexpected source, poetry. The poet shares many concerns with the scholar who seeks to study international relations critically. Both know that reality never is. Reality happens. It must be opened up to multiple ways of seeing. And it is this opening up, the process of questioning linguistically embedded ways of looking at the world, that creates possibilities for social change. A poetic creation, Octavio Paz argues, is above all an act of violence done to language. It 'is revolutionary by nature'.[4] Likewise, a critical look at global politics is an act of violence done to the linguistic and discursive framework through which we have come to perceive, internalise and objectivise the realities of global politics. Expressed in Robert Cox's words, critical international theory is an approach that stands apart from the prevailing order and explores the range of possible alternatives to it.[5] Language, this book argued, is a central aspect of this task.

The East German literary scene at Prenzlauer Berg illustrated how local acts of dissent may transgress and challenge the existing spatial logic of global politics. Much of the poetic work produced by the younger generation of East German writers highlights the intricacies of interfering with links between language and social reality. Because poetry is self-conscious about the substance of form and the metaphorical structure of language, it is able to shed light on processes by which the use of language can become a viable form of discursive dissent. It demonstrates how it is possible to reveal the grey shades of domination and resistance, how potential for human agency can emerge from questioning linguistically entrenched ideas, assumptions and social practices that have been placed beyond scrutiny.

The poets at Prenzlauer Berg were subversive because they succeeded in naming that which had no name before: the daily realities,

---

[4] Octavio Paz, *The Bow and the Lyre*, tr. R.L.C. Simms (Austin: University of Texas Press, 1973/1956), p. 3.
[5] Robert W. Cox, 'Social Forces, States and World Orders: Beyond International Relations Theory', in *Millennium*, 10, 2, 1981, 130.

mundane and suffocating as they were, of life in the industrial and urban wastelands of East Germany. They were transversally subversive because they challenged, as a central motive, the spatial logic of international politics, the division into two fundamentally distinct spheres of life, a domestic and an international one. Much of their poetry was about the recognition of painful boundaries, and about the desire to break out of them. As it turned out, this transversal engagement was only the beginning of an intricate, frustrating and lengthy process. The infiltration of the Prenzlauer Berg scene by the State Security Service revealed how deeply rooted and how complex transversal power relations are in today's world.

Poetry cannot solve the problem of linguistic domination, but it is unique – and offers valuable insight – insofar as it makes this problem the vortex of its existence. Poetry also reminds students of global politics that languages are not just mediums of communication or ways of representing the world. Languages embody the social relationship between people and their environment. They are disguised political practices, for they silently frame, enforce and entrench systems of domination.

To recognise that language is politics is to acknowledge that form and substance cannot be separated. The manner in which a text is written, a speech is uttered, a thought is thought, is integral to its content. There is no neutral form of representing the world, a form that is somehow detached from the linguistic and social practices in which the speaker or writer is embedded. Science and philosophy, empirical analyses and literature, mathematics and poetry, are all bound by the form through which they convey their ideas. Being built on specific grammatical and rhetorical structures, all of these stories and accounts, Michael Shapiro points out, implicitly advance political arguments. All of them, 'no matter how much their style might protest innocence, contain a mythical level – that is they have a job to do, a perspective to promote, a kind of world to affirm or deny'.[6] This is not to say that every account of social dynamics is equally insightful or valid. But it is to accept that linguistic practices are metaphorical. Some tropes, however, have been so extensively rehearsed and are so deeply entrenched in linguistic and cultural traditions that they

---

[6] Michael J. Shapiro, 'Introduction' to *Language and Politics* (Oxford: Basil Blackwell, 1984), p. 2.

appear as authentic representations of the real. Dissent in global politics is the process that interferes with such objectifications.

Transgressions, transitions, circularity

Transversal forms of dissent cannot succeed overnight. An engagement with linguistically and discursively entrenched forms of domination works slowly and indirectly. The effects of such interferences are difficult to see or prove, especially if one approaches the question of evidence with a positivist understanding of knowledge. But transversal dissent is nevertheless real. It enters the social context in the form of what the East German poet Uwe Kolbe called 'a trace element'.[7] It does not directly cause particular events. It engenders human agency through a multi-layered and diffused process, through a gradual transformation of societal values. This process has no end.

No matter how successful they are, discursive forms of dissent, even if they manage to transgress national boundaries, are never complete. There is no emancipatory peak to be climbed. Dissent is the very act of climbing, daily, doggedly, endlessly. It is not an event that happens once, a spectacular outburst of energy that overcomes the dark forces of oppression and lifts liberation into an superior state of perpetual triumph. 'Everything becomes and returns eternally', Nietzsche says. 'Escape is impossible!'[8] Even the most just social order excludes what does not fit into its view of the world. Inclusiveness lies in a constant process of disturbing language and rethinking meaning, rather than in an utopian final stage.

If we are to gain and retain a viable understanding of human agency in global politics we must embrace the transversal and the transitional as inevitable aspects of life. Human agency not only engenders transition, it is itself transition. The role and potential of agency, its ability to open up new ways of perceiving global politics, can be appreciated once we accept, with Rilke, and as a permanent condition of life, that we always 'stand in the middle of a transition where we cannot remain standing'.

---

[7] Uwe Kolbe, interviewed by Robert von Hallberg, *Literary Intellectuals and the Dissolution of the State: Professionalism and Conformity in the GDR* (Chicago: University of Chicago Press, 1996), p. 255.
[8] Friedrich Nietzsche, *The Will to Power*, tr. W. Kaufmann and R.J. Hollingdale (New York: Vintage Books, 1967), § 1058, p. 545.

A discursive notion of human agency is grounded precisely in this recognition that there is no end to circles of revealing and concealing, of opening and closing spaces to think and act. Revealing is always an act, not something that remains stable. Anything else would suggest a static view of the world, one in which human agency is annihilated, one in which the future can never tear down the boundaries of the present. Just as the interaction of domination and resistance has no end, efforts at coming to terms with them will never arrive at a stage of ultimate insight. Because discursive dissent operates through a constant process of becoming something else than what it is, a theoretical engagement with its dynamics can never be exhaustive. It can never be more than a set of open-ended meditations. An approach to understanding dissent and human agency thus remains useful only as long as it resists the temptation of digging deeper by anchoring itself in a newly discovered essence, a stable foundation that could bring the illusion of order and certainty to the increasingly transversal domain of global politics.

Index

academic disciplines, function of, 17–21,
    276–7, 224–5, 230–1, 276–7
Adorno, Theodor
    and avant-gardism, 235–6, 267
    on language, 227–9, 231–9
    on modernity and identity thinking,
        106, 140, 227–8, 232, 235
agent–structure debate, 6, 9–16, 20, 37–9,
    49–50, 211, 274–6
ambivalence, repression of, 106, 110 ,115,
    260
anarchy
    and radical dissent, 85–7, 94–5
    and international relations theory, 4–5
Anderson, Sascha, 255, 262–3, 264–6, 269
aphorisms, as a strategy of dissent, 22,
    237–8
Ashley, Richard, 7, 16, 224
Atwood, Margaret, 156, 202
avant-gardism,
    problematic nature of, 235–6, 256, 263–
        4, 267–8
    as radical dissent, 181, 253, 263

Bakhtin, Mikhail, 46, 203–5, 222, 239
Barthes, Roland, 65, 223, 241, 243, 255
Bathrick, David, 183, 246, 260
Baudrillard, Jean, 97, 110–13, 141, 255
Beck, Ulrich, 131
being
    constituted dimensions of, 24, 194–6
    and domination/resistance, 41, 196–
        200, 206–7, 210–11, 277
    and language, 215
Benhabib, Seyla, 36
Benjamin, Walter, 46, 238
Berlin Wall, collapse of
    events leading up to, 41–2, 130–4, 177–
        84

and gender, 34, 147, 160–72, 185
lacking anticipation of, 48–50, 255
linguistic representations of, 216–17
role of domestic politics, 130–4, 178–83
role of external/transversal factors,
    118–19, 122, 130, 180–2
role of literature/poetry, 41–5, 186,
    244–72
role of media, 33, 44, 119, 125–6, 178,
    180–2, 246, 259
role of popular protest, 1–2, 32–4, 121–
    7, 161–4, 173, 178–9, 185–6, 216–17
Biermann, Wolf, 164, 248, 250, 263, 268
Bodin, Jean, 76
Bohley, Bärbel, 162, 164, 166
Bondurant, Joan, 102
Bourdieu, Pierre, 13
Braidotti, Rosi, 148–50, 159, 198
Brown, Chris, 20
Brown, Judith, 91
Butler, Judith, 38, 39, 149–50, 197

Calvin, 69
Campbell, David, 2, 6, 7, 15, 44, 246
Caputo, John, 94, 102
Carter, April, 102
Case, Clarence Marsh, 97, 99–101
Castoriadis, Cornelius, 36
causality
    and human agency, 27, 40, 247
    and international relations theory, 4–5,
        14–15, 19, 182, 211
    problematic nature of, 40, 45, 211–13,
        271, 277
de Certeau, Michel
    on everyday forms of resistance, 201–2,
        212–14
    on operational schemes, 39–40, 209
    on tactic versus strategy, 212–14

283

Freire, Paolo, 233

Gandhi, Mohandas
  and Indian independence movement,
    31, 89–92, 104, 153
  influence on radical dissent, 31, 91, 93,
    95, 89–90, 101, 104–5, 114
  and masculinism, 92–3, 152–5
  on power and nonviolent resistance,
    27, 87–93
gender
  and being/identity, 147–50, 153, 208–
    14
  and civil society, 34, 169–70
  and consent, 153–5
  and discourse, 84, 147–72
  and German unification, 34, 147, 160–
    72, 185
  and history, 155–60
  and international relations theory, 8
  and language, 47, 149–50, 224
  and popular dissent, 84, 92, 147, 151–5,
    204–5
  versus sex, 147–51
genealogy, as a method of inquiry, 24–9,
    51–2, 82, 97
George, Jim, 16
Germany, East
  gendered aspects of politics, 34, 147,
    160–72, 185
  and literature/poetry, 41–5, 186, 244–
    72
  and media, 33, 44, 119, 125–6, 178, 180–
    2
  political context of collapse, 41–2, 118–
    19, 130–4, 173–4, 177–84, 216–17
  and protests/dissent, 1–2, 32–4, 121–7,
    161–4, 178–9, 185–6
  unification with West, 34, 160–72
  see also Berlin Wall, Prenzlauer Berg
Germany, West
  domination of unification process, 161–
    2, 164–7
  media and other influences on East, 44,
    180–2, 246, 248, 259–60,
Giddens, Anthony, 10–11
globalisation
  and changing role of dissent, 1–12, 52,
    74, 87, 93–5, 96–7, 113–19, 185, 273–9
  definition of, 31–2
  and everyday life, 31–2, 42, 187–8, 270,
    278–9
  and language, 42, 215–16, 222, 239–40,
    278–9
  and media, 1, 23, 31–2, 110–14, 137, 141

God
  death of, 23, 29–30, 45, 67, 73, 83, 106,
    109, 115–18, 138–40, 144, 146, 244,
    275
  and early modern thought, 29, 53–4,
    57–8, 66–70, 72–3
Gorbachev, Mikhail, 119, 131
Gramsci, Antonio, 90, 174–7, 184, 192–3,
    232
grand theories of dissent
  and modern thought, 99, 105–6, 109–10
  problematic nature of, 33, 106, 115–18,
    127–9, 133–4, 136–8, 146
Gregg, Richard B., 97, 99–101, 104
Grünbein, Durs, 258–60, 261

Habermas, Jürgen, 33, 108, 122, 164, 240
Hager, Kurt, 126, 268
Haraway, Donna, 156, 197, 200
Härtel, Heidemarie, 42–3
Hartsock, Nancy, 137
Harvey, David, 141
Hegel, G.W.F., 30, 88, 92, 108
hegemony
  and discourse/dissent, 174–6, 183–4,
    188–93, 206–7
  and state/civil society, 175–9
  in East Germany, 179–83
  thick theory versus thin theory, 192–3
Heidegger, Martin
  on Being and ontology, 12, 24, 194–8,
    200, 211,
  and deconstruction, 24–5, 197
  and feminist theory, 196–8, 200
  on language and poetry, 215, 223, 244
  on revealing/concealing, 276–7
heroism
  alternatives to, 42, 120, 200–6, 256, 278
  and dissent, 96–7, 120, 170–1, 183–5,
    258, 278
  gendered aspects of, 147, 151–5, 170–1
  and romanticism, 81, 83–5, 89–90, 94,
    152–5
Hindess, Barry, 127
Hirschmann, Albert O., 122
Hirschmann, Nancy, 154
history, political dimensions of, 24–5, 38,
    42–3, 55, 143, 155–60, 223, 260
Hobbes, Thomas, 77, 104
Hollis, Martin, 48, 49, 118
Holsti, K.J., 5
Honecker, Erich, 122, 124–5, 131, 132,
    178, 180, 247
Horkheimer, Max, 18, 106
humanism, 54–73, 77–8, 93–4, 107–9

voice, forms of protest, 121–7, 168
Voluntary Servitude, 26, 63–5, 90, 100,
    129–30, 153–4

Walker, R.B.J., 20, 25, 43, 206, 231
Waltz, Kenneth, 49
Weil, Simone, 87
Welsch, Wolfgang, 97, 143–4
Wendt, Alexander, 6, 11, 15
Wittgenstein, Ludwig
    on aphorisms, 22, 138

on epistemology, 39, 225
on language, 41, 217, 219–22, 231, 236,
    255, 266
Writing
    and clarity of expression, 232–7, 241–2
    methodological aspects of, 17–21
    as a practice of dissent, 84, 119, 186,
        227–43, 244–72, 279–81
    as representing language, 217, 226–7
    style, significance of, 232–43, 244–62,
        267
    versus speech, 226–7

CAMBRIDGE STUDIES IN INTERNATIONAL
RELATIONS